Senate Office Building, have a confronta-
tion with Lyndon Johnson when he was the
all-powerful Majority Leader, challenge the
group promoting the wasteful Supersonic
Transport, poll the voters back home to find
out what they are thinking...all in the interest of getting "Uncle Sam—The Last of the
Bigtime Spenders" back on the right road.

Senator Proxmire has written a powerful,
important book—one that may well influence this country's future.

Senator William Proxmire is one of the
best-known figures in the U.S. Senate. Even
his recent successful struggle against losing his hair made front-page headlines. He
prides himself on never missing a roll call
and on staying in close touch with the voters back home in Wisconsin. He was first
elected to the Senate in 1957 to fill the seat
left vacant by the death of Senator Joseph
McCarthy, and since then his effort to
make sure that peo... money...
wasted has become s...

Uncle Sam— The Last of the Bigtime Spenders

WILLIAM PROXMIRE

SIMON AND SCHUSTER · NEW YORK

First printing

SBN 671-21432-2
Library of Congress Catalog Card Number: 72-83908
Designed by Eve Metz
Manufactured in the United States of America

ACKNOWLEDGMENT

I want to thank my administrative assistant, Howard E. Shuman, without
whose efforts far above and beyond the usual researching, advising
and suggesting, this book could not have been written, and my executive
secretary, Arlene Branca, for her work on the manuscript.

Contents

Preface

Proxmire's Complaint: Everything You've Always Wanted to Know About Government Waste but Were Afraid to Ask

Most of your work in the Senate revolves around a going-to-school process. The classroom is the committee session. And the faculty is really whizz bang.

How can you miss learning when you have the chance I have had as chairman of the Congressional Joint Economic Committee?

Consider our teachers: Nobel Prize–winning economist Paul Samuelson, Harvard's John Kenneth Galbraith, present and former heads of the President's Council of Economic Advisers like Walter Heller, Paul McCracken, and Gardner Ackley, labor leaders like George Meany and Leonard Woodcock, present and former Budget Directors like Charles Schultze, and men as diverse and famous as Robert S. McNamara, Dean Acheson, Ralph Nader, General James Gavin, Barry Goldwater, and the heads of the National Association of Manufacturers and the Chamber of Commerce.

And we don't just sit at their feet in a large lecture hall. Repeatedly I have been the *only* Senator present—the only pupil in a one-to-one challenging and learning session with these men.

But of course all this can be theoretical, impractical, useless. The Chinese do many things wrong; one thing I know they do right is to make their executives get right out with the rest of the boys and work day after day on the assembly line, or in the grease pit with the mechanic.

They have their reasons which are probably wrong. The reason the results are good is that the direct, personal, earthy experience keeps you from getting lost in the broad generalities.

Unlike most elected officials, I was anything but a natural people's choice. My constituents could not possibly consider me as one of them. From the beginning I was an outsider, an interloper. I carpetbagged into Wisconsin with about every political liability in the book. I had no degree from the University of Wisconsin. I had one from Yale and two from Harvard, all of which were political liabilities. My last employment had been not just on Wall Street, but with J. P. Morgan and Company. How do you like that for a "liberal Democrat"!

My wife wasn't a Wisconsin dairy princess. The only thing we had going for us in this regard was her first name and Borden advertising. She was Elsie Rockefeller at a time before Nelson and Jay had come on the scene and when the name Rockefeller meant corporate cruelty at its meanest.

So I needed some identification. What I did and what I have been doing since is the reason why I have learned something about the waste that makes Nils Torgeson so mad he'll kick your butt right off his place when you ask him to sign your nomination papers.

I wanted to win election under these circumstances. I was desperate. I just had to get elected. How do I identify?

Well, there's only one thing left: go out and make friends. Here's how I did it.

I picked out the state legislature as my first goal. For six months I went personally—no friends, no relatives—to house after house in that assembly district of about ten thousand families. I talked and especially I listened. We won the election. And, much more important, I learned something about what the people of eastern Dane County wanted, needed, hated and loved.

Two years later I ran for governor. That wasn't nearly as much as it sounds. We Democrats hadn't won for a generation, and I didn't disappoint. I lost by a near-record half-million votes.

But what an education!

I campaigned for the best part of 1952. And when you run with a constituency of four million you have literally one hundred times as many voters to see as I did in 1950 running in an assembly district. It would have taken me the best part of a hundred years to visit all the families in the state.

Does that mean you forget it? No—seeing the people is still the name of the game. You have to find a way to see more of them. You have to see them a lot faster.

This means, of course, you get a broader and wider education in popular concern.

But how do you do it? It means hitting the factory gates at 6 A.M. Factory workers have a marvelously illogical way of going to work. They're entirely different from office workers. Factory workers enjoy getting on the job well in advance of when they punch in. There's very little last-minute rush. If a thousand workers have to go through a certain gate by 7 P.M., they'll usually start coming in at six, and for an hour the regularity is astonishing. To go to a thousand homes would take days. To shake a thousand hands at the gate takes an hour.

Of course, the conversation is very limited indeed—a few seconds for each worker. But the worker who does have something bothering him will deliver his gripes. It's not a matter of trying to think of something nice to say to be neighborly. It's a matter of speaking up because he really feels something in his gut. And you listen to him—you learn.

After I was elected, this educational process went on. Unlike most Senators, I don't go home to speak to my constituents—except when the speaking engagements are unavoidable. They feel they hear too much of me on television anyway. I go home to hear them, to listen to them.

The plant gates aren't nearly what they used to be. They're still good, but a minority of workers work in plants. That marvel of the merchandising revolution, the shopping center, is a real dream for me. In a few hours I can meet thousands of my bosses and test their reactions. The Green Bay Packer football games, the Brewers, the Bucks, the University of Wisconsin and Marquette sports events attract thousands who flock in a beautifully organized rythmn to the entrance, where I meet them, shake their hands and get the occasional deeply motivated gripe or satisfaction. It's a down-to-earth counterbalance. And it's priceless.

And there's the playback from all this Wisconsin association. What makes Helga Schmidt mad stays in my mind. She gets furious when son Hans wastes their money on a new Vega that costs too much. And she'd throw a fit if she heard the Air Force is paying a fat two billion more than it was obligated to pay for a turkey of a plane like the C-5A. So when Ernie Fitzgerald, the Pentagon program analyst, testified to me as chairman of the Joint Economic Committee about the C-5A overrun, Helga helped magnify my outrage.

And what good would the supersonic transport do Casimir Jankowski? Casey lives on the South Side of Milwaukee. He works his tail off. He can afford to go to Schmidt's Tavern every night to brood over a beer. But how many times is Casey going to fly to Paris, or to Warsaw for that matter? Why should Casey have less beer money to make it possible for some family living in posh Whitefish Bay to travel three times as fast overseas? Casey didn't talk about priorities to me at the Allen Bradley gate. He told me to forget the SST and do something about Lake Michigan. He used to swim in it. He still fishes in it. But for how long?

Mary Finerty has a thing about Communists. She flies the flag every day—not just on holidays. She loves this country, and I love her. But she told me when I was shaking hands at the Holiday on Ice Show at the Milwaukee Arena what I could do with the Subversive Activities Control Board.

"Those bums get thirty-five thousand dollars a year, and for twenty years they've done nothing, absolutely nothing. What burns me up," she said, "is that it's my money. Either kill it or, say, Prox, get me one of those jobs. I could use thirty-five thousand dollars for doing nothing. It beats typing for peanuts at Northwest Mutual."

Well, I wrote this book not for Ralph Nader and Ken Galbraith and Paul Samuelson. I wrote it for Nils Torgeson, Helga Schmidt, Casey Jankowski and Mary Finerty.

Well, Nils, Helga, Casey, and Mary, I hope you like it.

1 · Priorities and American Needs

Once or twice a year I poll eighteen thousand Wisconsin voters chosen at random from phone books. I ask their views on everything from whether the wage-price controls are working to how I should vote on the nomination of Richard Kleindienst for Attorney General. (They were two to one against Kleindienst. I voted for him anyway, because I believe the President has a right to his own man in his Cabinet unless there is overwhelming proof of wrongdoing against him.)

This is no phony poll where they load the questions, as the opposition often did when Harry Truman was in the White House ("Are you against the President's policy of being soft on Communism?"). Instead I tell them, "You be the Senator. How would you vote on the McGovern-Hatfield resolution to get out of Vietnam? Should the government become the employer of last resort and provide direct jobs for the unemployed?"

One of my biggest questions is on spending. In a table giving the amounts proposed in the budget for health, education, the Pentagon, the National Aeronautics and Space Administration (NASA), Social Security, and other major items, I ask Wisconsin voters to check a column indicating whether they would increase, decrease, or keep the proposed spending at the same level for these programs.

In my latest poll, the number-one targets for cuts were foreign aid, space, and national defense. That has been the overwhelming opinion, year in and year out, of Wisconsin citizens for over half a decade. But before the ink was dry on the tabulation of results from a recent return, the White House announced a series of actions which was directly opposed to these overwhelming views.

In the course of a single week the Administration decided to proceed with the space shuttle, to raise the military budget by several billion dollars, and to establish a U. S. presence in the Indian Ocean by sending in an attack carrier fleet. Simultaneously, as a sop to the $38-billion budget deficit, a freeze was placed on $200 million for food stamps for the poor. That's what you call "reordering priorities."

These relatively unnoticed actions portended a spectacular increase in federal spending. Even with no overruns, the space shuttle will cost $5.5 billion over the next six years, plus a $1-billion contingency fund to handle unforeseen events. The Pentagon, not to be outdone by NASA, proposed that its share of the federal budget go up by over $5 billion in a single year. While the immediate costs of an American naval presence in the Indian Ocean are comparatively insignificant, the ultimate costs are staggering. The Navy, without doubt, will rush to justify a new attack carrier, plus its supporting fleet, on the grounds that it has a responsibility in one more ocean of the world. That will cost another $2 billion.

The consequences are clear. The President chose the space shuttle, aircraft carriers, and Pentagon procurement over money for schools, health, housing, mass transit, the environment, and other needed programs. With the freeze on the food-stamp money, he also cut a vital program already starved for funds. He reordered priorities, but he reordered them in the wrong way.

Big Spending Ahead

He did this at a time when the demands for new funds to meet immediate needs are overwhelming. For example:

Many people have suggested that the federal government should pick up the costs for welfare now borne by the states. This would cost $7 billion a year.

Even modest proposals for a comprehensive American health program total $40 billion a year, of which the federal share would come to at least $20 billion.

Proposals for revenue sharing will cost a minimum of $5 billion a year, and leading spokesmen for the program such as Governor Nelson Rockefeller of New York argue that $10 billion is not enough.

Even if present housing costs do not rise, the annual federal subsidy to build five to six million new low- and moderate-income housing units in a decade would average $2.5 billion to $3 billion annually and cost at least $5 billion a year by 1978.

There are serious proposals to establish a minimum family income for families of four at $4,000 a year, and to raise that amount to $6,500 by 1976. Even by modest calculations, a $4,000 guarantee for a family of four would cost $40 billion. A $6,500 guarantee would cost the federal government between $75 and $80 billion a year by 1976.

According to a Brookings Institution study, the annual costs of primary and secondary treatment of all waste water in the United States—from manufacturing, municipalities, and livestock —will come to $18.5 billion in 1973 and to $27.5 billion by 1980. The federal share will be a minimum of $10 to $15 billion.

New funds for mass transit, air pollution and other environmental controls, elementary and higher education, manpower training, poverty programs, vocational education, and aid to the aged, to name only a few pressing needs, will cost billions more.

Thus, even a modest estimate indicates that such programs will cost $100 billion a year in the near future. But the U. S. government just does not have the money to finance all of these needs. Charles Schultze, former director of the Bureau of the Budget, has estimated that existing government programs will take every dime of new federal revenues for three years into the future. This is true even if unemployment is reduced to 4 percent.

Must Cut Frills, Fat, and Waste

The time has come, therefore, for cuts in the frills, fat, and waste in the military programs, which now take more than two thirds of the controllable budget funds. Unless there is a decisive shift from military to civilian spending, there is no major source of funds on which to draw even to begin to pay for the great unmet needs of the country.

But cuts in the frills, fat, and waste in the civilian programs are also needed. Great Society programs have grown from $1.7 billion in 1963 to $35.7 billion in 1973. Meanwhile, the civilian programs in the budget have increased from 47 percent to 66 percent of the total. Too often they fail to do what they were designed to do. Often they take highly productive resources from the private sector and spend them inefficiently in the public sector. Programs designed to help the weak and the poor end up going to the powerful and the wealthy.

Making such cuts will not be easy. Big spending for the military, space, public works, and highway programs are all darlings of the conservative forces. In fact, it can be charged fairly that "the conservatives are the big spenders." Unlike the 1930s, it is they who now benefit the most from federal actions—direct spending, tax loopholes, direct and indirect subsidies, government loans and guarantees, and the issuance of special privileges, permits, and franchises.

But liberals have their pork barrels, too. Big budgets for urban renewal, foreign aid, and education have become the sacred cows of the liberal establishment. They should be examined much more critically.

It is not enough merely to attempt to reorder priorities between military and civilian spending. Priorities must be established *within* the military departments—for example, between spending for the U. S. submarine-launched nuclear deterrent, which is invulnerable, and spending production money for a new manned bomber, which is highly vulnerable and utterly wasteful.

In the same way, spending priorities must be established within the civilian agencies. Merely to shift funds from the B-1 bomber or the ABM to the federal highway program or subsidies for the big farmers would continue to distort budgetary priorities.

To establish a hard-nosed, critical examination of *all* government programs will be as difficult to achieve as it is necessary. One of the many reasons why this is so has to do with the past advice of economists.

Past Policies of Spend, Spend, Spend

The economics profession has been gravely lax in its willingness to look critically at individual programs. Economists have been so involved with the big picture and general spending levels, that they have failed for years to consider the quality as well as the quantity of the stimulative programs they advocate. In times of recession or unemployment, all spending was good and all cuts were bad. The phrase most commonly heard was "The public sector is starved," and the transfer of resources from the private to the public sector was always considered good. "Spend! Spend! Spend!" was the cry.

But we now find that this has had unfortunate consequences. The war in Vietnam, men on the moon, Lockheed bail-outs, sugar subsidies, highway demolitions, military foreign aid, and excessive Medicare payments distort American priorities as much as boondoggles for the C-5A's or the TFX.

One reason we face such great dilemmas today is that we have no proper system within the public sector for making tough choices. A. C. Pigou was a pioneer when in 1920 he published *The Economics of Welfare*. But even as late as 1960, when we on the Joint Economic Committee carried on our seminal study of employment, growth and prices, it was virtually impossible to get reputable economists to criticize the quality of federal spending. They were concerned either at looking intently at less and less, as they did in their microeconomic studies on the theory of the firm, or at looking intently at more and more, as when they pontificated on their macroeconomic studies and economic growth.

Now political figures and informed public opinion have at last led the economists back to their more traditional ways, a tradition established in classical economic theory by the writings of Adam Smith, David Ricardo, William Stanley Jevons, and Alfred Marshall in their work on value theory and the marketplace.

Paul H. Douglas, both a great Senator and a great economist, often complained that most of his liberal friends reacted like Pavlov's dog: say "spend" and they salivated. They were for every spending proposal and for every tax cut. Their reaction to spending proposals for the public sector—any public sector—was a vision of a flow of dollars that would fill the Atlantic Ocean. In reaction to this automatic response, Paul Douglas coined the phrase "To be a liberal one need not be a wastrel."

Causes of the Conditioned Response

What were the causes of this Pavlovian, knee-jerk conditioned response?

One cause was that many of the services provided by government could not be measured by the standards of the marketplace. You could not, for example, measure the value of education, the price of the life of a combat Marine, or the social importance of a police department. And without such an objective measurement system, it was easier to support programs automatically than to criticize them constructively.

Another cause was the effect of the Great Depression on the traditional belief in economy and on the careful traits for which New England Yankees and the old economists were famous. In the late 1920s, the intellectual proponents of economy confused their traditional views with a paralysis of government, and they became unwilling to do anything for an economy which was flat on its back. As the trauma of the depression grew worse, their criticism of government spending not only seemed completely out of touch with the times but became equated with the kind of puerile opposition shown by the mossbacks in the thirties.

Spending thus became good and economy was discredited. And things were so desperate that it was true that almost any spending was better than the paralysis of the country and the tragedy inflicted on the human spirit by the ravages of the depression that saw unemployment rise to over one quarter of the work force and that lasted for almost ten years. One cannot cry "economy in government" with unemployment at 26 percent.

The experience of the depression was followed by the experience of the war. Once again, spending was good. It produced guns, planes and tanks to defeat Hitler and Tojo. The emphasis was on spending and production, and damn the economic consequences.

As a matter of record, we did not do too badly. About a third of the costs of the war were paid for in higher taxes, another third by borrowing, and a final third by inflation. While not perfect, it was a far better record than that of paying for wars in the past.

In the immediate postwar world the fear again was that we would return to a period of recession, depression, joblessness, and idle resources. Full employment and economic growth were emphasized. The expansion of the money supply became the first chosen instrument of economic policy to achieve these ends. This lasted until the Treasury–Federal Reserve accord of 1954. Fiscal policy, a shelf of public works, a massive highway program, and expansion of the military became the touchstones of public policy to achieve economic growth and relatively full employment.

Both Guns and Butter Brought Inflation

It was therefore a combination of intellectual argument and practical experience which brought us to the unfortunate state of affairs of the mid-1960s, when we discovered that we could not have guns and butter without serious inflation. Sharply increased spending on both the Vietnam War and rapidly expanding social programs at home combined to plunge us into a crisis that still plagues the nation. In the absence of resources to meet our growing and pressing public needs and of any willingness to pay for an unpopular war through higher taxes, the country finally had to face some tough, hard, unhappy choices. Uncle Sam could not continue to be the last of the bigtime spenders.

Spending was not all good. Some of it—that on wasteful and unneeded weapons systems, the excesses in the space program, and highways rammed through public parks and black neighborhoods—was clearly bad.

Bad, too, was sloppy spending on housing or health or other essential programs. We were beginning to realize that the era of all this and heaven too was over—that we had little enough for our essential needs and therefore we could not afford to waste any of it in careless spending on *anything*.

I have seen many times how commitments we make to meet temporary problems often become permanent and then eat up resources which should be committed to more important programs. We need therefore to become far more discriminating in saying yes to the good programs and far more emphatic in saying no to wasteful programs.

The belief that most federal programs, subsidies, loans or spending are good is still held by many with noble and idealistic intentions. That this is dangerous, from both an economic and a social point of view, can be shown by citing a few examples.

The Distorted Purpose of Foreign Aid

Since President Truman proposed his Point Four program, most idealistic and forward-looking people have supported foreign aid. But there has been a massive shift in its nature. The bulk of it, both within and outside the foreign-aid budget, is now spent for military purposes. Even a great program such as Food for Peace, which combines the self-interest of how to reduce massive domestic food surpluses with the idealism of getting vast quantities of it to those who are hungry in the world, has been converted in part to military purposes.

As much as $150 million a year of funds generated from the sale of American surplus farm commodities abroad has been so used. Yet the official description of the program in the U. S. budget contains not one word about the use of Food for Peace funds for military purposes. It states merely: "This program combats hunger and malnutrition, promotes economic growth in developing nations, and develops and expands export markets for U. S. commodities." The use of these funds in this way is a corruption of the original ideal. It should remain a food-for-peace, not a food-for-war, program.

Meantime a large proportion of the funds for multilateral economic aid which are funneled through the international-development banks are for big projects—big dams, highways, mining, and power plants. A very small proportion goes for schools, for housing, or for medical or humanitarian purposes. The military-industrial complex and the highway lobby are almost as active abroad as they are at home.

It is therefore ironic that among the general public the foreign-aid program is largely supported by idealistic persons and traditionally opposed by the right wing. When the program is looked at in its totality the bulk of the funds go either for military aid or for huge public-works projects which benefit the haves both at home and abroad. Only a tiny proportion goes for social or humanitarian projects in support of the have-nots. It is entirely possible that instead of redistributing income from the wealthy in the United States to the poor abroad, the foreign-aid program taxes relatively modest-income groups in the United States and distributes the revenues or balance to powerful economic forces at home and wealthy groups abroad. The banks, road builders, shipping firms, cement makers, and military industries get the AID contracts. Their counterparts are the direct beneficiaries abroad.

While some former advocates and defenders of foreign aid, such as Senators Fulbright and Church, have sensed this irony and have acted accordingly, it has yet to penetrate the awareness of many otherwise knowledgeable individuals and groups. Altogether some $10 billion or more of American resources—the overwhelming proportion of it in military aid—is involved in this program which appears now to defeat the purpose for which it was originally designed.

Excessive Costs for Reclamation

Let's take another example. Over $300 million a year is spent on water-reclamation programs. The federal government builds dams and irrigation ditches and funnels water onto arid land. Over the years, some $6 billion has been spent on big reclamation dams. Under reclamation, which applies only to seventeen Western states, the principal is paid back but the funds are interest-free. But the amounts paid back are placed in a reclamation fund which is used for more reclamation projects. Traditionally it was required that desert land irrigated with public funds must serve a public purpose, namely to help establish the family-sized farm and the social goals it promoted. To do that, the government limited to 160 acres the holdings on which federal reclamation water was supplied. In practice, because both husband and wife, as well as children, were eligible, the effective limit was 320 or more acres. Such a holding, especially if dedicated to growing oranges in California or apples in the Yakima Valley, provided a decent family income.

But this massive interest-free loan program, as well as the funds provided for the huge dams on the Trinity and Feather Rivers and the Upper Colorado, are under fire for a variety of reasons. The federal government is paying farmers to withdraw production in areas of high rainfall while subsidizing farmers to open up new productive lands in areas of low rainfall.

Costs are excessive. On some Upper Colorado River projects, it cost over $2,000 per acre to reclaim land worth $100 per acre, upon which only hay and forage crops were to be grown.

In many of the new projects, especially those in California, the traditional 160-acre limitation has been negated either by amendment to the initial legislation or through lax administration. Ordinary taxpayers now contribute hundreds of millions to subsidize a few of the wealthiest farm corporations in the world, whose lands are worked by migrant labor instead of a family operator. This defeats the public purpose for which the initial subsidy was justified.

Finally, reclamation is having disastrous effects on metropolitan water tables and on the land itself. Such vast quantities of underground water have been sucked out of the ground to irrigate farmlands—which account for only 10 percent of the production of states like Arizona—that local community water supplies are endangered. Are these the proper uses of public funds? Do they benefit the right people? Do they carry out intelligent public policies?

Few Space-Shuttle Benefits

A further example that spending per se is not necessarily good is seen in the example of the space shuttle. What will it do? What benefits will we be getting for the massive spending of $6.5 billion?

I addressed a letter to the head of the space program and asked for the justification for the space shuttle. Specifically I asked what tangible benefits we could expect from the program. Here is the key justification in the reply: "The basic premise leading to the conclusion that this nation should proceed with the development of a space shuttle system is that the U. S. should and will continue to have an active space program from now on." In simple words, the main rationale for the shuttle is that it will keep the space program going. But it also means a steady drain on the U. S. Treasury.

The agency also asserted, without proof, that the program would save costs. The space program now uses exceedingly costly, expendable boosters. Obviously, a reusable shuttle will be cheaper than expendable boosters if enough trips are made. But a study by the Rand Corporation prepared for the Air Force demonstrated that the shuttle would have to carry more than $141 billion in traffic over its thirteen-year lifetime before it would become cost effective. But what are the payloads for? What is a space transportation system going to carry? Is Congress going to have to appropriate $141 billion over the shuttle's lifetime in order to make worthwhile the shuttle's $6.5-billion development cost? I shall return to these questions in a later chapter. Here I merely offer them as an example of why all federal spending should be closely examined.

The Legitimate Objects of Government

Abraham Lincoln defined the legitimate objects of government as doing for the people "whatever they need to have done, but cannot do at all, or cannot so well do for themselves, in their separate and individual capacities."

There are many goods or services which the private sector is unable to produce. Among them are national defense and the security of the nation, police and fire protection, a judicial system, the printing of money, and the control of floods.

Where there is monopoly there is a legitimate purpose in public intervention to help allocate resources more efficiently. It is clear that the federal government should regulate the transmission of electricity over national grids and of oil and gas through pipelines, because of the monopoly nature of the product. Where the private sector cannot produce needed goods because costs are higher than consumers can pay, as in housing for the poor, there must be some form of public subsidy.

These are proper functions of government. Broadly stated, they fall into three major areas: (1) the production of public goods and services; (2) to compensate for the inability of the market to allocate resources because of frictions, monopoly, or burdens that the production process places on society (e.g., the spewing of pollutants into the air or the water, which imposes costs on society not borne either by the producer or the consumer of the specific product); and (3) to achieve equity through a redistribution of income to reduce the harshness of society and to make it more humane.

Civil Rights

Since the Great Depression there has been very little controversy that these are the proper functions of government.

There are also less tangible goals of society that are the proper function of government to promote. They are found in the great documents of our nation, the Declaration of Independence, the Preamble to the Constitution, the Gettysburg Address, and in the music, writings, and poetry of our leaders and artists. They also include the Bill of Rights and the Fourteenth Amendment to the Constitution, which provides that no state shall "deny to any person within its jurisdiction the equal protection of the laws."

It took more than a century, from Lincoln's Emancipation Proclamation in 1863 to the Civil Rights Act of 1964, for that constitutional right to be implemented in law. That failure brought one hundred years of segregated schools, "White Only" signs on the restrooms, the banning of blacks to the back of the bus, separate but unequal facilities, and poverty, humiliation, and degradation for tens of millions of brown, black, and Indian

Americans. For them the promise of the Bill of Rights and the post–Civil War amendments remained unrequited.

The aroused public conscience that led to the legal fulfillment of the Fourteenth Amendment in 1964 and the Fifteenth Amendment in 1965 has since given way to deeper divisions than before. The assassination of Martin Luther King, the murders of John and Robert Kennedy, and a coalition of negatives constructed from the poison of the Vietnam War, the inevitable inflation, and ensuing unemployment, have made a bad situation worse. Some embittered blacks have answered the siren call of their most radical and irresponsible leaders. While the cities burned, white middle-class suburban America reacted by tightening even tighter the white noose around the black urban centers. The government responded not by enlightened leadership but by obfuscation, delay, and denial of rights previously won. America has come a long way. But America has a long way to go.

There are other goals as well. They include not only what we are as a country at home but what we do abroad. As Senator J. William Fulbright put it in his testimony on national priorities before the Joint Economic Committee:

Your hearings focus on the question all Senators and Congressmen should have uppermost in their minds in approaching their responsibilities—what do we want our nation to be? Do we want it to be a Sparta or an Athens?

Do we want a world of diversity where security is founded on international cooperation, or do we want a Pax Americana? Do we as a people place a greater value on trying to mold foreign societies than we do on eliminating the inequities of our own society?

I believe that, contrary to the traditions which have guided our nation since the days of the Founding Fathers, we are in grave danger of becoming a Sparta bent upon policing the world.

Unfortunately, the primary instrument by which great decisions are made, priorities determined, and goals carried out, is the dull, dry, boring, opaque, obtuse and ponderous document called

"The Budget of the United States Government."

As Senator Fulbright said, in the budget we chart the nation's course for the future. It represents the collective wisdom of two of the three branches of the government. It reflects the sense of values of the political leaders under whom it is prepared and the values of the dominant elements in the Congress by whom it is approved.

Shortcomings of the Priority Document

But that document has great shortcomings. It is too voluminous for any one man to understand. That is true whether that man is the President of the United States, the director of the Office of Management and Budget, or the chairman of the House or Senate Appropriations Committee. As Max Frankel wrote in *The New York Times:*

The budget, in other words, is something less than either scientific analysis or artistic prophecy. It is a political melange of Presidential expectations, calculations, hopes and demands, offered in the immutable language of the statisticians and with the clinical pretense that no responsible person could carve the pie very differently. And it offers little help to the few in Congress who would try.

As an instrument which sets our priorities, it has other impossible shortcomings as well.

More often than not there is no explicit statement in the budget document as to the specific purpose of each particular outlay. If there is one, it is misleading, or inadequate, or designed for public-relations purposes. That explains why funds designed to help low-income farmers end up in the pockets of absentee owners of corporate farms. That is why the $7.3 billion authorized for the Export-Import Bank, according to a brilliant study prepared for the Joint Economic Committee, has no relationship to the amount of American exports.

In fact, a close student of the political process will note that the stated purpose of many programs is the opposite of its actual effect. Bail-outs for Lockheed Aircraft and tax loopholes for the wealthy are supported on the grounds that they aid the unemployed or provide an incentive for charitable giving.

But advocates of programs which genuinely aid the weak and the poor are often ashamed to argue for them on idealistic grounds. Instead the appeals are made to self-interest, crude profit-and-loss motives, or fear. For years foreign-aid programs were sold on the basis of stopping Communism. There is a much greater impetus for the food-stamp program in the fact that it will help rid us of surpluses than that it will feed needy children. Wheat for hungry people in India or tractors for Ethiopian farmers gain their political clout because the wheat is in surplus, the tractors are produced in Peoria, both will be carried in American ships, and the financing will be done by a Manhattan bank, rather than from any humanitarian argument.

It is an unfortunate but a cardinal rule of political debate that bad programs are supported by idealistic arguments and that good programs draw their support from appeals to self-interest.

The budget—our number-one priority instrument—not only fails to define the fundamental purpose of expenditures but gives no quantitative statement of the programs' objectives either. Who benefits? Who pays the costs? If $1 million is appropriated to help poor farmers, how much goes to poor farmers? Do the subsidized housing programs actually house lower-income families or do the funds go to builders, bankers, and financiers?

Which costs more—to allow industries to use the major rivers of the nation as public sewers and provide treatment plants to clean them up, or to tax industry through an effluent charge at a high enough rate that it becomes uneconomic for them to pollute? And who actually pays for the work under the alternative proposals? In the one it is the taxpayer through the incidence of the federal tax system. In the other, it is the consumer through an increase in the price of goods necessary to cover the costs of pollution-free production.

These kinds of specific facts are neither given to us in the budget document nor provided by the great departments of the government in justification of their programs. But how much the alternative programs cost and who bears that cost are the kinds of intelligent facts needed to make good public choices and establish priorities. In fact, that is what the question of priorities is all about.

The Economics of the Environmental Problem

Because of the importance of improving the environment as a national priority, it is worthwhile to examine the economics of the problem in greater detail.

We on the Joint Economic Committee have held days of hearings on the economics of national priorities. In those hearings the best testimony on the economics of the environment was given by Professor Robert Haveman of the Department of Economics at the University of Wisconsin, former staff economist to the Joint Economic Committee itself.

Haveman pointed out that numerous reasons have been given to explain why we have an environmental problem. Some say it is because we have too affluent a society. Because we produce so much, we must dispose of so much. Others say it is because we produce the wrong things—too many automobiles, not enough mass transit; too much primary paper, not enough recycled paper; and too many tin cans, beer bottles, and plastic containers.

But Haveman insists that while each of these provides some explanation, the basic cause of the environmental problem is economic. He charges that the problem exists because the market economy fails to place a price on the use of environmental resources—public watercourses, the air mantle, and public lands.

The major factors of production, labor, capital, and land each have their price in the market economy. Because of these prices, the system tends to do an efficient job of allocating scarce resources to the production of goods and services that have the highest value to the people. But environmental services have no price. They are treated by everyone as free goods.

Haveman points out that the fact that people who live downstream suffer great abuse—they can no longer fish or swim in the river and during periods of low stream flow the river becomes anaerobic and smells—does not really affect the polluters. The polluters are not required to bear the costs that their actions generate. Environmental services are like a free lunch to them. But society has to pay for their free lunch.

Use Price Formula

Haveman argues that a way must be found to price environmental resources. They have to be brought back into the economic system. Federal policy has failed to recognize this simple fact. After two decades under environmental programs the waste-assimilative capacities of rivers remain "free goods." Government has refused to set prices to keep these resources from being diverted to low-valued uses. Instead of the market and price mechanism, rule enforcement and subsidies have been used as the key policies to improve water quality.

"This policy strategy has been a dismal failure," Haveman charges. He points out that after spending $5.4 billion to construct waste-treatment plants, industrial pollution has continued to grow. Pollution in the rivers is worse. He cites a General Accounting Office study indicating that in one river basin $7.7 million was spent for treatment works, eighteen plants were subsidized, and waste discharges equal to 147,000 people were treated. But during the same period industrial waste in the basin increased to the extent of 2.4 million people. He concludes that the "continued spending of taxpayers' money to clean up after polluters—along the lines of the current strategy—is going to be an enormously expensive and relatively fruitless venture."

Haveman proposes a user charge on polluters. He would impose a user or effluent charge on waste discharges which would require polluters to "pay by the pound." The user charge would be high enough to stop the pollution. The revenues could be used to finance those environmental measures that are properly public functions.

Haveman calculates that the net cost over five years of an effective effluent-charge program which I introduced as the Proxmire Regional Water Quality Act would be $4.3 billion. This is almost $10 billion less than the $14-billion five-year cost of the Muskie bill strategy which follows the traditional waste-treatment grant program. It is $8 billion less than the Nixon Administration's proposal along lines similar to those of the Muskie bill.

The effluent-charge strategy can provide a far more effective means to control pollution at a much smaller cost than the present ineffective system. It is not only right in theory, but it works.

Specific economic data on costs of pollution and other programs are seldom provided to Congress by the departments. Most often the departments do not have such information. And when public agencies do have it, as was the case with the systems analysis documents for the C-5A and a new attack aircraft carrier, it is considered internal information and explicitly denied to the Congress and the public. In the case of the Department of Transportation, it is prevented by the terms of its enabling act from analyzing the benefits and costs of the federal highway program. The act reads: "The Secretary . . . shall develop and . . . revise standards and criteria . . . for the formulation and economic evaluation of all proposals for the investment of Federal funds in transportation facilities or equipment, except such proposals as are concerned with . . . (6) grant-in-aid programs authorized by law."

The key "grant-in-aid programs authorized by law" is the highway program. No economic evaluation of the investment of funds in highways can be made. This was the price the highway lobby extracted for its support to establish the new department, out of fear that such studies would lead to more funds for mass transit and less for highways.

More Weaknesses in the Priority Document

The budget as THE priority document suffers from many other weaknesses as well. Billions in federal benefits, subsidies, and expenditures are entirely outside its compass. The Export-Import Bank is one example, housing mortgage institutions are another. The decisions of the federal regulatory agencies and their economic effects are not reviewed at all. The granting of a television franchise, the discontinuance of rail service, or the price of gas at the wellhead are wholly outside even the existing inadequate system of budget priorities. Yet these are all proper subjects of government regulation and intervention and have vast economic consequences not only for the producers or owners but for the American public as consumers of products and as taxpayers.

Some subsidies can be seen and are in the budget. But their weakness is that they are not subjected to a rigorous cost examination at either the executive or the Congressional level. These cash subsidies amount to at least $10 to $13 billion. They include payments to build ships and to operate them, to encourage farmers to produce or not to produce, to encourage students to attend college, to build fishponds and irrigation systems, to get business firms to hire certain types of workers, to fly airplanes, to compensate beekeepers for dead bees, and for many other purposes.

To some degree, at least, these cash subsidies can be counted and judged. But many other subsidies are virtually impossible to comprehend, let alone evaluate. There are tax subsidies, credit subsidies, subsidies which take the form of benefits-in-kind, and purchase subsidies. Some are paid out of revenues. Others represent tax money not collected.

Some, like the housing subsidies, were designed to be obscure. Because public opinion was unwilling initially to support vast sums for housing the poor, the method of achieving the end was designed to be complicated. The underlying thrust was that if no one understood them no one would complain about them. But in the process, the few who did understand them grabbed the greatest proportion for themselves and left only a few crumbs for those in need.

They were made complex and obscure for a second reason. There are no "capital budget" and figures "below the line" in the U. S. budget, as there are in every business firm's balance sheet. Funds which private industry treats as a long-term capital asset and depreciates over a thirty-year life are treated in the U. S. budget as a liability and charged against the budget in a single year. To avoid the fiscal consequences of such a perverse accounting system, the supporters of government housing programs designed them to do one of two things. The fiscal method to support them had either to minimize the immediate budget consequences or get funds outside the budget process entirely. As a consequence the ultimate costs of the program skyrocketed in order to preserve a small annual cost. In this way costs rose while control over the programs was lost.

Tax Expenditures

Another vast area of ill-defined and hence uncontrollable expenditures are the tax subsidies. They are probably the worst offenders against a proper system of priorities. They amount to almost $40 billion a year. They escape entirely even the cursory budget review afforded direct expenditures. There is no ongoing analysis of either their aims or whether they meet them. They often fail to meet the test of equity or of taxation according to ability to pay. In fact, in some cases they redistribute income upward.

Philip Stern, author of *The Great Treasury Raid,* testified before the Joint Economic Committee that the tax expenditures amount to a huge welfare program for the rich. The thirty families with income in excess of $1 million a year get a tax-expenditure "welfare payment" of $720,448 a year each, or $13,854.78 a week. The families with income below $3,000 a year get a tax-expenditure "welfare payment" of $16 a year or 31 cents a day. This is the effect of the special preferences, exemptions, deductions, credits and exclusions in the tax laws. The benefits for the recipient of the special privilege are exactly the same he would receive if he got a direct government payment. The effect on other taxpayers is also the same—namely, they have to pay additional taxes to make up for the amounts that are not collected because of the tax preferences, privileges, or loopholes.

They are exactly like budget expenditures. This is why they are called "tax expenditures." But there is even less scrutiny over them than there is by the Budget Bureau or Congress for the least examined direct expenditure or subsidy. Neither their costs nor their benefits are described in any official document. They are not examined to determine if they do what they were established to do. No one asks if some other method would be less costly or more efficient. Their "equity" or distributional effects are not examined. If they were, it would be found that they are highly regressive and inequitable. At long last, the Mansfield-Mills proposal will do this.

Congress Has Lost Control of the Purse Strings

Not only are matters like tax expenditures outside the budget and therefore entirely outside an annual Congressional scrutiny, but Congress does little more than give a perfunctory examination to those items that are in the budget. This means that the instrument by which priorities are determined or reexamined —the budget—is essentially outside the purview of the Congress.

There are reasons for this. Little more than half of the budget is "controllable." Veterans' payments, interest on the national debt,

Social Security and Commodity Credit Corporation (CCC) pay-ments, and unemployment compensation are not subject to change except through administrative rulings or amendments to the basic laws or fundamental economic policies. Neither the Budget Bureau nor Congress examines these annually.

The action of Congress, even when it cuts or reorders programs, is often ineffective. Congress has cut the President's budget re-quests every year for the last quarter of a century, but its cuts affect only a minute proportion of the total. In addition, what Congress appropriates and what the President spends are only indirectly related. For example, in the four-year period from fiscal year 1969 through 1972, Congress cut more than $16 billion from President Nixon's military-budget requests, but the actual amounts spent remained at precisely $77 billion in three of those four years; the $16 billion in Congressional cuts were translated into less than $4 billion in Pentagon cuts in military spending. There are complex reasons for this, including a $40-billion back-log in Pentagon funds and the fact that outlays and appropriations are different things. But the essential fact remains that the budget document and hence American priorities are essentially what the President says they should be in his annual budget.

Congress needs both a method by which the budget can be examined properly and the means to make its judgment effective.

A Complex Problem

In summary, America has great unmet needs. These needs can be met only by a reordering of priorities—but that is a far more complex issue than most people imagine. It does not mean merely increasing the amount of funds spent in the public sector. It means making choices—hard, tough, difficult choices.

It means cutting back on redundant and inefficent existing pro-grams in both the military and civilian budgets.

It means closing the tax loopholes and making choices between tax expenditures, on the one hand, and direct expenditures over which there is some control, on the other.

It means cutting back on contradictory programs such as paying one farmer to take land out of cultivation while subsidizing another farmer to plant crops.

It means devising a system to make certain that programs are examined from the bottom up every year.

It means that Congress must begin to do its job, and must hire the experts to do the job.

Until these things are done it would be irresponsible to raise federal taxes—as many people have advocated as a means of meeting our needs—except in the gravest national emergency. To burden people with higher taxes while powerful interest groups have their nose in the federal trough, receive subsidies, or gain from egregious tax loopholes would be a failure to carry out the public trust, particularly at a time when neither the President nor the Congress has even the most elementary system to examine the benefits and effectiveness of billions of dollars of tax money already spent. To raise taxes frustrates policies to bring full employment, which would increase federal revenues by more than $25 billion a year.

The President and Congress should first find out where the bodies are buried and then deal with them. But the increased revenues from reducing unemployment to 4 percent, the net gain from closing tax loopholes, and the realistic cuts that can be made in the military budget are insufficient to pay for even modest proposals for welfare reform, aid to the cities, a health program, mass transit, anti-pollution, education, and other urgent needs. That is why a top to bottom examination of existing programs, their benefits and costs, is imperative.

This means finding out where the wastes and inefficiencies are and then how to analyze them, how to rid our system of them, and finally how to use all these wasted resources to meet our gigantic needs.

And that is the subject of this book.

2 · The Economy, the Number-One Domestic Priority

In the summer of 1971 unemployment was 6 percent of the labor force, where it had hovered for eight months. Two million more men and women were out of work than only two years before. Industry was operating at less than 75 percent of capacity. Corporate profits were off. But the dull and dreary economic statistics gave little meaning to the human aspects of recession and unemployment. To put flesh and blood on the bare-boned figures and to give the general situation some personal significance, we on the Joint Economic Committee called a number of unemployed men and women to testify at our hearing.

Henry Wulforst was a highly skilled plumber. At age fifty-three, he had worked more than thirty-three years at his trade. In June 1971 he worked four days. Of the twenty-six weeks since the first of the year, he had spent ten out of work. Of the 925 men in his local, 170 to 200 were unemployed. For the first time in thirty-three years—since 1938—Henry Wulforst had to leave town to get work.

Louis Lantner was in a bigger fix. A college graduate, a three-year Navy veteran who had spent a year in Vietnam, he was discharged as a lieutenant junior grade. He scored 101.5 points out of 100 on a civil-service exam, having got five extra points for veteran's preference in addition to his grade of 96.5. But with all his background and qualifications Louis could not get a government job. His wife, Karin, held a master's degree, was trained as a computer linguist, and had worked for two years in her skill. She had been unemployed for five months. Both were actively seeking work in their skills. In desperation they had moved in with her family to save money.

If Louis and Karin Lantner could not find work with their education, background, skills, and initiative, imagine the problem those with far fewer qualifications have.

One such man was Jules Fabre, age twenty-eight, married, black, and unemployed. He had been laid off by General Motors in March 1970, fifteen months before. As a young man he was not qualified for severance pay from the company. His wife taught school, but was unemployed in the summer. Because he took a part-time job paying eighty-five dollars a week, he could not qualify for unemployment compensation. Because his wife worked as a schoolteacher, he could not get food stamps. He was driving a cab, but when there is a big layoff everyone drives a cab. Jules sat for hours waiting for calls. In any case, what he wanted was a full-time job, not part-time cab work, not food stamps, not unemployment compensation.

These are the human costs of unemployment. They are far worse than the dollar costs. Unemployment is the biggest waste of all, since the time lost by the unemployed can never be regained. It is gone forever. That is why the stories of these people tell far more than the raw statistics can ever say. And that is why Congress needs to hear them.

They illustrate why the United States can do more to combat social ills, to provide funds to solve problems, and to reorder the nation's priorities through a fully employed, growing economy than in any other way.

Full Employment Without Inflation

It is possible with sensible policies to achieve a high and sustained rate of economic growth, a high level of employment and a low rate of unemployment, and to do this with relatively stable prices without either creeping or galloping inflation. Both economic theory and the history of the United States demonstrate that this is true.

The economy is the number-one domestic priority because all the others—housing, health, education, antipollution, and our ultimate security—depend on it.

The human, social, and economic costs when we fail to achieve the goals of economic growth, full employment, and stable prices are tragic. They are epitomized by the prolonged panics of the nineteenth century, the Great Depression, and the recessions of the post–World War II era.

The Employment Act of 1946 is the Magna Charta by which the country's economic goals are pursued. Actions taken under it have not always been ideal, because of human error or imperfect perception, but it has nonetheless had one great, signal success: in the more than a quarter of a century since its passage there has been no nationwide depression. Every major war in our history and some minor ones as well were followed by a depression—if not immediately, then within a decade—but with the passage of the 1946 Employment Act and its emphasis on growth and "maximum employment," a post–World War II depression did not happen.

While successful in avoiding a depression, the U. S. economy has not avoided recessions. The numerous downturns in economic activity—those in 1949, 1953–54, 1958, 1960, and 1970–71—have inflicted painful and unnecessary hardship on millions of American people.

The Costs of Recession

Take just one example—the recession of 1970–71. Two million more men and women were out of work in 1972, with unemployment at mid-year at 6 percent, than in 1969, when it was below 4 percent. Not only those who lost their jobs suffered. In an economy where industry functions at only 75 percent of its capacity other hardships are imposed as well.

Millions of people are underemployed both in the number of hours they work and in the skills they perform. Recession promotes underemployment. When the highly skilled engineer loses his job it is wasteful and traumatic; it is only somewhat less so when he pumps gasoline or clerks in a store, using only a third of his potential capacity.

Millions who wish to change jobs fear to do so. Millions more forgo upgrading or promotion. Millions lack the overtime work that they need in order to bring in enough income to make life worthwhile.

Construction workers, blacks, women, and teenagers suffer especially. The returning veteran finds it more difficult to get a job than others of his age and circumstances. The productive skills and resources of millions of Americans are lost when they are forced to retire early.

Unemployment is cruel and harsh punishment to inflict upon those seeking jobs in our society. But it inflicts enormous penalties on society itself. Consider these:

Excessive unemployment at 6 percent added at least two million to the number of those living below the poverty level. If we had had full employment instead, the number and proportion of those in poverty would have been reduced.

The gap between the potential gross national product and the actual gross national product in the years affected by the recession amounted to almost $200 billion. We lost this much in production. It can never be regained.

The loss in government revenues is astounding—more than $80 billion in the period of the recession and its aftermath and more than $27 billion a year with unemployment at 6 percent.

Government spending foi unemployment compensation, Social Security, and welfare payments attributable to the rise in unemployment amounted to about $8 billion in fiscal year 1972.

The government deficit rose by $85 billion over the period of the slack economy.

Floating All the Boats

Returning to full employment would provide funds to pay for many public and private needs. It would add $35 billion to payrolls and $15 billion after taxes to corporate profits.

State and local revenues would increase far more than the $10 billion requested for federal revenue sharing.

Schools and colleges not only would get more resources from additional state and local revenues, but would get increased private support as well.

The tremendous importance of economic growth in providing resources can be seen by a simple example.

If the economy should grow at its potential of 4.3 percent in the four years 1973–76, instead of at the 2.5 percent rate of the 1969–72 period, the gross national product would grow in real terms by $226.8 billion more than at the lower rate. The simple calculations are given in the table below.

Difference in Gross National Product If Economy Grows at 4.3 Percent
Instead of 2.5 Percent (in billions)

Year	Real Growth 2.5%	Real Growth 4.3%	Difference
1972	$1,145. (estimate)	$1,145. (estimate)	
1973	$1,173.6	$1,194.2	$ 20.6
1974	$1,202.9	$1,245.6	$ 42.7
1975	$1,230.0	$1,299.2	$ 69.2
1976	$1,260.8	$1,355.1	$ 94.3
			$226.8

As John F. Kennedy was fond of saying, "A rising tide floats all the boats."

Compared with 6 percent unemployment, full employment would provide jobs and incomes for two million more Americans. On a personal level, it would boost millions out of poverty, feed the ghetto child, insure higher education for tens of thousands of teenagers now unable to attend, keep a northern-Wisconsin farmer out of bankruptcy, make it possible for an aerospace engineer to change jobs, provide employment for women who wanted to work, and make it easier for blacks and other minority groups to attain the income and equality they so richly deserve. Corporate profits would add to investment and productivity. At least $40 billion in federal-government revenues lost or used for expenditures imposed by recession would be recouped. Full employment would also provide the means to reorder some of the priorities and reduce frictions in the functioning of the economy. Here are some of the goals we could achieve.

Because of the fear of a further loss in jobs, it is almost impossible to cut the military budget when unemployment is at 6 percent. With full employment and alternative jobs available, military spending can be cut.

It is equally difficult to cut tariffs, reduce subsidies, and stop wasteful expenditures when five million men and women are out of work. This can be done when there is high production and high employment.

With unemployment at 6 percent it is often futile to upgrade the work force through job training, because there are no jobs at the end of the training. Equally, there is no reason to increase the mobility of the work force when there is no job for the man who moves. These programs are necessary to reduce frictional blocks to competition, productivity and economic efficiency. They are necessary to sustain economic growth and full employment at stable prices. Once full employment is obtained, we can negotiate automation in plants, workers will not lose their jobs, and we will get a great increase in productivity. All this is necessary to reorder priorities and meet essential needs. But they are impossible to achieve with an underpowered economy chugging along on only five cylinders.

How did the economy get where it is?

Wrong Diagnosis, Wrong Remedy

The recession of 1970–71 was brought about deliberately through a misreading of events. When the Nixon Administration took office there was a high level of employment but a rampaging inflation. The inflation was caused initially by an attempt to have both guns and butter and the failure either to cut spending or to raise taxes to pay for the added outlays of the Vietnam War. The big inflationary pressures came in the years 1966 to 1968.

But by early 1969 the nature of the inflation had changed. It was no longer a demand inflation where too much money was chasing too few goods. Instead it was an administered price inflation which was sustained by the market power of big industries and big unions who were capable of raising prices and wages without regard to competitive conditions.

Misreading the nature of the inflation, as the experts in the Eisenhower Administration misread them a decade before, the Nixon economic experts followed a policy of restraint on demand. They described it in the 1970 Economic Report of the President as "...a policy of firm and persistent restraint on the expansion in the demand for goods, services, and labor." But the country did not then suffer from demand inflation.

Having diagnosed the problem wrongly, they proposed the wrong remedy to solve it. They advocated a rise in unemployment, which they confidently predicted would be "small and temporary." Instead it was sharp and prolonged.

The fact remains that the Nixon Administration followed a deliberate course of inducing unemployment as a means of reducing inflation.

The unemployment was created by a curtailment in government orders and a reduction in demand. But after more than two years of these restrictive policies, inflation remained unabated and elaborate wage and price controls were imposed. In the end we got the worst of all worlds—high unemployment, low growth, rising prices, and wage and price controls. It was a situation of both economic stagnation and price inflation. This was first described by the British as "stag-flation."

It was bad enough to cause the high level of unemployment. It was even worse to do little or nothing about it. Micawberish statements were issued month by dreary month in the hope that something would turn up, but nothing did.

Shooting the Messenger

Over the years the Bureau of Labor Statistics (BLS) built up a reputation for absolute impartiality, high professional competence, and a completely nonpartisan approach.

They need it. Every month the Bureau puts out the unemployment figures—the most politically sensitive figures the government collects. They also gather and release the Consumer Price Index. Most people call it the "cost-of-living index." Millions of dollars in pay raises for industrial workers, government employees, and retirees ride on its absolute accuracy.

Since 1947, except during the Korean War, a monthly press conference has been held to release the cost-of-living figures. Since 1959 the unemployment figures have also been released at a monthly press briefing. But on March 19, 1971, this practice stopped abruptly.

When the unemployment figures for February were released early in March, the unemployment rate showed a drop from 6 percent in January to 5.8 percent in February. Secretary of Labor James D. Hodgson rushed to the White House. There he pronounced this decline of two tenths of one percent as "heartening" and of "great significance." But at the monthly BLS press conference the independent professional expert Harold Goldstein referred to the figures as only "marginally significant" and as "sort of mixed." When asked about the contradiction between his and Secretary Hodgson's views, Goldstein courageously replied, "I am not here to support or not support the Secretary's statement. I am here to help you interpret the figures."

Result: the monthly BLS press briefings were canceled. A Labor Department spokesman said the decision to cancel was made "jointly with the White House." A Labor Department statement rationalized the change by saying it would "avoid the awkwardness of subjecting the professional staff of the bureau to questions with policy implications."

Because the integrity of the entire process was at stake, I decided to do something about this. On April 2, 1971, the day the March unemployment figures were due, I called a hearing of the Joint Economic Committee. I called both the Commissioner of the BLS, Geoffrey H. Moore, who is an appointed official, and Harold Goldstein to testify. In my opening statement I said:

When the long-standing practice of a monthly news conference was stopped last month, I felt that a forum was needed whereby the Congress, the press, and the public could receive both the details of the employment and unemployment figures and the public, truthful, and unvarnished explanation of them which has characterized the experts at the Bureau of Labor Statistics in the past.

Then I questioned Mr. Moore about who was responsible for canceling the press conferences.

Chairman Proxmire: Did they initiate the decision, the Secretary and the White House?

Mr. Moore: . . . the immediate action that was taken on this occasion I did not initiate, no, sir. . . . The Secretary and the White House made the decision themselves. I was, as I say, consulted about it. And I support the decision.

When pressed to state whether or not the press conference was canceled because of Mr. Goldstein's honest comments, Commissioner Moore replied, "There have been some implications or insinuations that the Secretary was not pleased with the way the BLS staff was performing. That is not the case."

At the end of that first hearing, Commissioner Moore, in an attempt to put down the press and to justify calling off the press conference, told us, "I do think, too, that the kind of questions that this committee has put before us are a little more penetrating than the ones that we typically get at a press conference. I am very happy to have the opportunity to answer them." But what Commissioner Moore didn't know was that I had solicited questions from the press table. Many of the "penetrating" questions he thought were superior to the ones he usually got came directly from the press.

In late September the White House and the Labor Department dropped the other shoe. Peter Henle, the chief economist at the BLS, was given "a leave of absence." Harold Goldstein's job was chopped in two. He no longer worked with the monthly figures—he got the part dealing with the "long-term" trends. He was not only no longer there to hold the press conferences but no longer there even to interpret the monthly figures.

To make certain that some public forum existed where the press and the public could get the unvarnished truth, the Joint Economic Committee continued to meet month after month through 1971 and into 1972 on the day the unemployment figures were released. But month after month, even without the press conference, unemployment remained at the general level of 6 percent.

Shooting the messenger who bore the bad news did not solve the high-unemployment problem. The White House, like King Canute, could not hold back the sea.

Public Relations No Substitute for Action

Unemployment cannot be reduced by public relations. It must be attacked by a constructive program. Fatuous remarks by those in high places that we should pay more attention to the doughnut (employment) than to the hole (unemployment) are examples of a Pollyannaish view toward the problem.

It is no answer to say merely that there is more employment now than ever before. As Arthur Okun, former chairman of the Council of Economic Advisers, testified before the Joint Economic Committee:

> The experience of the last year [1971] illustrates how the movement of *employment* can be a misleading indicator of the changing state of labor markets. Unless employment rises rapidly enough to match the growth of the labor force, unemployment keeps rising. In the same way that, with a rising population, heroin addiction can be a growing problem even though the number of nonaddicts continually increases, so unemployment can be a growing problem while the number of jobs is increasing.

With a growing population and a rise in productivity, which characterizes a period of recovery, the economy must run merely to stay in place. One million three hundred thousand new jobs must be created each year merely to employ those entering the labor force. Many more jobs must be created to reduce a high level of unemployment.

Another tack in the public-relations ploy to obscure and minimize the high level of unemployment is to downplay the importance of the parts composing the total. The argument is that the high level of unemployment is neither as significant as it once was nor as important to alleviate, because a somewhat higher proportion of women and teenagers are in the unemployed totals.

This is a scurrilous attempt to excuse the inexcusable. Women, teenagers, and blacks are better educated and better trained and have higher skills than male whites a decade or so ago. Because of this there should be a significant reduction in the numbers and proportions of these categories who are unemployed. The fact that unemployment in these groups has risen dramatically does not excuse the high general level of unemployment. It is a damaging admission of failure when unemployment rises as the skills and productivity of major segments of the society increase.

This analysis overlooks numerous other problems as well.

Severe unemployment was not confined to women and teenagers. Adult male unemployment doubled in the 1969–72 period. Many women are heads of households, and their jobs are as important to their families as are the jobs of male breadwinners. Further, why shouldn't society provide a job for every individual in the country who is willing and able and is seeking work?

Finally, relatively full employment is defined at roughly 4 percent unemployment, not at zero or 1 or 2 percent of the labor force. The unemployment figures already make generous allowances for those moving between jobs, those temporarily out of work, and groups that move in and out of the labor force. Unemployment significantly above 4 percent is serious whether occasioned by out-of-work women, blacks, teenagers, or white male adult heads of households. And 4 percent is too high. In Western Germany it is .07 percent. A 4-percent level might lead to revolution.

Defense Cutbacks Not the Cause

Another argument used by the apologists for high unemployment is that it was caused by the reduction in defense spending and the discharge of military personnel as the Vietnam War wound down.

But the facts belie the apology. While unemployment among veterans was about 1.5 percent higher than among other men in the same age groups, that fact accounts for no more than one tenth of one percent in the overall unemployment rate. Unemployment held steady at the general level of 6 percent through mid-1972. If there had been no unemployment occasioned by the reduction in the armed services of one million men and women, the unemployment rate for the year would have dropped to only 5.9 percent.

It was not minor cutbacks in defense spending that occasioned the increase in unemployment. The Administration first determined to cut back demand to fight inflation. It then determined to use defense expenditures as one of the main vehicles to accomplish this aim. In fact if cuts had been applied elsewhere instead of defense even higher unemployment might well have resulted. This is so because of the relatively large number of highly skilled and highly paid workers in defense and aerospace industries who lost jobs. The same cutbacks applied elsewhere would have resulted in more lost jobs for the same reduction in outlays. As Arthur Okun testified:

> The Administration chose deliberately and consciously to use the defense cutback as a vehicle for fiscal restraint in order to fight inflation, and worked hard to ensure that it was not offset by increased civilian expenditures. The economic malnutrition that resulted was a consequence of that overall fiscal decision and not of the defense cutback. . . .
>
> To be sure, the defense cutback has affected the composition of unemployment. If we had the same overall fiscal policy but no defense cutback surely Seattle would have lower unemployment today, but Detroit and Chicago would have higher unemployment.

There is no excuse for any unemployment occasioned by the cutback in Vietnam. The cutback was deliberate. It was carried out gradually over a period of almost four years. In these circumstances plans for the conversion of swords into plowshares and for soldiers and defense workers to make the transition to civilian employment should have been made and executed.

At the end of World War II we faced a real problem. In the two-year period from fiscal year 1945 to 1947 military spending was cut by a total of $66 billion. Almost 10 million men and women were discharged from the military services. Millions more were transferred from military to civilian work. But unemployment at the end of the transition in calendar year 1947 was a low 3.6 percent. In the three-and-a-half-year period from January 1969 to July 1972, the military forces were reduced by only 1.1 million, not 10 million. The overall annual defense budget declined by less than $3 billion, not $66 billion. But unemployment rose by more than 2 million.

The job of reconversion should have been much easier in the

1970s than in the 1940s. We did a much poorer job. But the experience of 1945–47 remains to prove that defense spending can be cut significantly without inducing unemployment, provided it is planned for.

If the Vietnam veterans had come home to a fully employed economy, industry would be standing in line to hire both them and the engineers making the transition from aerospace and military plants to productive civilian work. The high level of un-employment cannot be talked out of existence or accounted for by the change in the structure of the work force or the reduction in Vietnam spending. A deliberate policy to fight inflation by reducing demand and inducing unemployment was imposed. The solution got out of hand. It did not work.

Can We Have Full Employment and Price Stability?

What, then, is the answer to the problem of achieving at the same time a high and stable rate of employment, a high rate of growth in national output and productive capacity, and a high degree of stability in the general level of prices? Specifically, can unemployment be reduced to an interim target of 4 percent, real economic growth increased to a long-term average of 4.3 percent, and inflation limited to a range of 2 to 3 percent a year?

The answer is that it can be done. By closing the gap between low actual performance and the potential performance of the economy, we could generate more than $60 billion a year of additional growth which private citizens and governments at all levels could use to meet the nation's unmet needs.

It is not enough to assert that this can be done. One must pro-pose constructive and workable policies to bring it about. One must not only criticize the policies of the past but prescribe recommendations for the future. Here are the policies needed to reduce unemployment, increase real growth, and to do so with relatively stable prices.

Along with proper monetary policies, the full-employment

budget is the main instrument of economic policy. Prior to the modern concept of "countercyclical" budget policies, a balanced budget was the touchstone of policy in good years and bad, in times of prosperity and recession. But reducing government spending to the level of revenues in times of recession merely made the recession worse, and spending every dime taken in inflationary periods merely exacerbated the inflation. Clearly a policy of balanced budgets every year conflicted with the budget as an instrument of economic policy.

In place of the balanced-budget fiscal policy, the countercyclical fiscal ideas evolved. In times of recession, the policy was to spend, spend, spend. In times of inflation, the theory was to pile up surpluses. But a primitive and unsophisticated countercyclical policy did not work very well. Among the principle problems were these:

1. There were a great many deficits and very few surpluses.

2. There was a time lag between the moment a recession got under way, when it was recognized for what it was, and action taken through the executive and legislative branches to do something about it. Most often a big fiscal stimulus or tax cuts were put into effect after the recovery period began. Their full force was often felt at the peak of the recovery and did little more than provide excessive demand and stimulus and provoke inflation.

3. The composition of the spending stimulus was often wrong. Small expenditures for dams, highways, or weapons systems during a recession translated themselves into massive spending which could not be shut off when prosperity arrived.

For all of these reasons the countercyclical budget policy was great in theory but largely failed in execution.

The Full-Employment-Budget Concept

Out of these experiences evolved the concept of the full-employment budget. It is a far more refined version of the countercyclical policy and imposes much more rigid disciplines on fiscal policy.

The concept is relatively simple to state. Establish the level of revenues that the government would collect if the economy were functioning at relatively full employment, or at about a 4 percent unemployment level. Then limit the expenditures for that year to the revenues that would have been collected at a full-employment level. Spend that much and no more or no less. In times of recession this provides an automatic deficit that, in theory at least, should stimulate the economy. In times of prosperity it provides an automatic surplus that should help bank the fires of inflation.

That is the concept. Its greatest asset is that in times of recession it combines a deficit and fiscal stimulus with a rigid discipline over total spending.

But it has weaknesses. The economy does not function on a merely mechanical basis. There are "impetuous" forces at work as well. When a recession or an inflation gets under way the mere neutral action of piling up automatic deficits or surpluses may be insufficient to turn it around. The full-employment deficit in times of a recession actually has no net stimulus.

To offset this weakness and yet retain the discipline over total spending which the full-employment-budget concept provides, at least two refinements are necessary: Within the total of the deficit, carefully select those spending projects which produce a large number of jobs. Next, and still within the spending ceiling, choose those stimulating expenditures which are temporary in nature and which automatically phase out as recovery occurs.

As Arthur Okun put it:

> The federal budget can and will become an engine of inflation in future years if we adopt massive new permanent expenditure programs as a means of promoting recovery. . . . We must avoid action that would commit us to inappropriate and inflationary deficits when full employment is restored.

The major instruments selected by the Nixon Administration in the 1973 fiscal-year budget to stimulate the economy offended against both these principles. The major chosen instruments were an increase in defense spending and an increase in public-works and reclamation projects. Neither is temporary. Neither can be turned off or phased out quickly. Neither creates many jobs.

In the case of reclamation and public works, the money is spent in large proportion in the rural and desert areas of the country, where the unemployment is low, and avoids the urban and industrial areas, where it is especially high. Furthermore, economists agree that these are among the least efficient and most costly federal outlays.

In the case of the $299 million in long-lead-time items for a new carrier, the $942 million for the ULMS (underwater long-range missile system), the $474 million for AWACS (airborne warning and control system), and the $445 million for the B-1 bomber, which were put into the fiscal 1973 budget as stimulants, these amounts are not temporary. They set in motion ultimate outlays of $3.0 billion for the carrier, its planes, and escort ships, $30 billion for a 30-ship ULMS, $20 billion for AWACS, and a minimum of $12 billion for the B-1 bomber. They mortgage budget outlays for years into the future. Yet they were justified on the grounds that increases would stimulate the economy.

The Correct Stimulative Programs

If these are the wrong stimulative programs, what are the right ones to carry out during a recession?

We should increase the amounts and expand the coverage and time eligibility for unemployment compensation. This stimulates the economy but is phased out when recovery returns.

We can also provide public-service jobs for work in state and local governments. There is much useful work to be done, and there are many who are unemployed. A public-service-jobs program combines the two and puts idle men to work providing needed services. As the economy recovers and additional state and local public-service jobs open up through both attrition and expansion, those individuals originally paid by federal outlays can be put to work full time at state and local expense.

We could provide countercyclical aid to state and local governments. Revenues for state and local governments decline heavily during periods of recession and unemployment. This is true especially of those states which rely heavily on a progressive income tax. When unemployment exceeds some specific figure, say 4.5 percent nationally, we could provide a general-purpose federal grant to state and local governments based on population, the severity of unemployment, and the extent of the reliance on a progressive income tax. The size of the grant would increase with the severity of unemployment but would return to zero when unemployment went below 4.5 percent. The program has the merit of being both intensively job producing and temporary.

We should use temporary tax cuts as a means of fiscal stimulus. A tax cut in the nature of a $100 income-tax credit, for example, is highly stimulative and yet temporary. Most of it would be spent for immediate consumption, would provide a multiplier effect of about three times the total amount, and yet would not mortgage billions of dollars of future federal income as public-works or military-weapons spending would do.

Finally, the government should become the employer of last resort. A program to create 100,000 new jobs per month, and then to be phased out as unemployment returns to the 4.5 to 5 percent level, could greatly speed up the process of recovery.

U. S. taxpayers rightly have an aversion to increased welfare payments or a guaranteed annual income except to the aged, the blind, the lame, or those incapable of working. But there should be no aversion to providing a job for everyone who is willing and able to work.

Jobs for Those Willing and Able to Work

Here is how the proposal would work if it had been instituted in January 1972.

Then unemployment was at the 6 percent level. The forecast for real economic growth for the year was 6 percent. Since a 4.3 percent growth rate is needed merely to provide jobs for the new entrants into the labor force, the 6 percent growth rate would have reduced the existing unemployment level by about 540,000 workers, or by 6/10ths percent. As a result, unemployment at the end of the year would fall to 5.4 percent. At this rate it would take at least three years for unemployment to return to 4 percent, even with a growth rate of 6 percent a year, which is well above the long-term-trend line of 4.3 percent. Meanwhile, billions would be lost in GNP and federal revenues and in added expenditures for unemployment compensation, higher welfare costs, and added Social Security payments.

Given the same circumstances, under a federal program to provide 100,000 new productive jobs a month, full employment could be attained within the year.

At a cost per job of $500 per month, or $6,000 per year, the first year's cost would be $3.9 billion. At the end of the year there would be a real-unemployment level of 5.4 percent, 540,000 new jobs having been provided by the 6 percent growth rate. Another 1.2 million jobs provided by the government as the employer of last resort would reduce the unemployment rate to the 4 percent zone. In this way there would be full employment at the end of one year rather than three years.

In the second year, a growth rate of 6 percent would reduce real unemployment to about a 4.7 percent level. At the end of the year the government as employer of last resort would employ about 600,000. The annual cost would be $5.25 billion, up from the first year because average employment for the year would be larger even though the end-of-the-year total dropped.

By the end of the third year, unemployment would return to the 4.0 percent zone. All those employed by the government as employer of last resort would then be removed from the federal payroll. The cost in the third year would come to $1.65 billion, since 275,000 would be the average employment for the year.

The following table gives the calculations.

	Projected Unemploy- ment Rate (6% real economic growth)	Jobs Provided by 6% Growth	Jobs Provided by Government as Employer of Last Resort	Unemploy- ment Rate As a Result of Growth Rate and Govern- ment- Provided Jobs	Annual Cost
January 1, 1972	6%		0*	6%	0
January 1, 1973	5.4%	540,000	1,200,000	4%	$3,900,000,000
January 1, 1974	4.7%	1,080,000	600,000	4%	$5,250,000,000
January 1, 1975	4.0%	1,620,000	0	4%	$1,650,000,000

*At the end of the first month, 100,000 would be employed; at the end of the second month 200,000, etc. The average number of jobs provided is: first year, 650,000; second year, 875,000; third year, 275,000.

How to Pay for the Program

Over a three-year period, the average annual cost of the program would be $3.6 billion. How should this be paid for?

First of all, the cost of such a program would be offset by a major drop in the costs of unemployment compensation, welfare, and Social Security cost increases induced by the high level of unemployment. In fiscal year 1972 these were estimated at $8 billion. One could argue that the savings in those costs would be sufficient to pay for a program of the government as the employer of last resort. That is probably true, although there would probably be a time lag before the savings were realized.

But I would prefer to pay for the program by cutting other programs which create very few jobs. Placing a firm ceiling on the payments to any one farm or farmer, cutting back on the sugar subsidy, reducing the massive waste in military procurement, cutting foreign military aid, or insisting that federal spending meet rigid cost and benefit tests would save enough to more than pay for a constructive and creative job program.

Unfortunately, neither the Office of Management and Budget nor the Treasury Department has made any study of the job-producing potential of various government expenditures. To make the full-employment-budget concept work, there should be a shelf of job-inducing expenditures. These should be temporary, ready to be substituted for existing spending programs when there is a high level of unemployment. It is in this way that when there is major unemployment the big deficit that accompanies a full-employment budget can become stimulating rather than merely neutral.

One of the reasons the whopping $26-billion deficit in fiscal 1972 and the $27-billion projected deficit in fiscal 1973 provided such small relative stimulus is that they were caused in the main by a reduction in receipts rather than by a step-up in spending. In these circumstances substituting high-job-inducing temporary programs for existing low-job-inducing government programs can create stimulus where little existed before.

Because of the impetuous forces at work in the economy, such job-stimulating programs are not only desirable but also a necessity to provide an adequate stimulus to turn the economy around during a recession. In this way we can provide a stimulus while keeping within the spending discipline of the full-employment-budget concept.

Reduce Inflationary Bias

In order to provide a rate of sustained growth that is close to the economy's potential, we must also reduce inflationary bias in the economy. We should not have to make the cruel choice between growth and stable prices. To make the economy grow at a high rate without galloping inflation, there are certain general policies which should be followed. These, which have been detailed in numerous reports of the Joint Economic Committee, include the following.

1. The final money demand for goods and services should grow at a rate equal to the increase in the potential supply of them. There have been numerous times in the past, principally during the 1957–58 and 1960 recessions, when the Federal Reserve Board money managers refused to supply the economy with an adequate supply of money and helped induce and prolong the recessions.

2. The instability which plagues the economy must be reduced. This includes both the number and extent of the postwar recessions and the unnecessary severe inflation of the 1966–68 period. We need sustained growth, not a policy of feast or famine.

3. The structure of the economy must be improved if it is to grow without inflation. The government must play the largest role in this endeavor through reducing the concentration of economic power, increasing the mobility of resources, providing the climate in which the genius of competitive forces can operate, and putting its own house in order by a series of actions which would reduce prices and increase the competitive climate.

4. The growth and the productive capability of the economy must be increased by investment in both physical capital and human capital, by raising the productivity of the labor force, and by improving the mobility of resources. If we are to grow without serious inflation we must devise a long-term incomes policy which does not suffocate the competitive spirit through elaborate bureaucratic peacetime controls. If rigid bureaucratic controls are imposed permanently, we will kill the free, flexible, mobile economy that has been so successful in improving efficiency and productivity. And unless productivity continues to grow there will be no fiscal dividend, no extra federal revenues generated by economic growth, and no way to meet our most urgent needs.

We must substitute for elaborate controls—which stifle the spirit and efficiency of the economy—wage-price guidelines for the limited number of big businesses and big unions that have such concentration of economic power they can set prices and wages outside the working of competitive market forces. An incomes policy should be limited severely to this small group. Under the Phase II program, more or less the opposite took place. The Pay Board gave in to those with great market power, as in the coal and dock settlements. Meanwhile every small competitive businessman in the country was involved in an elaborate and silly system of price posting, cost determination, and mathematical productivity analysis.

A proper incomes policy of wage-price guidelines for the administered-price industries and for some special areas, such as construction and health services, where there are special problems would make it possible to do two things. First, by reducing inflationary forces it would allow the government to take more positive action in putting into effect stimulating and job-producing programs than would otherwise be the case. It thus would make full employment and economic growth easier to attain. Second, it also becomes easier for the government to crack down on the frictions and inefficiencies fostered by the actions of both private enterprise and government programs.

What the Government Can Do to Stop Inflation

Government itself can do a great deal to reduce the inflationary forces in the economy.

It should cut back on inappropriate, wasteful, and inefficient federal spending and federal programs.

A vigorous and effective antitrust policy should be pursued. Everyone gives lip service to competition. Few giant businesses actually are willing to live under it. The Anti-Trust Division of the Justice Department must make certain that a competitive climate is fostered and preserved.

A thorough attack on conglomerates and mergers is long overdue. According to the Federal Trade Commission, by 1968 the 100 largest corporations held a greater share of the manufacturing assets of the country than the 200 largest in 1950. The 200 largest manufacturing corporations in 1968 controlled a share of assets equal to that held by the 1,000 largest corporations in 1941, when the seminal study by the Temporary National Economic Committee entitled "Investigation of Concentration of Economic Power" was submitted to the Congress.

Special emphasis should be placed on promoting new technology, on basic research, on improving the education and skills of the labor force, in establishing productivity councils throughout industry, and in promoting collective-bargaining agreements which make entrance into unions simpler for the poor, minorities, women, and the less skilled.

We must pay special attention to areas of intense shortages such as those in medical-care services, where costs have risen sharper and faster than in almost any other area.

Priority must be placed on improving productivity in the "service" industries, for they now make up a much larger share of the total economy than ever before.

Tough standards must be followed in deciding what government spending programs should be undertaken. As economist Norman Ture told the Joint Economic Committee, ". . . unless every dollar of appropriations can be justified on the ground that their value productivity is greater than in other uses, the economy would be far better served by allowing appropriations to expire and/or allocating the funds to constructive tax reduction." That is precisely why the SST, the space shuttle, the Lockheed bail-out, and pork-barrel spending for dams and reclamation projects are wrong. The same funds would yield very much more if spent elsewhere.

The federal government can also reduce its stockpile of strategic metals when shortages in the private markets occur. This would reduce prices.

Through a study of productivity in the federal government by the General Accounting Office, which I initiated, we can determine where efficiency is high in the bureaucracy and where it is low, and we can attempt to apply the efficient methods universally. In the past the possibility of greatly improved productivity in government has been overlooked. A study initiated by Kermit Gordon, then head of the Budget Bureau and now president of the Brookings Institution, indicated that government agencies, like private business, were susceptible to major advances in efficiency. Why couldn't there be a speedup in the Urban Renewal program, in processing passports, in paying government workers in the billion-dollar buying program of the General Services Administration, in running government institutions, in processing Social Security or unemployment benefits, and in thousands of other government activities? Government productivity is an untapped field which could save tens of millions of dollars. That is why I initiated the new General Accounting Office study. That study is too dull to get much attention even in Congress. But it represents a highly promising—I think exciting—way for the taxpayer to get more service for the same tax dollar.

Government Action to Reduce Prices

Government actions which raise prices to the consumer at home and add to inflationary pressures include the import quotas on oil and gas and the restrictions on imports of steel and chemicals.

Fostering competition through freer trade would lower prices, fight inflation, and aid consumers. Meanwhile we should vigorously enforce the laws against dumping by foreign firms.

Breaking up international shipping cartels which discriminate against American goods would also reduce prices.

Cutting back on sugar subsidies and removing support from the coffee cartel would help the fight on inflation. Through subsidies, quotas, production payments, and other devices, the price of these basic commodities to the consumer is raised by government action.

Bringing competition into Pentagon procurement and nonmilitary government purchases would also help.

The Buy America Act, tied foreign-aid loans, and shipbuilding subsidies all raise prices, foster inflation, and reduce competition. Reforms are needed here.

Bringing more competition into the government-bond market, shifting surplus government cash from demand to time deposits, and imposing user fees for government services to relatively affluent citizens could save money, raise revenues, and reduce inflation.

Removing or reducing the frictions imposed on the competitiveness of the economy through government subsidies and actions is a fundamental requirement in the fight against inflation. It is of great importance because of the vast number of such inefficiencies and because the government itself can lead in doing something about them.

Improving consumer information plus establishing vigorous programs to protect the consumer against shoddy merchandise, misleading advertising, and outrageous charges not only are in the public interest but improve the workings of the economy.

Number-One Domestic Priority

A prerequisite to meeting many of the nation's most urgent needs is a fully employed, growing, noninflationary economy. It is a key to reordering priorities. It is also the key to Henry Wulforst, our part-time plumber, working full time again. It would provide a job for both veteran Louis Lantner and his skilled wife Karin. It means that Jules Fabre can return to work on the General Motors assembly line instead of hacking his cab at odd hours.

3 · Military Spending— A Surfeit of Excesses

In an Associated Press story the Baltimore *Evening Sun* reported that a new Navy F11F1 Grumman jet fighter shot itself down by flying into cannon shells it had fired seconds before. The paper said the accident occurred while a test pilot was testing the plane's four cannons at thirteen thousand feet above the Atlantic Ocean. It reported that the pilot fired two bursts of shells at 880 miles per hour and then flew into the shells, which pierced the windshield and knocked out the jet engine.

While this unique accident appears to defy the laws of physics, it is not unique for the Pentagon to mock the laws of fiscal responsibility.

War Down, Spending Up

At the same time that the Vietnam War was being wound down, the military budget was going up. The opposite should be the case.

How does the President justify new spending authority for national defense in fiscal year 1973 of $85.4 billion when that figure is $4 billion more than the government spent for national defense in fiscal year 1969 at the height of the Vietnam War?

At its peak the incremental cost of the Vietnam War added $26 billion to the Pentagon budget. Now the war is almost over, and the incremental costs are less than $5 billion a year. But where has the $20-plus billion gone?

Why does the Pentagon budget continue to rise even though the number of active-duty personnel in the services has dropped from 3.5 million in 1969 to less than 2.4 million today, or by almost one third?

What happened to the economies from the 215,000 slash in civilian employees at the Pentagon?

Where are the reductions from mothballing countless Navy ships—announced several times over by the Pentagon propaganda machine—and the savings from the alleged cuts in procurement?

What happened to the efficiencies gained from the new "Fly Before You Buy" policy?

Where are the savings from the "Milestone" procurement policy which preceded the "Fly Before You Buy" procurement policy?

Where have the billions gone? Where are the benefits to the long-suffering taxpayer?

Pentagon apologists say the money goes for pay raises and was eaten up by inflation. But even generous allowances for pay and price increases account for less than half the amount.

The remainder has not been returned to the civilian budget. The Pentagon usurped $10–$12 billion. It is substituting new weapons for old, poor-mouthing our relative strength compared with the Soviet Union, and claiming, as they have claimed countless times before, that we are in deadly peril if we reorder our priorities and return to a pre-Vietnam level of defense spending.

The Pentagon stole the peace dividend. It presented it to itself. But we are not stronger as a result.

Personnel Excesses

Instead, the military is surfeited by excesses. In the field of personnel alone, the statistics are a joke.

There are more three- and four-star generals and admirals in uniform now than at the height of World War II. Then there were 139 (with 12 million men and women under arms). Now there are 190 (with only about 2.5 million).

The comparison for the grades of colonel, lieutenant colonel, navy captain, and commander is even more startling. Although there are 900,000 fewer officers now than there were in 1945, there are 6,000 more officers in these four grades.

At the height of the Vietnam War, when there were 3.5 million men on active duty, there was one officer for every eight enlisted men. There was one officer or one noncommissioned officer for every two enlisted men. The ratio is even worse today, because the big cuts in manpower have been in enlisted personnel. This is called reordering priorities. Fewer enlisted men, more brass.

In its report on the 1972 military authorization bill, the Senate Armed Services Committee was highly critical of this state of affairs and alluded to yet another problem:

The Committee feels that much of this proliferation of high-ranking officers results from the assigning of military men to traditionally civilian jobs. . . . A case in point is the Defense Supply Agency, which is authorized 21 general officers. In addition, hearings with DSA revealed that while DSA's employment will have dropped by 5,355 during the last two years, the organization will have added 127 more colonels and above during the same period.

The statement concluded: "A further case can be made that DSA does not require any general officers. This continual upgrading of personnel apparently is happening throughout the entire Defense Department."

Not only are the fighting forces surfeited with this kind of manpower excess, but the same holds true with respect to civilians at the Pentagon. While the number of troops has been cut from 3.5 million to less than 2.4 million, the ratio of civilian to military personnel has gone up. That means less muscle and more fat; fewer fighting men but more bureaucrats. In 1969 there were 35 civilians working for the Pentagon for every 100 men or women on active duty. But at the end of fiscal year 1972, there were 42 civilians for every 100 active duty personnel, a rise of 20 percent.

As we pulled back from Vietnam and shortened the supply lines, the ratio of support and logistic personnel to combat troops should have gone down. Instead it went up.

Buying Excesses

The excesses are not limited to personnel alone. They are particularly scandalous in the field of Pentagon buying. As a result of the fight I made over military waste, the General Accounting Office reports to me annually on the cost of major weapon systems. In early 1972 they sent me some astounding figures. The cost overruns—the amount by which costs exceeded their estimates—were a whopping $35.2 billion on only forty-five major systems.

Just a year before, the same forty-five programs showed an overrun of $28.2 billion. Thus, in one year the overruns alone grew by $7 billion, or 25 percent. There was no letup in the spiraling costs of weapons. The overruns on only nine of the forty-five programs amounted to $15.5 billion, or 44 percent of the total. Among the nine were the biggest and most expensive weapons systems—the Safeguard ABM, the B-1 bomber, and the Minuteman missiles.

As one pundit put it, "While weapons program performance is poor and deliveries are late, costs are overrunning right on schedule." And these astronomical increases are not due to inflation. Pentagon contracts provide a generous annual allowance for that.

Former Deputy Secretary of Defense David Packard admitted that "we have a real mess on our hands," and argued that in defense procurement "we don't need more people in the act—we need fewer people. We overorganize, overman, overspend, and underaccomplish." Even such an out-and-out Pentagon supporter as Gilbert Fitzhugh, who headed the famous Blue Ribbon Defense Panel, charged that "Defense Department policies have contributed to serious cost overruns, schedule slippage, and performance weakness."

Among the reasons for the excesses was the lack of competition and the concentration of big Pentagon contracts in the hands of a very few companies. The 100 biggest defense contractors got $21.5 billion of defense prime contracts, or 72 percent of the $29.8 billion total according to the latest reports. Over half of all Pentagon prime contracts go to twenty-five companies.

Five giant contractors, Lockheed Aircraft, General Dynamics, American Telephone and Telegraph, Grumman, and General Electric, got $6.3 billion, or 21.3 percent of the total.

One reason for this appalling situation is that only 11 percent of all military-procurement awards are made through formally advertised, competitive methods. Thus, only one dollar in nine for military procurement is spent through this most accepted and efficient method used by both industry and government. While a few of the remaining contracts contain vestiges of competitive conditions, in almost 60 percent of Pentagon contracts there is no competition at all. Nineteen billion in Pentagon contracts are awarded either as follow-on contracts or on a sole-source, single-bidder basis.

One result of this system is a huge stockpile of excess and surplus supplies sold off for only a few cents on the dollar. The latest figures show that the Pentagon generated $9.7 billion a year in excess supplies, an amount more than half that spent on new-weapons procurement.

Old-Boy System

The concentration of contracts, sole-source awards, and surplus supplies results in part from the old-boy system in defense contracting. I reported in 1969 that the 100 largest military contractors employed almost 2,100 retired or former military officers of the rank of colonel or navy captain and above. Lockheed Aircraft and General Dynamics, the number-one and number-two defense contractors, had respectively 210 and 113 retired high-ranking officers on their payroll. Almost ten years before that, Senator Paul Douglas made a similar survey. In 1959 he found 721 retired high-ranking officers in the pay of the 100 biggest military contractors. In a decade the numbers had almost tripled.

As a result of these disclosures I got an amendment adopted to the Military Procurement Bill of 1969. It required the Secretary of Defense to report each year the number of high-ranking officers in the pay of the big Pentagon contractors who had been hired in the previous three years.

At the end of 1971, or almost three years from the time I revealed that 2,100 retired officers were on contractors' payrolls, the Secretary of Defense reported to Congress under the terms of my amendment that an additional 993 retired or former military officers had been signed on by the big Pentagon contractors. He also revealed under the terms of my amendment that some 108 high-ranking Pentagon civilian employees had gone to work for big Pentagon contractors. Further, 232 former civilian employees or consultants to defense contractors were hired by the Pentagon at salaries of $19,000 or more.

It was President Eisenhower in his farewell speech who warned the nation against "unwarranted influence, whether sought or unsought, by the military-industrial complex." I have carefully refrained from charging that these companies, the retired officers on their payrolls, and the procurement officials at the Pentagon are engaged in a gigantic conspiracy designed to bilk the American people or to place key members of the military-industrial complex in dictatorial positions. I have charged no general wrongdoing on the part of these groups.

As I said when I first disclosed the vast exchange between the personnel of the Pentagon and its suppliers:

We should eschew even the slightest suggestion of any conspiracy between the Pentagon and the companies who hire former employees. There is not a scintilla of evidence that it exists. But what can be said, and should properly be said, is that there is a continuing community of interest between the military on the one hand and these industries on the other. It is not a question of wrongdoing. It is a question of what can be called the "old-boy network" or the "old-school tie."

It is a dangerous and shocking situation. It makes imperative that new weapon systems receive the most critical review and that defense contracts be examined in the most microscopic detail.

But the procurement officers, who are also about-to-retire officers, tend to be influenced by how their procurement actions will affect their retirement prospects.

Duplication and Waste

Waste at the Pentagon is so excessive that the security of the United States is endangered. Military procurement is plagued by duplication and interservice rivalry. The way in which the military procures planes, tanks, ships, and guns is in such a sad state that one can look in vain for a major weapons system that cost what the military estimated it would cost, was delivered on time, and works according to its specifications.

Some weapons, like the ABM or AWACS, both of them $10–20-billion systems, are not needed at all. The same is true of a new carrier. Others, like the proposed new ULMS, are not needed now even if there is some justification for them later. A project like that to build the F-14 fighter plane at $15–20 million a copy, is an example of a gold-plated Cadillac bought to do a compact Chevy's job. Costly lemons like the Cheyenne helicopter duplicate the close-support mission of the Army's A-X and the Marine Corps's Harrier aircraft. Three planes are bought to do the job of one. The carrier-based S-3A ASW (anti–submarine-warfare) plane, at an estimated cost of $2.95 billion, is a duplication of the land-based P-3C anti-submarine plane which can do the ASW job better. The infamous Main Battle Tank, finally scrapped by the Congress, was a $1-million-a-copy lemon which was no better than its M-60 predecessor.

Waste and duplication in procurement result from these and other shortcomings. The absence of prototypes, the concurrent development and production of a weapon, the provision of single weapons for multiple missions in which none of the missions are performed well, the addition of complicated and complex avionics or black-box systems, and the failure to hold contractors' feet to the fire on cost estimates are all reasons why procurement is a mess, costs escalate, and spending is out of control.

Interservice rivalry, tradition, outmoded missions, and empire building are further reasons why the defense dollar is wasted.

Some detailed examples will show how we can get more bang for a buck and how this country can be stronger by spending and wasting less.

Obsolete Carriers

The high Navy brass continues to insist on building new attack carriers. Since the time the Washington Naval Disarmament Treaty of 1921 limited the United States to fifteen "capital ships," the Navy has pressed for fifteen "capital ships."

Until World War II the queen of the fleet was the battleship. When it became obsolete it was replaced by the carrier. Routinely, year in and year out, the Navy deploys fifteen attack carriers. Using a yardstick of a thirty-year useful life, the Navy goal is a new attack carrier every two years to replace the old ones.

But since World War II, the carrier has been a ship in search of a mission. In addition, it costs too much and is highly vulnerable.

Sensing that carriers needed a "strategic" mission to justify their survival at the end of World War II, the Navy justified their existence on the grounds that a carrier's planes could shower nuclear devastation on a potential enemy. But with the advent of land-based missiles, even this tenuous justification became entirely obsolete. The carrier has no strategic mission.

In addition, its tactical mission has been vastly limited. The job of protecting the World War II type of Marine Corps landings is largely obsolete. There have been none since the Inchon landing in Korea more than twenty years ago. Fifteen attack carriers are not needed for that job. There are only a limited number of times and places requiring offshore air support for troops already ashore. They are limited to situations where the U. S. has virtually complete air and sea superiority and where no land-based aircraft can operate. That the U. S. will intervene to carry out its treaty commitment where its ally refuses us access to its terrain is highly questionable. Before we are required to do that we should reexamine our commitments. In any case, fifteen attack carriers are not required for these limited threats.

In the absence of absolute dominance of the sea and the air, the aircraft carrier is a sitting duck for attacks from submarines, planes, and modern missiles. The sinking of an Israeli destroyer by an Egyptian PT boat with a single STYX missile, now outmoded by new missiles, is a case in point. The aircraft carrier is highly vulnerable, especially in relatively confined areas. We can shoot down intercontinental missiles traveling seventeen thousand miles an hour. It is nothing to hit a carrier steaming at forty knots. As Senator Stuart Symington remarked, with modern weapons "it is as easy to knock them out as it is to hit a bull in the butt with a bass fiddle." But the Navy argues that the loss of U. S. overseas bases justifies a fifteen-carrier fleet and the building of new attack carriers.

The Air Force denies this. In a reply to Senator Mark Hatfield's question whether the loss of overseas land bases had jeopardized the Air Force's tactical air capability, the Air Force stated that "the capability of USAF tactical air has in no sense been diminished by land base deactivations."

"There are enough land air bases in Southeast Asia and Europe," the Air Force wrote Hatfield, "to base all the tactical fighter aircraft which the Joint Chiefs of Staff estimate are required to meet a major contingency in those areas."

Excessive Carrier Costs

If no justification exists for a fifteen-attack-carrier fleet on the basis of its highly limited mission, even less justification exists if one examines costs.

A new attack carrier, its supporting fleet, and its air wing cost about $3 billion. But because the Navy insists that an attack carrier can spend no more than four months on station and must be rotated for overhaul and leave for its crew, it takes three carriers to do the job of one. The effective capital cost to put one carrier on station is therefore nearly $9 billion.

The operating costs for new attack carriers now run as high as $125 million a year. This means that another $350 to $375 million must be added annually to finance one carrier on station.

With a fifteen-carrier fleet, nine assigned to the Pacific and six to the Atlantic, the effective force on station numbers only five. Yet the estimates are that 40 percent of the Navy budget goes to the carrier fleet for capital costs and operating costs, including personnel, planes, maintenance, fuel, repair, home bases, housing ashore and the rest. It is also estimated that a carrier wing over a ten-year period costs at least $1 billion more than does a land-based air wing.

In addition to these astronomical costs for limited potential missions, virtually half the cost for an attack-carrier task force is spent for the defense of the carrier itself. Its planes, guns, escort ships, helicopters, radar sonar equipment, and Phoenix missiles are dedicated in large part to keeping the carrier afloat and viable against attacks from enemy submarines, planes, and missiles.

In justifying new carriers the Navy fails to note that to carry out its limited mission one new carrier has the firepower of two old ones. We should therefore need fewer. It is unwilling to adopt the interchange of crews and fighter pilots, methods used successfully by the submarine fleet, instead of taking the carrier off station.

This would make them more efficient. And it is unwilling to face the fact that our potential enemy, the Soviet Union, is not building a single attack carrier for its expanded fleet, because attack carriers are both too vulnerable and too costly for the expenditure of the vast resources they require.

As Senator Walter F. Mondale said during the fight he and Senator Clifford P. Case led against funding the CVA-70, "the time when we could afford the luxury of such 'eternal verities' as a fleet of fifteen carriers has long since passed. I fear our children will observe in the future that our blind adherence to fifteen attack carriers was as absurd as was our failure to recognize the demise of the horse cavalry."

$1 Billion in Claims Against the Government

Carriers are not the only Navy excesses. Take the destroyer escort (DE) program.

The destroyer escorts, along with the cruisers, destroyers, and frigates, provide protection for the carrier. Among the better-known destroyer escort procurements is that for the DE-1052s. The major mission of this class of ships is anti–submarine warfare. Through elaborate sonar and helicopter equipment, the DE-1052s are designed to protect the carrier, its escorting fleet, and other shipping against an enemy submarine menace.

In 1964 the Navy began the award of a series of contracts to three shipbuilders—Todd, Avondale, and Lockheed—for forty-six DE-1052s. The total price for the contracts: $510.2 million. The cost of the total program, including items not in the ship contract, was $1.285 billion.

All three contractors had trouble meeting their price and delivery schedules. Huge claims for their excessive costs were filed against the government. Furthermore, there were serious concurrency problems. The sonar, helicopter, and other systems to be provided by other contractors adversely affected the ship's performance.

Because of Navy accounting practices, the way the sonar and helicopter were budgeted and the issue of how much should be paid on the claims, it is difficult to estimate either the final cost or the size of the overrun. Here are some of the problems and issues brought out in the hearings I chaired on the DE-1052 program:

The added claims filed by the shipbuilders were for $300 million, or 60 percent of their total contract price. The Todd claim of $114.3 million was settled for $96.5 million. This effected an increase in the Todd contract of 64 percent. The General Accounting Office, at my request, investigated the claim. Its report criticized the Navy for failing to substantiate the claim before settling it.

The admiral in charge of the program agreed to a settlement with the Avondale builders, but the claim is still pending. The chief Navy claims officer charged publicly that the admiral settled it without having in hand a legal memorandum of entitlement substantiating the items and amounts. That stopped payment. The third claim by Lockheed is also pending.

Among other claims pending is one for Litton Industries alone for $450 million. Whether it is justified or not, Litton claims it will go bankrupt if it does not get the funds. The total claims now amount to at least $1 billion.

Technical Problems Too

Claims were not the only problem.

The sonar system, called the SQS-26, was delayed because of technical problems. The current cost estimate is $119.6 million, or $25 million more than the $95.7-million planning cost.

The unmanned drone helicopter, called DASH, was a colossal failure. Of 750 built, 411 crashed in tests before the Navy canceled the program. $275 million was spent on DASH.

In a fiscal sleight of hand, two cost items which totaled $100 million were transferred out of the DE-1052 program although they were costs of that program.

The Navy's official cost estimate is now $1.4 billion. But this vastly underestimates the total. The claims, the sonar, the helicopter, a contingency fund of $192 million, and the $100 million transferred out of the DE-1052 budget were not counted. The overrun is therefore more than $500 million, not $100 million. This does not include the amount of the pending settlements or the cost of a new helicopter to replace DASH.

The first ship delivered under the program, the U.S.S. *Knox*, was delivered twenty months late, and the others were still undelivered at the beginning of 1972.

The DE-1052 is a classic example of military waste and mismanagement. There were not only large cost overruns, serious schedule delays, and questionable practices in settling the claims. There were also serious technical questions.

When the *Knox* was delivered to the Navy, Admiral John D. Bulkeley, president of the Navy's Board of Inspection and Survey, conducted five days of acceptance trials and inspections of the ship. In a three-page report listing the defects in the ship, he concluded: "The Board finds that there are serious deficiencies in *Knox* that make her unacceptable for unrestricted fleet service in that these deficiencies significantly degrade her ability to carry out all of her assigned wartime mission and tasks."

Defects on Delivery

Among the deficiencies listed were:

Most of the *Knox's* operations and electronic installations are unsatisfactory. The height-finding radar does not acquire targets at design ranges or heights and, at times, not at all.

The IFF (friend-or-foe indicator) is inoperative.

Approximately 50 percent of the high-frequency and ultra-high-frequency transmitting systems are significantly below standards in output and strength.

The ECM (electrochemical-machining) equipment is marginal on two bands, out of a total of nine bands. There is a thirty-degree blind spot aft in coverage.

There is a significant radio frequency interference problem on the mast. The ECM antennas are located in a high-radio-frequency environment-caused by the two radar and UHF transmitting antennas. During the trial the high-radio-frequency environment burned out the crystals in one of the operative tuners.

The sonar interferes with the operation of the fathometer.

The underwater telephone is blanked out by the sonar when transmitting.

The sonar has excessive self-noise levels. The cause is presently unknown.

There is also pitting on the exterior of the sonar dome which could lead to earlier failure of the dome. This condition will probably occur on follow-on ships also. The solution to this problem is presently not known.

The fin stabilizer crosshead (tiller) locking pin (lug) broke during the trials, being inadequate in strength and other factors. There is also a deflection of the power ram assembly foundations which must be resolved or it will fail.

The ASROC loader is not entirely satisfactory, but probably can be fixed. It is the best seen by the Board thus far.

There is no variable-depth sonar installed, as called for by the ship's characteristics.

There is a hanger and landing deck for a DASH installation. This same installation is being built into oncoming ships at this yard and is done in varying degrees already in the *Whipple,* the *Gray,* and the *Roark* (DE-1062, DE-1054, and DE-1053). A substitute for DASH has not been determined.

There is no vertical replenishment capability for the ship, since the DASH helo deck is not certified and also there is a large whip antenna at the landing deck area creating a major interference to any helo operations.

The underway replenishment capability is very limited. The two RAS (replenishment-at-sea) kingposts are too heavy (860 pounds) to be portable, and the present intent is to stow the kingposts in a folded position at the RAS stations. This places a seventeen-foot obstruction between the ASROC launchers and mount 51 forward and in the middle of the DASH helo deck aft.

The probe refueling installation appears satisfactory, but the arrangement for conventional ROBB fueling is unsatisfactory.

The task lights are mounted on a sponsor on the mast atop the MACK on the starboard quarter. Any intelligence from these lights, to indicate that the *Knox* is not able to maneuver to ships crossing ahead, being engaged in replenishment or otherwise, is lost through an arc forward from about 30 to 270 degrees (relative). In addition, the radar antenna is in front of the task lights and results in a flashing effect.

There is also a quantity of missing electronic equipment. Certain change orders are pending which will rearrange electronic equipment and antennas. Both of these factors will undoubtedly have an impact on the RF (radio frequency) envelope of the ship. Thus, this trial could not evaluate the total electronic suit as called for in the ship's characteristics. As a matter of fact, some items considered less significant during this trial could very easily become major as the result of completion of the installation and/or rearrangement of antennas. This was vividly demonstrated in the case of the ECM antennas which were recently relocated from the MACK to the mast and resulted in the RF interference problem which the Board noted. Unless the Board can observe a complete electronic installation with all systems operating at "full power," so to speak, the major and minor electronic deficiencies cannot be fully documented. In this day of "electronic sophistication," it would seem that the goal of a complete electronic installation should be made attainable.

In addition to correction of the deficiencies listed, an early resolution of the requirements for helo operations and installation of the variable depth sonar is required to fulfill the desired ship's characteristics.

Is this ship in this shape worth millions of your tax money? The DE-1052 is not unique. Late delivery, cost overruns, and technical failures are the rule, not the exception, in Army, Navy, and Air Force procurement. Its saving grace, unlike many weapons systems, is that with a new helicopter it may actually be able to perform its mission. And the ASW mission is one that actually should be performed.

The F-14 Navy Fighter Plane Lemon

The F-14 Navy fighter plane is another example of excessive costs, huge overruns, delays, and technical imperfections.

When Congress killed the ill-fated F-111, the Navy insisted on building a multimission fighter plane in its place. Therein lies its problem. The F-14 has too many missions for it to carry out any one of them well. It is scheduled to be the Navy's new chief tactical fighter plane. It is designed also for fleet air defense—to interdict Russian bombers, a threat which does not seriously exist, and to interdict Soviet missiles. It does none of these missions well and costs far too much. In simple terms, it is a lemon.

The most costly and sophisticated fighter plane ever built, its original cost estimate was $11.5 million a copy. After charges by me and other Senators that costs were over $16 million each, the Navy admitted they had grown to $12.7 million. But that figure failed to include $1.3 billion in research and development costs and a projected $367-million initial loss projected by Grumman Aircraft, its manufacturer.

As time unfolded, costs rose again. There were further delays, an $800,000 overrun per plane on its two engines, and a 65 percent overrun on the F-14's avionics when costs rose from $2.6 to $4.3 million per plane. At that point I confidently predicted that the F-14 buy of 301 planes would exceed $20 million per copy. That is now fact.

It is an absolutely outrageous price. The Russian MIG-21, which the F-14 would barely excel even if the bugs are removed, costs $1 million per plane. The French Mirage 5, flown by the Israelis, costs $1.5 million each. The F-4 Phantom jet, the F-14's predecessor, cost $2.5 million a copy in its original version, and even the F-4J with the addition of sophisticated avionics is produced at $4 million each.

The F-14 also carries six Phoenix missiles which cost $400,000 each, or a total of $2.4 million.

Here are some of the ironies about the F-14:

Its performance is no better than an improved model of the F-4 Phantom.

The successor to the MIG-21, the MIG-23, will no doubt exceed the F-14's performance.

Because of its small wing area, the F-14 has less hard-turn capability than a modified F-4 or the MIG-21.

Without the B engine, now dropped because of the high costs, the F-14's acceleration potential is greatly reduced. With the addition of leading edge slats, the F-4 Phantom would be able to outturn, outaccelerate, and outmaneuver the F-14A. It is an inferior fighter.

But the F-14's ability to perform its interdiction mission is questionable as well. Its six Phoenix missiles might be effective in protecting the carrier against an incoming bomber attack. But no one in his right mind believes that if the Russians decide to launch a nuclear war against the United States, they will send their over-age bombers or any new bombers they develop against the Navy's carrier fleet. That the Russians could use heavy bombers against U. S. carriers without starting a nuclear war is also highly questionable. More likely a carrier and other ships in the fleet would be attacked by missiles—showers of them from the new Russian cruise missile ships. The F-14 and its Phoenix missile might conceivably stop one or two incoming weapons, but it is incapable of protecting the carrier against a major missile attack.

If the F-14 is required to engage enemy fighters, it must drop its six Phoenix missiles in order to gain maneuverability. If it fails to use its Phoenix missiles, at the present time the F-14 is too heavy to land on the carrier with a full Phoenix load. Consequently the F-14 may have to dump missiles valued at $2.4 million in order to perform its routine missions as a carrier-based fighter plane. How do you like having $2.4 million of your tax money dropped in the ocean every time there is a rough sea? The cost of the missiles alone equals or exceeds that of the MIG-21 fighter, the French Mirage, or the original version of the F-4 Phantom which it is designed to replace.

The F-14 procurement illustrates why the United States is less secure while spending more. We need a new fighter plane. But we need a light, fast, maneuverable, simple, inexpensive plane. Buying the F-14 means we get fewer planes and less defense for billions more. At least five F-4 Phantoms in their most sophisticated mode could be bought for every one F-14.

As Forbes Mann, president of Ling-Temco-Vaught Aerospace Corporation, said in a speech before the American Ordnance Association in Fort Worth:

A . . . valid criticism of the aerospace industry might be that it has acquired the syndrome of incorporating the most advanced technology available into almost everything it builds. As a result, the unit cost of new aerospace products has consistently increased by a factor of four every ten years. This is true whether the product is commercial airliners, military fighters or space missions. One can show that in the case of a fixed defense budget, if this trend persists, we are only sixty-two years from the day when our Navy and Air Force will each consist of a single airplane.

Not only do we get fewer planes for more money, but we get an inferior final product. The F-14 is incapable of performing its fighter mission efficiently because it is also designed for interdiction. But it cannot interdict if it must first dump its missiles so that it can perform its fighter mission.

Its ultimate irony is that its basic mission includes the defense of the carrier which is now obsolete except for limited uses. We are asked to spend billions on the F-14 in order to protect the carrier, and billions on new attack carriers to carry the F-14.

The C-5A Turkey

The fat and waste found in the carrier, F-14, and DE-1052 programs are duplicated a hundredfold in other Pentagon policies and procurement practices. Consider, for example, the C-5A cargo plane scandal, a classic tale of waste and cover-up.

Originally the Air Force estimated that forty C-5A's were needed to carry the outsized equipment of an armored division during the first two weeks of a military crisis. Because of the estimated price of $28 million a copy, the Air Force argued that additional planes would be cost-effective and should be purchased to carry general cargo as well. Instead of 40 C-5A's, 120 were ordered.

But the costs rose by $2 billion, from $3.4 billion to $5.4 billion. The price per copy went up from $28 million to almost $60 million. Boeing's commercial 747, a plane which is essentially the same size with the same speed requirements as the C-5A, costs only $23 million each. As costs went up, the performance of the C-5A declined. Landing gears collapsed. Motors fell off. Wings cracked. Dozens of serious defects were detailed by the General Accounting Office study in March 1972.

But there is now also vast unused cargo-carrying capacity in the Air Force. New planes will remain idle. While commercial planes are used ten to twelve hours a day, and some use their cargo planes as much as fourteen hours a day the year round, the Air Force plans call for using the C-5A's on the average of only four hours a day.

The time to stop the C-5A program is now.

Reserve and Guard Forces Not Ready

Here is another example of Pentagon profligacy.

We have a National Guard and reserve units of the individual services whose job it is to be ready, in the case of an emergency, to augment the regular forces. We spend $4 billion a year to provide for a million men and women in the Army and Air National Guard, and for the Army, Naval, Marine Corps and Air Force Reserves. But these forces, whose purpose is to be ready during an emergency, were essentially not used in the recent emergency, the Vietnam War.

This is what the Senate Appropriations Committee said on this matter:

The limited use of National Guard and Reserve Forces to meet the manpower requirements of the conflict in Southeast Asia is a matter of great concern to the Committee. During fiscal years 1966 through 1968, the strength of our Active Forces was increased from 2,535,000 to 3,547,000, an addition of over a million. However, during this period only 36,972 National Guard and Reserve Forces personnel were called to active duty involuntarily.

We could save $4 billion by doing either of two things. If the National Guard and the reserve are not ready for an emergency, they should be disbanded. They certainly are not needed for ceremonial purposes, at these costs. If they are ready for an emergency, then the $4 billion could properly be saved from our regular forces. In either case, we could save money either by making certain these forces are ready to fight or by disbanding them if they are to continue on the basis that they are not to be used in an emergency.

Why a New Manned Bomber?

There are a series of other weapons which should be challenged and which are highly vulnerable to criticism.

The B-1 bomber is now in the research and development stage. But the basic question is, Why do we need a new manned bomber, not to be available until the late 1970s, in an age of sophisticated missiles? What possible reason is there for us to be building a new fleet of bombers at a minimum cost of $12 billion? The B-1 cannot be justified by its mission to gravity-bomb enemy cities or targets by penetrating their airspace. Many highly qualified experts believe that the B-52 bomber with standoff weapons can adequately perform the same bombing mission. In addition, we should remember that the Soviets have a modern air defense system. To spend billions on a new manned bomber designed to penetrate enemy airspace is wasteful by definition.

Why Billions for Bomber Defense?

AWACS is an airborne warning and control system designed to give early warning against a Russian intercontinental bomber attack. There are several reasons to question spending untold billions on the system.

In the first place, the Russians do not pose an intercontinental-bomber threat. The Russians have from 175 to 195 outmoded heavy bombers which, at best, could reach the United States but could not return. They are building no new long-range bombers. And 50 of the 175 to 195 are Bisons which are configured for tankers. In addition, we have spent billions already on the SAGE (semi-automatic ground environment), DEW (distant early-warning) line and Nike-Hercules systems which in the past have been touted as 100 percent effective against a bomber attack.

Thus the Air Force is proposing to spend billions for an early-warning bomber system when neither the Russians nor the Chinese pose a long-range bomber threat. In fact, the Chinese do not even have outdated long-range bombers. At best, they have a medium-range 1,600-mile plane which poses no threat to us.

We refused to build a thick defense against Russian missiles when we limited our ABM system to a few Minuteman sites. Isn't it absurd to spend $20 billion to erect yet another defensive system against outdated Russian bombers when we are not building a thick defense against far more destructive Russian missiles?

Unable to justify AWACS on the ground that it is needed as a bomber defense, the military is now trying to justify it by saying that it may have some tactical usefulness. This system has every appearance of being a major boondoggle.

Why Three Close-Support Aircraft?

There is now major controversy among the three services over the close-support aircraft. The Army is pressing for the Cheyenne helicopter. Due to serious technical troubles, the Cheyenne had its production contract canceled in 1969, but, like Old Man River, it keeps rolling along, and has now been revived by the Army. Meanwhile the Air Force is developing the A-X close-support plane and is also building several prototypes, and the Marine Corps has ordered the Harrier, a British-built plane, for use as a close-support aircraft.

Here is duplication at its worst. It is the kind of interservice rivalry supposedly done away with when the Defense Department was formed. But in the close-support program there are at least five and perhaps as many as seven different planes or prototypes competing against each other.

In the interest of the defense of the United States, it is time the Pentagon made a decision.

Duplication in Anti–Submarine-Warfare Weapons

The same problem of waste and duplication is presented by the anti-submarine-warfare issue. An ASW program is needed.

But the military is unable to decide which system is most effective and which system to use. Instead it is pursuing a series of contradictory actions which are excessively costly. The components of the present overlapping program and the present estimated costs include:

Weapon	Cost in Billions
DLGN-38 (guided-missile frigate)	$5.49
P-3C (land-based ASW and patrol plane)	2.61
S-3A (carrier-based ASW plane)	2.95
Mark 48 Torpedo (anti-sub and shipping torpedo)	3.78
SSN-688 (hunter-killer sub)	4.28
DD-963 (destroyer)	4.18
Total:	$23.29

The ASW program is out of control. The military is merely building everything it can think of as an anti-sub weapon. There is no reason to build both frigates and destroyers, to build land-based and carrier-based planes, to build hunter-killer subs as well, and to sink vast sums into the Mark-48 torpedo, which is now running four years late and is very expensive.

Someone has to bang some heads together and bring order out of chaos in this field.

Too Many Bases

Why do we need over four hundred major and some three thousand minor bases scattered in some thirty-one countries around the world? The need for these bases, many of them redundant but held since World War II, should be reviewed.

Why, a quarter of a century after World War II, should the United States be providing over 300,000 troops and $14 billion a year to the NATO alliance? Our European allies have a larger population than we do. They are now as wealthy as we are. They had to shoulder none of the costs of the Asian war. Yet we continue with this tremendous outlay of military expenditures for the defense of Europe.

We should reduce our forces in NATO by half. We should continue to provide the nuclear umbrella for the defense of Europe, but the Europeans should provide most of the manpower. It is time to Europeanize NATO as it is time to Vietnamize the Asian war. If the Europeans are unwilling to defend themselves against a Russian attack in the center of Europe, then there is no reason why we should bear the major share of that burden.

Cut Waste, Spend Only for Needed Weapons

If the military were not squandering such vast sums on the B-1 bomber, an unneeded AWACS program, duplicate close-air-support weapons, the gold-plated F-14 fighter-plane program, as well as the vast duplication in the ASW program, we could easily support the new weapons we need. We could also save billions for the taxpayer. We must soon end the all-this-and-heaven-too military-weapons policy in order that we can produce those weapons which we need most and which may be vital to our security, in line with the agreement reached at the Strategic Arms Limitation Talks (SALT).

For our future security, the following systems in my view should be funded in the research and development stage so that they can go into production if the need for them develops.

We need to continue with the ULMS, or underwater long-range missile system, in research and development, but must not proceed with a crash program. Laser research should continue. We should move forward with the submarine-launched Poseidon missile program even as we put a stop to the B-1 bomber.

We need to continue with an advance strategic warning and detection system—not AWACS, but infrared research and satellite-detection techniques. We need a major improvement in our communications system not so much in the mere technical relay of information as in the ability to act upon information when it is received. The *Pueblo* incident, where twenty-four hours passed before the military could even decide what to do—only to find that it was then too late—is typical of the present defense system in which highly sophisticated and technical systems are too complex for use.

All of these could be funded from a much reduced military budget if we were not wasting our resources on a series of overlapping programs, cost overruns, faulty procurement, and unneeded weapons.

Real Strength Based on Military–Civilian Balance

By reforming procurement, by doing away with unneeded and overlapping weapons, we could make great savings in the defense budget without endangering our security. As real security is based on a balance between military and domestic needs, and between the strength of our weapons and the strength of our economy, we would in fact enhance our overall security. If we persist in the present military excesses, we will weaken this country rather than strengthen it.

We should reduce our military expenditures rather than increase them as our military needs in Asia decrease. The charge of "neo-isolationism" hurled at those who advocate reform is badly misplaced. In fact, if the military fails to reform, it may so endanger its own credibility as to bring about the very neo-isolationism it claims to oppose. Instead of hurling epithets at those who would reform the system, those who really want us to remain strong and free should urge the Pentagon to provide this country with a leaner, stronger and far less costly and more efficient military force.

4 · Foreign Aid—
Perversion of Intent

The bundle of morning mail arrived in Suite 2311 of the New Senate Office Building. Among the five hundred or more daily messages were the usual proportion from servicemen seeking help, veterans inquiring about their rights, applications for the service academies, lobbyist–inspired mail, and crank letters typed in both red and blue ink and with messages in ornate handwriting on the margins.

One letter that day caught my eye. It was from a man named Charles Pettis, who was the project engineer on the Tarapoto–Rio Vieva highway project in Peru. The project was financed by the U.S. Agency for International Development (AID) and the Export-Import Bank. The American firm of Brown and Root Overseas, Inc., was the consultant to the project, and Morrison-Knudsen, Inc., was building it.

Pettis' charges of misappropriation of funds, deficient design, lack of proper authority for the work, and inexperienced personnel were shocking and serious.

I followed my normal custom on receiving serious charges which appear to be made by responsible persons. I asked the General Accounting Office, the fiscal watchdog for Congress, to investigate them in detail. These were the results:

Mr. Pettis alleged that "the consultant's [Brown and Root Overseas, Inc.] design for the Tarapoto road was deficient because, among other things, no core borings had been made to determine subsurface conditions . . ." The GAO confirmed this.

Pettis alleged that "the consultant's design had not called for proper placement of drainage pipes under the roadway." The GAO confirmed this.

Pettis alleged that "the consultant's regional engineer had ordered the contractor [Morrison-Knudsen, Inc.] to perform work totaling almost $1 million without having authority to do so from the Government of Peru or the U.S. Mission." The GAO confirmed this.

Pettis alleged that "during the early stages of the project, the contractor did not have employees experienced in road construction . . ." The GAO confirmed this.

Pettis alleged that "during the early stages of the project, the contractor did not have . . . proper construction equipment." The GAO confirmed this.

Pettis alleged that "a fellow consultant employee had improperly used contract funds derived from food payments for personal expenses and had charged the Peru contract for material and labor used to construct a private house for himself." The GAO confirmed this.

Pettis alleged that "the consultant changed its position [after meeting with the contractor] and authorized payment to the contractor for slide removal" which would have added $2.2 million to the cost of the project without the approval of Peru or AID. The GAO confirmed this.

After confirming Mr. Pettis' charges, the GAO attacked the lack of supervision by AID and the Export-Import Bank. The GAO report stated: "The U.S. Mission in Peru and AID/Washington were aware of many of the project's problems by early 1967 but did not take substantive action until the end of 1968."

What happened to Mr. Pettis? He was sacked! Instead of correcting the problem, they fired the man who blew the whistle. Unfortunately, in both government and big industry, this is par for the course.

Here was waste, corruption, and mismanagement Worse, it was a perversion of the original intent of the AID program.

President Truman's Intent

In Point Four of his inaugural address after his astonishing upset victory of 1948, President Truman said this:

We must embark on a bold new program for making the benefits of our scientific advances and industrial progress available for the improvement and growth of underdeveloped areas. . . .

Our aim should be to help the free people of the world, through their own efforts, to produce more food, more clothing, more materials for housing, and more mechanical power to lighten their burdens. . . .

This should be a cooperative enterprise in which all nations work together through the United Nations and its specialized agencies whenever practicable. It must be a worldwide effort for the achievement of peace, plenty, and freedom.

President Truman's charge to the American people received a warmhearted and generous response. In addition to more than $15 billion in immediate postwar relief, the American people subscribed $12.5 billion in Marshall Plan aid and at least $80 billion more in economic aid in the following two decades.

Now, almost twenty-five years after it began, the foreign-aid program is the most disliked major program of the federal government.

It is not opposed only by those who hold parochial or xenophobic views. The most thoughtful, generous, and compassionate men in the United States Senate—men like Mike Mansfield, Frank Church, Mark Hatfield and J. William Fulbright—vote against it. It engenders more Congressional mail in opposition than any other legislative issue. Year in and year out, the mail runs at least seven or eight to one against it. Not all of this mail is from organized anti–foreign-aid groups. It mirrors public opinion.

In my latest poll of my constituents, out of some eighteen thousand replies a whopping 81.6 percent said foreign aid should be cut. Only 2 percent favored increasing it. The remaining 16.4

percent favored holding it at existing levels. This result was not due to indiscriminate opposition to all government spending. Even during the high-tax, budget-crunch, and $40-billion-deficit period of 1972, this same cross section did not oppose spending for health, housing, education, Social Security, veterans, and public works.

Boos for Foreign Aid

Year in and year out, foreign aid gets more boos than any other program.

The political pundits give a number of reasons why this is so. It is claimed that foreign aid has no domestic constituency, which is not true. Its unpopularity is attributed to high local taxes, a natural selfishness, neo-isolationism, or political and international stupidity. While there is considerable truth in some of these assumptions, the big disenchantment stems mainly, in my view, from a perversion of the program's intent.

Its main thrust is now a corruption of the idealism by which the American people supported it so magnificently for so long with their faith and their checkbooks. Taken in its totality, the program is *not* now aimed at achieving peace. For every two dollars spent on economic aid, three support military aid.

President Truman's call to help the free peoples of the world to produce more food, more clothing and more housing is not the dominant purpose of the small proportion of it which goes to economic aid. Only about one out of every three dollars of economic aid goes for these purposes. The bulk of economic aid, already overshadowed by military support, is spent for the big projects—dams, highways, power plants, and mining endeavors. It can be said without fear of contradiction that the trickle-down theory now dominates the foreign-aid program, and that the highway lobby has followed it to the ends of the earth.

Foreign aid has fallen on evil days for another reason. It is not the "cooperative enterprise" which President Truman called for, in which all nations work together through the United Nations and its specialized agencies. Many programs are funneled through the UN or other multinational groups, *but,* in program after program twenty-five years after the end of World War II, the United States provides an excessive proportion of the funds—40, 50, 60, and even 70 percent—to the international agencies. These ratios, justified perhaps when the world was recovering from the ravages of war, are unjustified now that the free nations of Western Europe are economically as strong as the United States. These nations now shoulder a smaller proportion of the cost of peace and security in the world than their wealth and population should provide.

The foreign-aid program is opposed because many of its former champions believe that the great purposes for which it was designed have been betrayed. Its goals and priorities have changed, and the program can be saved only through restoration, redemption, and reform.

Bill of Particulars

Here is the bill of particulars why the program must be changed.

Because of excessive reliance on military aid, it is highly questionable whether foreign aid is now a "worldwide effort for the achievement of peace," as President Truman decreed.

Foreign aid was in enough trouble before it alienated its traditional supporters. It has always been one of the most controversial issues facing the Congress. Some believe that almost all economic aid is wasteful. Others oppose siphoning aid through the international organizations. But now those who supported a variety of forms of economic assistance have come to believe that the vast expenditures for military aid are excessive, promote war and fratricidal conflict, and are designed to create trouble in an already troubled world. In short, they believe, and I heartily concur in this point, that most of our military aid does little but create mischief around the world. That is why it is now beleaguered from both right and left.

One of the reasons the foreign-aid program has grown so large and has survived for so long is that the military-aid billions are obscured in the budget. They are scattered throughout numerous budget accounts and hidden deep in the inner recesses of the federal balance sheet. The money is shoveled out the back door.

Because of the paucity of information on just how much we do spend for military aid, I chaired a series of hearings by the Joint Economic Committee whose purpose merely was to determine the facts. Throughout most of 1970 Dick Kaufman, a very sharp young lawyer investigating the economic issues in military assistance, helped to prepare me for those early 1971 hearings.

I was interested in military assistance for two reasons: (1) President Nixon's State of the World message and other Presidential statements relating to the Nixon Doctrine had clear implications of a greater role for military aid in the conduct of our foreign and military policies, and (2) a study of budgetary information, together with data on surplus and excess military property, raised a number of questions about the actual level of military aid and the recent trends.

For example, under "National Defense" in the budget document a line item for "military assistance" showed only $685 million for actual outlays in fiscal year 1969 and an estimated $545 million for fiscal year 1970. This was ridiculous. I knew that military aid to South Vietnam alone exceeded this amount and that several hundred million dollars' worth of military property was being disposed of each year to foreign governments under the surplus-property program. I also knew that part of the foreign-aid program administered under the State Department was being used for military purposes. But how much was concealed? A few hundred million? A billion? Only God seemed to know, and he wasn't testifying.

A series of informal discussions were then held with persons in the State Department, in the Pentagon, and outside government. From these I found that the military-assistance program had been deliberately fragmented into several parts. This was partly the byproduct of our stepped-up involvement in the Vietnam War, partly because several programs such as Food for Peace had previously been diverted for military-aid purposes, partly because administration of the program was segmented and in a state of near chaos, and primarily, I am sure, to keep the Congress, the press, and the public in the dark.

I read the transcripts of the hearings before the Committees on foreign relations, armed services, and appropriations. I studied the budget document, and I began to get a picture of the full extent of military aid in its various forms. The amount really stunned me. No wonder Administrations had broken the aid package apart. They had plenty, and I mean plenty, to hide.

At this point I called on the General Accounting Office for help in ferreting out the numbers. Dick Kaufman literally drew GAO a picture of how the military-aid program worked, indicating which pieces were being handled by which agencies. He gave them his best estimates of what had been spent in the most recent fiscal year for each component and suggested that a number of tables be made up showing the official figures following GAO's investigations. Needless to say, Kaufman's estimates for 1969 of total military-aid spending indicated a level eight to ten times the official figures contained in the budget document.

Those meetings in the fall of 1970 with GAO led to another step. I began getting in touch with former high officials of the government who had experience in the military-aid program. Several, including Chester Bowles and Nicholas Katzenbach, gave the straight and shocking story. But even these brilliant men, who had been our principal officials in charge of these programs, were startled by the size of our military giveaways.

We found that foreign military aid is pervasive, omnipresent, and ubiquitous. It is found in virtually every place and everywhere. The estimated totals involved in the various programs are staggering.

No One Knows How Much We Spend

No one knew the total figures. The administrative branch should know. But its witness, Deputy Assistant Secretary of Defense Armistead I. Selden, and his entourage of generals were unable to provide an accurate total. As the committee and the press watched in amazement, he and his associates first gave one figure, then gave another, qualified the numbers again, and finally gave up the attempt. The spectacle of those in charge of military aid unable to tell us how much we spend in military aid was appalling.

The State Department witness, Undersecretary John N. Irwin II, was somewhat more precise, but his figures were very incomplete. The best estimates were made by Senator J. William Fulbright and Comptroller General Elmer Staats. Yet they are representatives of the legislative branch, which should at least be able to rely on the administrators for accurate figures.

Senator Fulbright, the first witness, estimated the magnitude of the outflow of military equipment, assistance, and sales at $7 billion a year. Exclusive of military sales, his estimate was $5.1 billion. In fiscal year 1971 the military-assistance portion (MAP) of grant foreign aid was $775 million. Supporting assistance totaled $570 million. The special credit for Israel came to $500 million. These funds are found in the foreign-aid budget. Support of international military headquarters cost $57 million. American military assistance groups and missions in some fifty countries abroad cost $167 million. Permanent military construction overseas was $190 million. Military-grant aid in the military budget, which goes by the name "Military Assistance Service Funded" because it is appropriated in the budgets of the individual military services, came to $2.3 billion. Economic assistance in the military budget was $117 million, and the acquisition value of excess defense articles donated under the grant MAP program came to $502 million. That is the makeup of the grand total of $5.1 billion.

Senator Fulbright also noted that foreign military sales totaled $1.8 billion, of which $1.2 billion was for cash, $235 was on credit from the Department of Defense, and another $416 million was provided through commercial sources. The actual cost of the sales items is the subsidy provided for the credit sales plus the administrative expenses.

The Comptroller General's Estimates

The Comptroller General of the United States, Elmer Staats, appeared next. He estimated the total at $6.25 billion. Exclusive of military sales, it came to $4 billion. The differences between the Comptroller General's and Senator Fulbright's figures are reconcilable and can be accounted for by differences in definitions.

Senator Fulbright included in his total some $200 million in military construction overseas, $500 million in excess defense articles granted to foreign nations under the grant MAP program, $117 million in economic assistance funneled through the Defense Department, and $50 million in military assistance hidden away in the military budget, not found in the Comptroller General's estimates.

On the other hand, Mr. Staats pointed out that a good many economic advantages to the recipient country from military aid are difficult if not impossible to calculate and are not included in his figures. They are nevertheless a part of the outflow of military equipment and support from the United States. They include such items as the subsidy involved in providing aid at official rather than actual exchange rates, in the labor provided by American forces to build roads, bridges, and other facilities abroad, and the direct transfers of weapons and equipment from the Department of Defense to foreign forces in the field.

In the period 1965 to 1970, for example, U. S. military purchases of Vietnamese piasters at official rates amounted to almost $1.5 billion. The overvaluation when computed as a subsidy to the Vietnamese economy was $680 million. In 1970 alone it was almost $200 million.

The Department of Defense reported that about five thousand American troops were used to build, rebuild, and maintain roads, bridges, and railroads in Vietnam. About 910 miles of roads and bridges were completed.

Neither the piaster subsidy nor the work-in-kind figures were included in Senator Fulbright's or the Comptroller General's total estimate. In addition, the Comptroller General included $90 million in Food for Peace funds used for military purposes, and $24 million in ship loans not included in Senator Fulbright's total.

The Pentagon Could Not Provide a Total

The unrevealed magnitude of military aid due to its diffuse and fractionalized nature was at least confirmed by the testimony of Secretary Selden, even though he was at a loss as to its total. The man in the Department of Defense in charge of military aid and the generals who accompanied him repeatedly gave divergent and conflicting total amounts for foreign military aid. They did not know how much we send abroad each year. At one point, after they took pencil and paper in hand, a figure of $4.8 billion was confidently announced as the grand total. Subsequently, Mr. Selden submitted figures for fiscal year 1971. This total came to $6.3 billion, but did not include some items in Senator Fulbright's calculations. Excluding export sales, his total was about $4 billion.

When we asked the State Department for its figures, Undersecretary Irwin corroborated many of the general estimates developed by the other three witnesses. His total was $6.4 billion for all international security assistance and about $4 billion when military sales were excluded.

By sifting and sorting the totals, we estimated that the cost of all foreign military aid was at least $6.25–7 billion a year, and that when military sales were excluded the total was $4–5 billion.

But one must add to these amounts other directly identifiable figures. One of them was uncovered during hearings I chaired on the 1972 Foreign Aid Appropriations Bill. We sensed that not all the military-aid figures were provided. As a result I wrote to the Defense Department requesting the dollar values of military assistance not included in the Foreign Assistance Act or under Military Assistance Service Funded (MASF). In a late and reluctant reply the deputy for the comptroller of the Pentagon wrote that with one exception

> there was and is no provision of law which requires that a value be assigned to property made available to MASF recipient countries when such property is excess to the needs of the United States Armed Forces, and consequently no records have been maintained in the headquarters of the Department of Defense on the basis of the value of such property . . .

"Being interpreted," this means that equipment paid for with taxpayers' money was given away and no records were kept. They nevertheless supplied me with a figure for transfers of unaccounted-for real and personal property to South Vietnam, Thailand, Laos, and Republic of Korea forces in Southeast Asia. The amounts: $321 million in fiscal year 1971 and $701 million in fiscal year 1972, or almost $1 billion. How much was shoveled out at the height of the Vietnam War may never be known. In addition, the letter acknowledged that almost $160 million more in equipment was turned over to the Republic of Korea forces by departing U. S. forces in these two fiscal years.

In my view the figures for direct transfers to forces in Vietnam are gross underestimates. Instead of "almost $1 billion," a more accurate description would be "untold billions."

Total Military Aid Exceeds $6 Billion

From the figures we have, we can now make a rough estimate of the total for military aid. When the $90 million for Food for Peace military aid, the $701 million for direct transfers, the $200-million piaster subsidy, and ship loans are added to Senator Fulbright's estimate of $5.1 billion, the grand total for fiscal year 1971 exceeds $6 billion.

This total excludes military sales. It also does not include the $14 billion we spend for American forces in NATO, Vietnam, or other places abroad in support of U. S. activities.

In tabular form the total included the following amounts in fiscal year 1971.

	Amounts in Millions
Military portion (MAP) of foreign aid, including supplemental request for Cambodia	$ 775.0
Supporting assistance	570.0
Special credit for Israel	500.0
International military headquarters	57.0
Military assistance groups, missions, etc.	167.0
Permanent military construction overseas	190.0
Military Assistance Service Funded (MASF)	2,260.3
Defense Department appropriations for economic assistance	117.0
MAP-grant excess defense articles (acquisition value)	502.0
Food for Peace, military aid	90.0
Direct transfers to MASF countries	710.0
Piaster subsidy	200.0
Ship loans	23.8
Total:[1]	$6,162.1

[1]Does not include dollar-value estimates for Work-in-kind and $1,824,500,000 in foreign military sales. Later figures are not available.

Until the Joint Economic Committee held its hearings, neither Congress nor the American people had any conception of the general magnitude, let alone the precise amounts, of military aid sent abroad. The program is accomplished by roundabout and surreptitious means. A conscious effort is made to avoid putting the details in one place at one time where they can be looked at and sensible judgments made about them. Instead the program is fractionalized and scattered among a dozen or more departments and agencies.

Some programs are authorized by legislative committees and funded by direct appropriations. In others, such as Food for Peace, the sale of excess and surplus commodities provides hundreds of millions in military stores which are supplied at bargain-basement prices under general authority without direct appropriations. In still others, billions are provided absolutely free and without any accounting whatsoever.

The consequences are clear. The money goes out bit by bit and piecemeal. No one either sees or acts on the overall amounts. No one, neither the President nor Congress, has any effective control over it. No one has made rational or intelligent judgments about it.

Even now we do not have an accurate account of how much is involved, although we are inching toward a final tabulation as we delve deeper into the problem. But it is clear from the cold figures we have that foreign military aid is out of control. The program is unmanaged and unmanageable.

The cloak of secrecy has not only been wrapped around the total figures. In the past the State Department has insisted that the amounts in the direct-aid programs going to individual countries be kept secret until a year after they are funded. That was changed in 1971 when I made them public after the State Department could give no national-security reason why they should remain secret.

Whether in the form of grants or loan subsidies, the military goods are no real bargain for poor countries. When developing countries have military weapons thrust upon them that they would never buy under the discipline of their budget restrictions and priorities, we are doing them no favor. The cost of maintaining weapons or of training the forces to use them often takes desperately needed funds in poor countries from programs to feed, clothe, and house their people. It is a cruel gift.

Issues of War and Peace

Foreign aid should be reformed not merely to bring order out of chaos or to provide an accurate balance sheet. What is involved are the great issues of war and peace. We are confronted with a moral problem and not merely a classroom exercise.

Foreign military aid is used to rain down death and destruction on men, women, and children in hamlets and villages throughout Vietnam and Southeast Asia. The funds provide massive technical instruments of war which have pulverized portions of Laos, Cambodia, and North and South Vietnam. Under the Nixon Doctrine it is proposed that gigantic future funds be used to arm the South Vietnamese and others as we withdraw from the conflict. While the citizens of the United States remain relatively safe in their homes and communities with very little physical risk to themselves, millions of people abroad are suffering the consequences of these policies and fifty thousand Americans have given their lives in Vietnam as a result of them.

There is great division in the nation over whether we should be doing what we are doing or what it is proposed that we do. Even if these acts are absolutely justified, no thinking person can welcome them when he contemplates the suffering they inflict. But with the fractionalizing of foreign aid, we are providing billions for the weapons of war mindlessly, without either knowing the total amounts or considering the consequences of our actions. There is no single time when either the President or the Congress focuses attention on the totality of foreign military aid. There is no moment when decisions are made and judgments brought to bear on this momentous issue in a way which is worthy of a great people and a great nation.

When we shovel out billions of dollars in weapons of destruction without questioning the amounts or the purposes for which they are used, the citizens of this country and the lawmakers of the land abdicate their responsibilities. They cede power to the military which it should not be theirs to exercise except by the deliberate action of the American people through their elected representatives.

The Program Contradicts the Purposes

Not too long ago we witnessed a bloodletting between India and Pakistan. While it was not of our immediate making, through our military-aid program we set forces in motion which culminated in the catastrophe. We aided and abetted it by our actions.

For the purpose of helping them defend themselves against Russian or Chinese attacks, we had given military aid to both countries. But the Pakistani government used that aid to put down the independence movement in East Pakistan (Bangladesh). Through the force of arms, much of it supplied by the United States, they killed, burned, raped, tortured and devastated an entire countryside. They drove ten million people from their homes. They murdered and slaughtered others. Some were driven into the sea. Others escaped to refugee camps in India, where thousands remained uncared for. India retaliated and drove the West Pakistan Army from Bangladesh. Weapons for both sides had been supplied by the United States. In the budget we call that "international security assistance."

The world is complex and difficult enough when facts are known and judgments made deliberately. When the threat of nuclear extinction hangs over all of our heads, it is suicidal to set military events into motion through the unthinking exercise of power. But that is done in our foreign military-aid programs and was done specifically in the case of India and Pakistan.

Measure the military-aid program against President Truman's call for "the improvement and growth of underdeveloped areas . . . to help the free people of the world," and "a worldwide effort for the achievement of peace, plenty, and freedom."

We provide military hardware to forty-six countries of the world. That does not establish peace.

We give military aid to dozens of dictatorships, including especially Greece, Spain, and Brazil. This does not aid freedom.

We provide $30 million a year to support the internal police forces of some twenty-five nations of the world under so-called "public safety programs." Among them are South Vietnam, Brazil, and Pakistan. That does not help the free peoples.

There are other contradictions. After supplying India and Pakistan with the arms to make war on each other, we then provided $225 million to care for the refugees of that conflict.

The administrator of the AID program, John Hannah, warned after the Senate voted down the AID program in October 1971 that one of the dire aspects of that action would be the cutoff of AID funds to the refugees in Laos. Only a few weeks later, dispatches from Laos warned that American bombing hampered the AID program and quoted a local Laotian leader who pleaded for the U. S. to "stop the bombing" so that his people would not have to flee again.

Military aid is a mess.

Redeeming Qualities

What about economic aid? While there are few redeeming qualities in the $6-billion-plus military-aid program, many of the great purposes and priorities outlined under President Truman's Point Four are actually carried out under portions of the $2-billion annual economic-aid program.

The Peace Corps, whose annual costs are less than the cost of one Main battle tank or four F-14s, has won the admiration of those at home and abroad for its selfless programs and economical operation. But, under the military-assistance aid program, we spend almost as much each year ($74 million) to train foreign military personnel as we authorize for the entire Peace Corps

($77.2 million). Under AID, funds are supplied for Arab refugees, exiles from the Iron Curtain, and the victims of famine and genocide in Bangladesh. Children are fed through UNICEF. Food production has increased due to the technical knowledge provided by teams of American university experts who have gone to less developed countries. Funds for population control have begun to attack that critical problem abroad. Project HOPE, the American University in Beirut, the Weizmann Institute in Israel, the American Research Center in Cairo, and the American Hospital in Rome are all supported by American contributions under the AID program.

But economic aid also needs critical examination to determine if its priorities are desirable and if its ostensible goals are reached. Among the major issues and questions which must be raised are the following.

Emphasis on Big Development Projects

The first is the nature and size of the "development" program. Well over half the funds for all economic aid are spent for "development" as opposed to technical assistance or humanitarian purposes.

In the United States bilateral AID pipeline alone, development loans make up almost 80 percent of the $2.5 billion total. What's wrong with that? The development-loan program is predominantly a big-project program under which roads, dams, fertilizer plants, and electric-power plants are built. The proportions are wrong. Only one third of the development program goes for nonproject loans such as those for education, training in skills, health, housing, small cooperatives and similar programs.

Big-project development is not only a continuing problem under the U. S. bilateral program, it is a universal problem in the international financial institutions for which the Senate appropriated $261 million in 1972. Through the end of 1970, about 77 percent of all World Bank loans had been made for transportation, electric power, industry, and mining. Housing, education, health, water and sewer projects got less than 3 percent. Even the International Development Agency (IDA), the World Bank's soft-loan, no-interest-rate window, made 54 percent of its loans for big-project items. The Inter-American Development Bank through 1970 made 73 percent of its loans for highways, power, industry, and mining. Housing, health, and education got the crumbs from the table.

Reverse Distribution of Income

With the bulk of development loans through the United States AID program—as well as those from the World Bank and the Inter-American Development Bank—going to big projects, it is probable that the major thrust of economic aid effected a reverse distribution of income. Instead of the poor profiting, the opposite took place. In the absence of clear evidence to the contrary, it appears that relatively modest-income Americans were taxed to provide funds for foreign aid which went to those with relatively high incomes both at home and abroad.

The $6 billion or more in military aid does not help the weak and the poor; it not only makes no positive contribution to a poor country but often draws limited resources from the poor nation to back up the military aid. The more than half of economic aid which goes to development programs and for the big projects does not directly aid the poor. The remainder—for technical assistance, the Peace Corps, refugees, etc.—is directed at the original purposes of Point Four, but it is less than one seventh of all foreign aid.

Yet over the years the idealists who support foreign aid on the grounds that it succors the weak and feeds the poor have provided what effective public opinion there is in support of the program. It is a very small tail wagging a very big dog, because the big money has gone to powerful economic interests for the military programs and development projects.

This realization has prompted the great disenchantment among the program's original sponsors. As one of their Senate supporters aptly described the situation, "We gave them an orchard and they gave us an apple."

Year in and year out there *is* a certain irony in the nature of the support and opposition to foreign aid. There is always the bitter right-wing mail fostered by the Liberty Lobby and the John Birch Society, demanding that the entire foreign-aid program be killed. The volume of pro-foreign-aid mail never equaled that in opposition, but it is made up of letters from church groups, members of the League of Women Voters, and citizens with a humanitarian or selfless view. But the right wing never realized that the bulk of the funds did not go to the UN or to feed the Hottentots, the issues which aroused their hostility. Instead it went to Chiang Kai-shek, Syngman Rhee, Vietnam, and the military juntas in Greece, Spain, or Brazil. The idealists were also misled in their view that it was largely a program in support of the forces they revered. The effect was that each of these groups unwittingly supported the other's basic interests. Both were misled as to the reality of the foreign-aid program. Both allowed their vision of it to obscure its substance.

Export-Import Bank: High Costs, Few Benefits

There are other items in the foreign-aid budget which would bear detailed scrutiny. One agency over which the Congress exercises responsibility but little control is worth special note. In the 1972 Foreign Aid Appropriations Bill, the Export-Import Bank was authorized to use $7.3 billion to finance exports from the United States. These borrowed funds are now, unfortunately, outside the budget of the United States, although authorized by the public.

This arrangement violates every principle of proper budget responsibility, for it means that the Export-Import Bank can function outside the general control of the President or Congress whatever the economic needs or budgetary circumstances may be. For example, the Ex-Im Bank now has the authority during periods of tight money, when funds are insufficient for housing, small business, or state and local government needs, to tap the credit markets without let or hindrance up to its vast statutory authority.

In a seminal study done for the Joint Economic Committee during its comprehensive review of subsidy programs, it was shown that there is no statistical relationship between the amount of exports financed by the Export-Import Bank and the volume of American exports. The Ex-Im Bank does not generate additional exports. But it has large costs. It provides a large interest-rate subsidy financed by the taxpayers of the United States. It has significant administrative costs. The costs also include the opportunity costs of the capital which might have been employed elsewhere and the increased demands on the money markets caused by an increase in government borrowing. It can also inhibit the effectiveness of countercyclical monetary policies. The Export-Import Bank involves all of these costs, but it provides few if any benefits, because, according to the study, it does not perform the function for which it was ostensibly established. The study concludes in specific terms that the Export-Import Bank has had no significant effect on U. S. exports.

But the Export-Import Bank is supported with great vigor by the economic interests it subsidizes, as an important part of our foreign economic policy. It has bamboozled Congress as well. It is a prime candidate for action under any program to reorder priorities.

Excessive Proportion of U. S. Contributions

There are additional proper criticisms of the economic-aid program. One is what appears to be the excessive proportion of the total contributions that the United States makes to numerous international institutions. We put up 66.7 percent of the money for the Inter-American Development Bank's Fund for Special Operations (soft loans); 78 percent for the UN Fund for Drug Abuse Control; 50 percent for the UN Population Program; 50 percent for the UN's Food and Agriculture Organization (FAO); 55 percent for the UN's Arab Refugee Program; 53 percent for Pakistani Refugee Relief; and 40 percent or more for the Inter-American Bank's callable capital, the UN force in Cyprus, and the Indus Basin Development Fund. Even when the amounts are not large, as the $7.5 million for UN population activities or the $2 million for drug abuse, the proportions are out of line.

As a general rule a "fair share" for the United States should not exceed 20 to 30 percent of truly multinational programs. These institutions would be better served and support of the program would be extended if the U. S. share of the total were cut, even if the actual dollar amounts were increased. In my view it would be healthier for the U. S. to give $15 million to the UN Population Program if that amount represented only 25 percent of the total than to give only $7.5 million which is half. By such a loaves-and-fishes formula the total program could be stepped up from $15 million to $60 million while the U. S. share of the total contribution was reduced.

Now that World War II is twenty-five years behind us, now that Europe has fully recovered and the UN has 133 members, a U. S. contribution to UN agencies in excess of the 20 to 30 percent range cannot be justified. It is neither good for the U. S. nor good for the UN.

There are numerous reasons why, even with all their shortcomings, we should move to multilateral aid programs. Even when the shares are not fair, other nations do have to put up some funds instead of none. That helps. It eases the U. S. burden. In addition, it does engender international cooperation. It is one way for nations to gain experience working with each other in useful ways for constructive ends. Finally, it greatly diminishes the charges of "Yankee imperialism" or "Uncle Shylock," the bane of American aid and foreign policies.

Powerful Forces Back Military and Development Aid

It is often said that the foreign-aid program is in trouble because it has no domestic constituency. That may be true for the humanitarian programs. It is decidedly not true for most of the others.

The military-aid program is backed not only by the Pentagon hierarchy but by the vast network of the military-industrial complex. How else does one explain the conversion of Truman's Point IV bootstrap program to one where 60 percent or more of the money goes for military functions?

Powerful economic groups also have a great self-interest in "development"—highways, dams, and electric power. That too accounts for the shift away from President Truman's program to produce more food, more clothing, and more housing. Billions now go for the so-called economic "infrastructure" instead. In this case the program has been as vulgarized as the word used to describe it. It proves once again what I call "Proxmire's law"— namely, that good programs have simple names, like Peace Corps, Children's Fund, and Project HOPE, while bad programs are described by euphemisms and barbarisms.

How powerful these economic interests are was clear during a key vote in the Senate when a motion was proposed to restore $100 million in cuts that my committee made in the big-project development loans for the Alliance for Progress.

The General Accounting Office reported to us that during four reviews of development assistance in Latin America the projects were found to be so lacking in objectives, goals, and targets that no objective measurement of their effectiveness could be made. No set times had been established for their completion. This was true of about 220 of the 259 specific goals reviewed.

In an effort to reorder priorities, force a change, and get the funds to the people who needed them, we cut Latin-American development funds. But we voted $125 million in the bill for population control which had previously come out of the de-velopment-program money. We also put back $121 million for the Inter-American Development Bank which had been cut out by the House Committee. In addition, the Alliance for Progress has a large backlog of unspent money. We thus, by these addi-tions, more than compensated for the cuts made in the develop-ment-loan program.

But with strong Nixon Administration and Senate Republican backing the $100 million for the big projects was restored. It was restored with votes from a number of vociferous anti–foreign-aid Senators. They voted to restore the big-project money and then turned around and voted against the entire foreign-aid bill. Three of those votes provided the margin by which the $100 million was added to foreign aid.

Who Gets the Gravy?

The foreign-aid program has survived against the over-whelming force of public opinion all of these years in part because of the powerful economic backing it has from essentially conservative forces. Here are some of the interests involved.

According to the AID agency itself, from 1962 through 1969, cargo financed under the Foreign Assistance Act ranged from 22 to 30 percent of the total cargo which moved on U. S.–flag ship-ping. In fiscal year 1971 one quarter of all U. S. fertilizer exports were financed by AID, as were 16 percent of exports of iron and steel mill products, 16 percent of railroad equipment, and smaller but significant percentages of exports of U. S. rice, textiles, petroleum, chemicals, papers, autos, and other products. For the commodities mentioned, AID spent $972 million in the United States in 1971. The military weapons bought with its funds added billions more.

The AID lobby is pervasive. When the Senate killed the AID authorization bill in 1971, I received more than a dozen calls from Wisconsin exporters of tallow urging me to reverse the Senate's action. They were urged to phone by the AID lobby.

When I criticized the Inter-American Development Bank in a Senate speech for making too many big-project loans, questioned why the money loaned out in Latin America at 3 to 4 percent was reloaned at 12 to 18 percent, and criticized the excessive splendor in which the bank conducts its annual meetings, I was questioned in great detail by one of the leading citizens of Wisconsin. Her letter was obviously drafted by the Inter-American Bank itself.

On yet another occasion, one of my mild criticisms of the bank drew a long letter to the editor in the Washington *Post* by a lawyer formerly a paid consultant of the bank. A long editorial-page article essentially defending the Inter-American Bank's questionable operations appeared as well.

I mention these not to object to the cut and thrust of argument or criticism, but to illustrate that the AID-supported institutions are not without strong friends and allies or the means to lobby for their interests. And as I watch the State Department and AID legislative-liaison officials buttonhole Senators in the Senate lobby prior to key votes, I visualize the groups and forces which stand behind them. I see a powerful road-building company in Texas, a Baltimore steelworks, a Michigan auto firm, a South Carolina textile company, a downstate Illinois tractor company, an Ohio research institute, and numerous nonscheduled airlines.

These are powerful economic forces. They pack a big political punch. They tell more than words why the AID program not only has survived but grows. They are also among the reasons its purposes have changed, its goals modified, and its original thrust reversed. They are the reason why AID priorities should be reordered and the totality of its military and big-project programs reduced.

5 · Setting Priorities — Cuts in Military and Foreign-Aid Spending

The United States must remain strong and free. We must retain military superiority over our potential enemies. National security must be America's number-one overall priority.

But what is security? What is more important to the genuine security of the German, Polish, or black American citizen of Milwaukee—that the police force be expanded and well paid or that we shovel out $112 million a year to Chiang Kai-shek's security forces on Taiwan?

Do not funds spent for heart and cancer research, health insurance, job training, and day-care centers enhance the security of Americans far more than the C-5A, the F-14, or the $117 million in military assistance to Greece?

How important is it to the real security of American citizens to spend $1 billion for the CVN-70 carrier, not counting its planes and escort ships? The same $1 billion would pay for 1.5 million public-housing units for an entire year. It would feed almost 6 million Americans under the direct food distribution program for a year. It would pay for the federal government's outlays for cancer research for the next three years.

In the view of the citizen of Milwaukee, is it not more important to his personal security that he have a policeman on the block than an armored U. S. division in Western Europe? Which poses the greater threat to his security—the repeated muggings in his neighborhood or the threat of a Russian invasion of Europe?

Annual Pentagon spending should be cut from $83.4 billion to $70 billion a year. This can be done without endangering national security. It can be done while retaining the U. S. commanding lead over the Soviet Union in overall military strength, in strategic weapons, in air superiority, and in naval power.

$70-Billion Defense Budget No Fantasy

A goal of $70 billion is no fantasy. In fact, a $60-billion figure has been endorsed by a number of responsible individuals and groups. One detailed analysis was done by the National Urban Coalition after the most extensive consultation with numerous former high-ranking Pentagon policy and budget officials, among them the former comptroller of the Pentagon, Robert Anthony. They urged a $60-billion budget in fiscal year 1972 even while $6 billion was still being spent for Vietnam. In a Brookings Institution report entitled "Setting National Priorities: The 1971 Budget," the specific strategic nuclear forces, general-purpose forces, personnel, and weapons to provide a Pentagon budget of $60 billion were detailed. Their third study, "Setting National Priorities: The 1973 Budget," projects one optional budget of $72 billion which includes a $3.5 billion incremental cost for Vietnam.

Senator George McGovern and his brilliant legislative assistant John Holum, according to the Washington *Star*, spelled out "in unprecedented detail" just how he would structure a 1975 defense budget if he were elected to the Presidency. The study was applauded, although not endorsed, by the *Star*'s able military correspondent, Orr Kelly, as a "superb job" and a "pioneering effort" in working out a force structure to match his vital assumptions. McGovern proposed a $54.8-billion Pentagon budget in 1975. I agree with Orr Kelly's description. I applaud the splendid effort of George McGovern and John Holum. But I do not endorse this deep a cut. I believe if we could reduce Pentagon spending to $70 billion that would be a significant effort.

It is not necessary here to spell out in each case the specific number of missiles, divisions, air wings, naval forces, and air and sea lifts that a $70-billion budget would provide. This is done admirably in the Brookings study, the Urban Coalition's "Counter-budget," and in Senator McGovern's unprecedented work. But the $70-billion budget I propose is based on a number of specific assumptions. These include a reduction of $4 billion in the $18-billion strategic budget, a cut of $1.5–2 billion in the $14-billion NATO budget through a reduction of 150,000 U. S. troops, a $4-billion reduction in the present costs of the Vietnam War (leaving a $2-billion residual for assistance), and a $2.5-billion saving in procurement by cutting out the duplication of weapons, excessive gold-plating, and genuine reform in procurement practices.

My proposal of a $70-billion Pentagon budget is a more modest cut than some of the others. This is true because it contemplates a continuation and improvement of the TRIAD deterrent—sea-based, land-based, and airborne strategic missiles—somewhat larger naval forces, and bigger allowances for pay in order to achieve an all-volunteer army and adequate and highly trained reserves. It is also true because one of the results of the SALT agreement negotiated in Moscow in May 1972 may be to substitute more sophisticated and hence more expensive versions for existing strategic missiles. And hence limit my proposed strategic savings.

False Charges Against Critics

Every attempt to make significant cuts in the military budget is met by charges that the budget cutters are neo-isolationists or believe in unilateral disarmament. These charges routinely appear in the syndicated columns.

In addition, a heavily financed outfit called the American Security Council is spending tens of thousands of dollars exaggerating the Russian strength, denigrating the power of the U. S. strategic forces, and charging defense critics with proposing suicidal policies. It is also widely distributing a "supplemental" report of the so-called Blue Ribbon Defense Panel which, incidentally, was produced after the report and was signed by only seven of the original seventeen members. Six of the seven happen to be right out of the top military-industrial-complex industries. The American Security Council is made up of some of the biggest financial angels of right-wing Republicans—men like Robert Galvin of the Motorola Corporation and James S. Kemper, insurance man and former Republican Party treasurer. In addition, its board and leading members include people like Robert Morris and Clare Boothe Luce, and almost a division of former high-ranking generals and admirals. Among them are General Earle G. Wheeler, General Nathan F. Twining, and General Lyman C. Lemnitzer, all former chairmen of the Joint Chiefs of Staff, as well as General Bernard Schriever, Admiral H. D. Felt, and General Albert Wedemeyer.

They charge, specifically, that due to cuts in military funds brought about by the efforts of myself and other Senate critics, "America is no longer the world's first military power. We are now second to Russia—and the Communists are widening their lead every week." What rubbish! As specific proof, they cite among other things the number of Russian super ICBMs and claim that we have none (what about the Titan IIs with their ten-megaton warheads?), the fact that Russia's total missile megatonnage exceeds ours by a six-to-one or eight-to-one ratio, that Russia has a missile defense system while we have none, and that "effective military spending" has been cut by about 25 percent during the first Nixon administration.

Among the favorite phrases used by members of the American Security Council is that the critics' policies would "leave us naked." These so-called facts are either untrue, misleading, or irrelevant. They are cited here as reasonably typical of the charges made against anyone who attempts to cut the military budget or seriously reform American priorities.

But they raise two important questions which should be answered because they are serious worries of the American people.

They are: (1) Can we significantly cut the American military budget without endangering the security of the United States? (2) Can we significantly cut the American military budget without knocking the economy into a tailspin and throwing hundreds of thousands of men and women out of work?

In the course of answering the first of these questions, the answers to the false charges and misleading information put out by the American Security Council will be clear. The second question has been answered in Chapter 2.

No Significant Pentagon Cuts

Our security has not been endangered by significant cuts in military spending. The reason? There have been no significant or big military cuts.

No case can be made that the bone and muscle have been cut from our military forces. The facts are that over the five years from fiscal year 1968 through fiscal year 1972, the Pentagon spent $3 billion more than the President requested. More outrageous, the Pentagon spent $21.6 billion more than Congress appropriated. The following table gives the facts.

President's Budget Request, Congressional Appropriations,* and Actual Pentagon Spending, Fiscal Years 1968-72
(in billions)

Fiscal Year	President's Requests	Congressional Appropriations	Cuts by Congress	Pentagon Outlays
1968	$76.2	$74.2	$2.0	$77.4
1969	$79.9	$74.4	$5.5	$77.9
1970	$78.4	$72.7	$5.7	$77.2
1971	$68.7	$66.6	$2.1	$74.6
1972	$75.6	$72.6	$3.1	$75.0†
Totals:	$378.8	$360.5	$18.4	$382.1

*The President's budget request for Department of Defense—Military includes funds for the Pentagon, military construction, family housing, and civil defense. Congress appropriates these amounts in three separate bills.
†Estimate from January 1972 FY 1973 budget.

Since the Pentagon spent $3 billion more than the President actually called for, unless the American Security Council is prepared to hold President Nixon culpable of malfeasance its charges do not hold up. Instead one should be shocked at how the Pentagon can spend some $21 billion more than Congress appropriates, or about $4 billion more, year in and year out, than it receives. The answer lies in the enormous $40-billion backlog of Pentagon funds, the way Congress has lost control of the purse strings, and the manner by which the Defense Department has usurped that power.

In fact, the American Security Council makes a devastating case against the stewardship of its leading members. It is telling us that even after spending about $400 billion in five years, or more than $76 billion a year, we are now second to the Russians and in danger of being overwhelmed. This has happened even though the Soviet Union's economy is half as productive as ours and her military spending was half or only slightly more than half of our military budget. If, in these circumstances, we are as weak as the American Security Council states, then waste and inefficiency at the Pentagon must be far worse than the critics have charged. Surely the ASC does not mean to imply that while Generals Wheeler, Lemnitzer, and Twining were in charge of the shop the American military hierarchy failed in its fundamental responsibility. Even the harshest critics of Pentagon profligacy have not made that wild accusation. All that can be said to these former chiefs of staff about that charge is that it is scandalous if true.

Ominous U. S. Strategic Power

In any case, it is not true. One reason the American Security Council and its allies are dead wrong is the power of our strategic weapons.

According to Secretary Laird's posture statement of February 15, 1972, the United States will have 5,700 "total offensive-force loadings," or strategic nuclear weapons, by mid-1972. The comparable figure given for the Russians in the Secretary's official estimate is only 2,500. The United States therefore has over twice the number of strategic nuclear weapons the Russians have. The issue is: Is this enough to deter the Russians from launching a nuclear war on us, or a preemptive first strike? Do we have sufficient "assured destructive capability" to deter them from that act? Will they be deterred from such folly by the sure knowledge that retaliation would destroy their country?

In his posture statement of January 1968, then Secretary of Defense Robert S. McNamara submitted a damage table giving the official Pentagon estimate of the proportion of Soviet population and industry which could be destroyed by various numbers of one-megaton equivalent of delivered warheads. The key figure indicates that four hundred delivered one-megaton warheads would destroy 30 percent of the Soviet Union's population and 76 percent of her industrial capacity. In the past the Pentagon has stated that the power to destroy 20 to 25 percent of the Russian population and 50 percent of her industry was considered sufficient to deter her from a first-strike attempt.

Secretary McNamara's Damage-Table Estimate of
Soviet Population and Industry Destruction
(assumed 1972 total population of 247,000,000 and urban population of 116,000,000)

1-mt.-equivalent delivered warheads	Total Population Fatalities (millions)	Percent	Industrial Capacity Destroyed (percent)
100	37	15	59
200	52	21	72
400	74	30	76
800	96	39	77
1,200	109	44	77
1,600	116	47	77

The 5,700 force loadings the United States had in its strategic arsenal in mid-1972 were more than fourteen times the number of warheads sufficient to destroy 30 percent of the Russian population and 76 percent of her industry. Not only that, but the 5,700 figure does not include some 3,000 to 4,000 tactical nuclear warheads which could be delivered from tactical land and sea planes stationed on the periphery of the Soviet Union; the Soviets consider these tactical nuclear weapons so significant that at one stage asked that they be included in the strategic calculations at the SALT talks. We therefore have in our arsenal now from 8,700 to 9,700 strategic *and* tactical nuclear weapons, or from twenty-one to twenty-four times the number needed to destroy 30 percent of the Soviet population and 76 percent of her industrial capacity.

But this is not all. The 5,700 strategic nuclear weapons in our arsenal are growing at a very fast rate. At mid-1971 the estimate was 4,600. There was thus almost a 25 percent increase in one year. By the 1974–75 period, the military planners expect to have almost 9,000 strategic-force loadings instead of the 5,700 in mid-1972. According to unclassified sources this number will be composed of the following estimated forces:

Launchers		Warheads
450 Minuteman II		450
550 Minuteman III		1,650
54 Titan II		54
160 Polaris A-3s		480
496 Poseidon launchers		4,960
450 heavy bombers		1,350
	Total warheads	8,944

The 3,000 to 4,000 tactical nuclear weapons can also be counted as part of our "assured destructive capability." Even without counting them we will increase our official strategic-nuclear-force loadings by almost 60 percent over the mid-1972 figures and by almost double the mid-1971 figures. We are doing this even though we now have more than fourteen times the nuclear warheads needed to destroy the capability of the Soviet Union to fight. Note that the doubling of one-megaton delivered warheads from 400 to 800 has only marginal additional destructive capability, increasing the population fatalities from 30 to 39 percent and the industrial capacity destroyed from 76 to 77 percent. This is nuclear overkill. We have an assured destructive capability in spades. None of this is affected by the 1972 Strategic Arms Limitation Treaty signed in Moscow. It freezes the number of land-based and sea-based missile launchers, but not the number of missiles each can carry.

Cut $4 Billion from Nuclear Overkill

The strategic deterrent costs us about $18 billion a year. We could cut back to $14 billion a year and easily provide by the 1974–75 time period some 7,600 strategic-nuclear-force loadings, or almost twenty times the number needed to inflict an unacceptable level of damage on the Soviet Union. That is a modest cut which would not endanger our security and which should be made. That can be made very clear by examining the destructive power of our weapons.

The Hiroshima bomb was a 20-kiloton bomb. Each of the thirty-one Poseidon submarines will carry sixteen missiles with MIRV ("multiple independently targeted reentry vehicle") warheads consisting of ten individual warheads each—a total of 4,960 warheads for the fleet. Each of these warheads is approximately fifty kilotons, or two and a half times bigger than the Hiroshima bomb.

The Minuteman-III missiles carry three 200-kiloton weapons, or three weapons each of which is ten times bigger than the Hiroshima bomb.

The fifty-four Titan-II missiles carry a 10-megaton warhead.

The bomb loads of the heavy bombers vary and are classified, but it is public knowledge that the B-52s can carry up to a 20-megaton weapon. They are more apt to carry numerous smaller ones. In light of these ominous weapons, to call a proposal that we limit the expansion of our nuclear arsenal to 7,600 force loadings, by the 1974–75 period, "neo-isolationism" or "unilateral disarmament," or to charge that it leaves us militarily "naked," not only is a misuse of the language but stretches the credulity of intelligent men.

By limiting the increase in our terror to that level we could save $4 billion a year and still have enough weapons to blow up the world many times over. Isn't that enough?

Misleading Megatonnage Argument

Nonetheless it is charged that the U.S. is in dire peril because Russia's total megatonnage exceeds ours by a six-to-one or eight-to-one ratio. Apart from the fact that this is not true, the use of megatonnage as a measure of strength is grossly misleading.

Years ago the United States rejected the big blockbuster in favor of developing far more numerous, far more accurate smaller weapons. We did this because they are better and more effective and add to our commanding nuclear lead.

The Russians have been far behind us in this respect. They have been required to go for the big-megatonnage bombs, which are far less accurate, require bigger boosters, and do only marginally more damage than the small bombs we have. A 25-megaton bomb does not provide twenty-five times the damage of a one-megaton bomb. Because it is less accurate, it may actually be of smaller potential danger to our land-based missile sites than a smaller, more accurate weapon.

Big megatonnage is also a sign of relative weakness because it signifies an absence of a MIRV capability. MIRVing weapons increases their potential terror. Whether this in fact adds to the security of any country is questionable. But as far as the military strategists are concerned, the fact that we have MIRV'd our Minuteman and Poseidon missiles is a major plus in the arms race. It was with some sense of relief, in fact, that Secretary Laird's February 1972 posture statement reported that the Russians had not yet tested a multiple independently targeted reentry vehicle.

MIRV means that the number of warheads on 550 Minuteman-III missiles will increase by a factor of three and that the warheads on the sixteen missiles aboard thirty-one Poseidon submarines will increase by a factor of ten, thereby increasing the number and the terror of the latter from 496 to 4,960. But MIRVing a missile decreases its total megatonnage somewhat, in some cases to about three-fifths its former power. When a one-megaton weapon on a Minuteman missile is replaced by three independently targeted weapons, the megatonnage is reduced to a total of six hundred kilotons, or three weapons of two hundred kilotons each. But three weapons targeted on a single or separate targets obviously cause more damage than a single bomb on a single target.

MIRVing increases the terror while reducing the megatonnage. Our smaller, more reliable, more numerous, more accurate weapons actually put us ahead of the Russians with their stockpile of blockbusters. In the narrowest strategic-weapons equation, instead of harming us, that helps us. But those who charge we are behind in "megatonnage" turn the matter upside down.

One wonders why the retired military men at the American Security Council keep denigrating and running down this country's military power.

When the Russians test a MIRV and begin to equip their SS-9s and Y-class submarines with multiple missiles, one can predict without fear of contradiction that the Pentagon and its allies will ask for a big budget increase to offset the Russian advance. They will do this even though one of the consequences will be to reduce Russian megatonnage. By such means do the Pentagon and its allies attempt to mislead the American people.

Keep the TRIAD

While we can safely reduce the rate of our nuclear-warhead deployment, we should continue with the TRIAD system of three separate strategic weapons. In spite of the Russian advances, our deterrent is still invulnerable. But the Russians are bound to advance relatively to the U.S., for no other reason than that the U.S. strategic deterrent is largely in place. Increasing it brings only marginal improvements at fantastic costs.

Even with their advances, the Russians do not now have the accuracy or reliability of weapons to knock out our land-based deterrent. While they may achieve such a capability within the future, it is not now the case. They do not now have the ability to stop all of our manned bombers. With the improvement in penetration devices, our B-52 bomber fleet can still rain great devastation on the Russians. Very soon, however, both land-based missiles and manned bombers may become "vulnerable" strategic systems. Meanwhile the Polaris-Poseidon fleet is absolutely invulnerable. No breakthrough threatening its invulnerability is in sight.

Nevertheless, in the absence of new agreements in future SALT talks, keeping a TRIAD of strategic-deterrent forces is the wisest policy. This is true even with the future vulnerability of two of our three strategic systems.

First of all, we have spent billions to put them in place. We have the TRIAD. There is no reason to junk it.

Second, it compounds the first-strike problem of the Soviet Union and hence deters her from attempting to gain a first-strike capability. If the Soviets have but one deterrent to concentrate on rather than three, a breakthrough might come more easily.

Third, even when components of TRIAD become vulnerable, the effort to knock out all three at once will cost vast sums of money and require great technical performance. Weapons of war do not work perfectly, and an in-place deterrent should not be scrapped. Even if each of the three separate deterrents becomes vulnerable, it does not necessarily follow that the entire deterrent is vulnerable.

Finally, unless the Russians make new and spectacular gains, there is no reason to move beyond deploying the existing deterrents by substituting new weapons. While marginal advances should be made in all three, there is no need to spend billions now on hardening the land-based-missile sites, producing a B-1 bomber, or moving the ULMS (underwater long-range missile system) out of the research and development stage.

We can vastly extend the time of our deterrent, not by building a new $12-billion B-1 system but by refitting the existing B-52's with the C-5A engine and the subsonic cruise armed decoy (SCAD) missile. This could transform our bomber fleet into a stand-off missile platform, vastly extend the life and relative invulnerability of the bomber deterrent, and do so at far less cost than building the B-1 bomber.

With respect to ULMS, the Russians are not even close to challenging the Polaris-Poseidon system. The paint is not dry on the latest Poseidon conversion. The production of ULMS at this stage is premature, because it could make ULMS, as well as the Polaris-Poseidon systems, vulnerable to any breakthrough the Russians might ultimately make in anti–submarine-warfare technology.

As I wrote to Admiral Rickover, on January 25, 1972:

> As you know, I support and believe in the underwater nuclear deterrent. It is still invulnerable, unlike the B-1 and the land-based missiles.
> But I do not understand why we are rushing into ULMS at such a fast pace. Where is the "fly before you buy?" Why is the IOC moved up from 1984 to 1978? Where is the supporting data showing that it is so superior to EXPO?
> We are inviting another procurement disaster if we move in this direction this fast. This is a minimum of $30 billion for this project.
> Can't we try to do this one right?

With respect to ULMS, we should keep our powder dry.

In any determination of how much we should spend on defense, one matter should be made clear. The cost of defending the continental United States, even including the strategic deterrent, is relatively small. Most of the defense budget is to help defend our allies or for deployment of weapons abroad. The calculation, based on the missions assigned to our various forces and the purposes of specific weapons systems, for the defense of the United States alone comes to about $30 billion. It is this amount which could be cut about $4 billion if the pace for the multiplication of our strategic terror were slowed down only nominally.

Cut NATO Costs

There are two remaining major factors which affect the necessary size of the military budget. The first is the amount necessary to defend our interests and our allies abroad. Included especially are the force levels and costs of military missions in Europe, NATO, Asia, and elsewhere. The second major factor concerns both the level and the management of the weapons systems really needed to carry out these objectives.

Another $1.5–2 billion could be saved by reducing U.S. NATO strength from 300,000 to 150,000 men. While continuing to provide the nuclear umbrella and the major sea support of the NATO alliance, we should Europeanize NATO's defenses just as we should Vietnamize the defense of Vietnam.

This is thoroughly justified. Our NATO allies spend roughly half the amount on defense that the United States does in terms of the burden and the effort. Collectively they are stronger economically and have a larger population than either the U.S. or the Soviet Union. Furthermore, such a reduction on the part of the U.S. could be made without endangering the security of Western Europe.

NATO has almost 800,000 troops assigned to the central front— troops in West Germany, the Benelux countries, and Denmark. Two hundred thousand of these are American troops. NATO countries exclusive of the U.S. have 3 million regular forces in Europe and trained reserve forces totaling 3.8 million. Opposite them, 685,000 troops are assigned to the Warsaw Pact, including almost 300,000 Soviet troops. Warsaw Pact countries have a total of 970,000 regular troops and another 1.9 million in the trained reserves.

In any conventional war the defense forces have a great advantage. It is easier to defend than attack key points, and the supply lines are shorter. A rule of thumb is that offensive forces must outnumber the defense by about three to one to be successful.

By any calculation, the North Atlantic Treaty countries outnumber the Warsaw Pact countries in terms of men on duty, total number of troops, and reserves. It is calculated that after fifteen days of warfare the Warsaw Pact countries, because of faster mobilization of reinforcements, would slightly outnumber the NATO forces, but that after thirty days the NATO countries would regain equality in numbers. In terms of quantity alone, NATO has more than the needed numerical forces to stop a Warsaw Pact attack. In terms of quality, NATO has a decided superiority in tactical aircraft, in tanks, and in antitank weapons.

If the Europeans are genuinely worried about their security, let them supply the additional troops to provide an actual defensive superiority. Meanwhile we should reduce our commitments by 150,000 men, hopefully through negotiation but directly if necessary. This would save $1.5–2 billion and leave NATO sufficiently strong to deter and stop a Warsaw Pact attack.

With respect to Asia and other overseas commitments outside Europe, the one-and-a-half-war concept, now official doctrine in the Pentagon, proposes sufficient forces to fight only one major conventional land war at a time plus the ability to respond to a minor contretemps such as the Dominican and Lebanon crises. As a result of our experience in Vietnam and the espousal of the Nixon Doctrine, it is unlikely that the United States will again provide troops for a ground war in Asia. Naval forces, land-based aircraft, and small amphibious landing forces will no doubt be the extent of our military participation once Vietnam is concluded.

The one-and-a-half-war concept has not yet resulted in any significant decrease in military spending. If actually implemented, it should result in a considerable reduction in the military budget. A $70-billion budget will provide very effective military forces. In addition to $14 billion for strategic purposes and $2 billion for Vietnam assistance, it would provide $54 billion for intelligence, research, reserves, personnel, and general-purpose forces.

I should enter a warning here that leading members of the military-industrial complex may succeed in their attempt to use the agreements reached at the SALT negotiations to justify even bigger and better military spending. They have already argued that any agreement which allows the Soviets to retain 950 submarine missiles to our 710 and which allows them to retain 1,618 land-based missiles to our 1,054 will lead to our inferiority.

In view of our MIRV capability which the Soviets do not have, the tactical weapons we have on the periphery of the Soviet Union which they cannot match, our vast lead in numbers of "force loadings," and the far greater accuracy and sophistication of our missiles, this is just plain nonsense. Our submarine fleet and its MIRV missiles are far more powerful than the Soviet submarine fleet. We routinely detect their noisy submarines with our anti-submarine capability, while they have never been known to track a single one of our strategic boats.

Nevertheless we will be pressed by writers like Joseph Alsop, groups like the American Security Council, and advocates of individual services to rush into a crash program for ULMS, fund the production of the B-1 bomber, build AWACS, move now to hard-site Minutemen, and step up our massive strategic deterrent. But when both sides already have enough weapons to blow each other to smithereens, and when our TRIAD and the present absolute unvulnerability of our submarine deterrent means that no Russian first strike can succeed, it makes far more sense to slow down the race to oblivion rather than to speed it up. In the modern nuclear age, there is still no place to hide.

Reform Procurement

Enormous additional savings can also come from the reform in procurement practices. Reforms should include but not be limited to the following.

There should be a vast increase in the proportion of contracts let by competitive bidding or at least partially competitive procedures. In a study done at the Pentagon by the former Assistant Secretary for Logistics and Supply, Thomas Morris, savings of twenty-five cents on the dollar were shown for every contract shifted from sole source to fully competitive bidding. Ten cents on the dollar was saved in shifts from sole source to more competitive circumstances, even when they were less than publicly advertised, sealed-bid procedures. Even shifting one third or one half of the present 60 percent of all Pentagon contracts let without any competition would bring savings of billions. Doubling the 10 percent now competitively advertised would save billions more.

An independent procurement agency should be established entirely outside the military to purchase defense weapons. In the present system, procurement is administered by the Army, the Navy, and the Air Force, who have a direct conflict of interest. Their concern is to get the weapons and hang the cost. This must be changed. The British Ministry of Technology, an independent agency which procures aircraft for the British military, could serve as a guide for such a new U.S. agency.

Concurrency of research and development, on the one hand, and production, on the other, must be stopped. It accounts for billions in overruns which have brought military-weapons procurement practices into disrepute.

Profit levels on negotiated contracts should be established on the basis of return on investment, not as a percentage of sales or costs. Now leading military contractors with billions in contracts a year have almost no invested capital of their own. Lockheed Aircraft, the number-one prime contractor, is the best example of this problem. Profits based on sales or costs impose no financial discipline on the manufacturing firm.

The new Uniform Accounting Standards must be implemented in both a tough and a fair-minded way. Some $2 billion of savings can be generated under the act if it is administered fearlessly.

The process of "zero-based budgeting," whereby every program is examined from the bottom up every year, must be implemented. Now this is seldom done. Once a program is under way, arguments center only on how much additional annual funding is necessary.

Simple, inexpensive, functioning weapons must be substituted for excessively sophisticated, high-priced, and malfunctioning systems. This will increase our might for far less money.

As a general rule, no merely marginally better new weapon system should move into production or be deployed. Only weapons with clear or massive superiority should be substituted for existing ones. Pentagon procurement patterned on the U. S. auto industry theory of obsolescence and a new model every year must be abandoned.

In determining the quantities of new weapons to be purchased, increases in firepower and effectiveness must be considered. New destroyers with twice the firepower of old destroyers and constructed of the size and tonnage of cruisers should be counted as the equal of two old destroyers. This is one way to reduce total procurement costs without reduction in military strength. Now the services demand two new ships or tanks or planes to replace two old ones even when firepower is vastly increased.

In determining the size of the military budget and the funds needed for procurement, there must be a thorough review of specific U. S. commitments. In numerous cases we are spending billions on sophisticated weapons to perform missions abroad for which there is no explicit American commitment.

Cuts in Wasteful Weapons

With respect to particular weapons and weapons systems, the following actions should be taken.

Carriers. No new carriers should be funded. The present number should be reduced from fifteen to twelve as they become overaged. When that level is reached, a further determination should be made as to whether the number should not be further reduced to nine. The $299 million in long-lead-times items for the CVN-70 should be cut from the 1973 budget.

F-14 Navy Fighter. The F-14 procurement and accompanying Phoenix missile procurement should end. They are costly lemons. The fiscal 1973 funding of $735 million for the F-14 should be reduced to a level to pay for termination costs.

ULMS (Underseas Long-range Missile System). Funding for the new undersea long-range missile system should be kept at the approximate level of 1972 funding of $140 million. The $942-million request for a crash program should be reduced to $380 million. ULMS should move into production only after the Poseidon fleet becomes overaged or becomes vulnerable to Russian anti–submarine-warfare weapons. Meantime, Congress should approve funds in the request for the ULMS-I missile and for research and development costs for the ULMS submarine.

AWACS. Production of the new airborne warning and control system should be scrapped. In an age when, wisely, we have chosen not to build a multibillion-dollar defense against intercontinental missiles, the expenditure of tens of billions on a new manned-bomber defense is ridiculous. This is especially so when the military has previously touted the SAGE and DEW lines as highly effective bomber defenses and while the Russians pose at best a token threat from outdated bombers. The 1973 increase from $142 to $474 million should be denied. Some development expenditures for communications and radar having more widespread application may be justified.

B-1 Bomber. The project should end. A fleet of new manned bombers in an age of sophisticated missiles is a luxury which even the wealthiest nation in the world cannot afford. The $445 million proposed for 1973 spending should be used to terminate the project and to provide for refitting existing late-model B-52s with engines and weapons to perform as a stand-off missile platform. This would provide for continuation of the TRIAD and an effective airborne strategic deterrent.

Safeguard ABM. Under the SALT agreement only two sites are now permitted. But research and development of hard-site defenses should continue. We can reduce the $1,483-billion 1973 request accordingly.

Minuteman and Poseidon MIRV Deployment. We should slow down MIRVing of Minuteman III and Poseidon weapons to reach 7,600 force loadings by 1975 instead of the contemplated 9,000 by that year. In view of the fact that U. S. force loadings increased from 4,600 to 5,700, or by 1,100 in the one-year period between June 1971 and June 1972 while the Russian force loadings went up by only 400—from 2,100 to 2,500—this is both possible and safe. As much as $500 million of the $1.6 billion in the budget for these purposes could be saved.

Cheyenne Helicopter. We should cancel development of the Cheyenne helicopter. The 1973 outlay should be reduced from $54 million to the level needed to terminate the project. Meanwhile, we should limit the Harrier buy to that already under contract and develop the A-X close-support plane for the close-support mission. Long-term costs of producing one instead of three close-support aircraft would be cut from $12 billion to $6 billion.

Anti–Submarine-Warfare Systems. We should shift the main emphasis for anti–submarine-warfare defenses from sea-based to land-based air systems. The ASW aircraft carriers should be retired. The carrier-based S-3A buy in the 1973 budget for $666 million should be ended. The ASW escort destroyers and other associated ships and weapons for the ASW carriers and retiring attack carriers should be cut.

All of these savings would make it possible to reduce the budget for "Department of Defense—Military" from $83.4 billion in new obligational authority to a $70-billion level of outlays. These cuts are both prudent and possible under the SALT agreement with the Soviet Union. While the agreement limits the number of submarine-based and land-based missile launchers, it does not affect the quality or sophistication of weapons.

We are significantly ahead of the Russians in MIRV technology, in sophistication, and in accuracy. If the Russians make significant gains in these areas we can offset them by converting additional submarines to the Poseidon configuration, MIRVing all of our Minuteman missiles, and proceeding with ULMS. Thus our sophisticated technology, plus the absence of an agreement limiting either bombers or tactical weapons, more than offsets any advantage the Russians have in somewhat larger number of authorized launchers or in megatonnage.

Cuts in Foreign Aid

It is equally important to cut and reform foreign military and economic aid.

The first need is to get adequate information. A list of what military aid the United States gives away, lends, sells, leases, or otherwise provides foreign countries should be compiled in a report and submitted to Congress annually. The American taxpayer who is footing the bill has every right to know what he's paying for. This principle is embodied in a Proxmire-Case bill which was accepted as an amendment to the 1972 Foreign Aid Authorization Bill.

Next we should demilitarize foreign aid. It is too important a matter for the military to run. We should place the responsibility for it—all of it—under the Secretary of State, where it belongs. In

Congress the responsibility for authorizing funds should be placed under the Senate Foreign Relations Committee and the House Foreign Affairs Committee. They should be the chief Congressional watchdog over foreign policy. This is the right policy. President Kennedy insisted when he took office that the ambassador in each country was responsible for the administration of American foreign policy abroad. When the Vietnam buildup came, massive foreign military aid was placed in the Pentagon budget and authorized by the Armed Services Committees. That policy should be reversed.

With respect to specific programs the following reforms should be instituted.

Reform Military Aid

The service-funded military aid—the $2.3-billion grant program for Vietnam, Laos, and Thailand now run by the Army, the Navy, and the Air Force—should be phased out and ended. Any residual amounts should be placed under the Secretary of State.

The military-grant program now under the Secretary of State—the grant MAP program—should be converted to a sales and credit-sales program. Instead of friendly countries having free military aid forced upon them, they should have to pay for it. This would force them to make hard choices and set their own domestic priorities as to whether the military equipment was needed or not. As long as we provide it free, they will take it. That should be stopped.

We should establish a series of "arms-free zones" where no weapons at all are allowed. Latin America, Africa, and the Indian Ocean area would be good beginnings. Meanwhile, as a starter, we should limit military aid to no more than ten countries instead of the existing forty-six.

Taken together, these reforms would represent an historic

shift in the nature of and control over the foreign military-aid programs. Such a shift away from the military and into civilian hands is long overdue.

We should also make public the names of foreign countries receiving military aid and the amounts of aid provided to them, instead of keeping a number of them secret, as the State Department insists. The right of the American people to make the great decisions of war and peace must not be denied on grounds of secrecy. Armed with facts, the people of the United States will make better decisions in the nation's interest than a group of Pentagon or State Department elitists in the secrecy of their war rooms. Arguments that publicizing country-by-country amounts would be embarrassing if made public make no sense at all. If we followed such logic domestically we would classify the entire military budget on the grounds that to reveal the amounts would embarrass the military services or the Joint Chiefs of Staff.

With respect to excess and surplus military supplies, they should no longer be given away free or disposed of abroad for a few cents on the dollar. A minimum of one third of their acquisition cost should be required, except for scrap items; in the latter case, the General Accounting Office and the recipient country should certify that items bought for scrap are used as scrap. The funds generated from sales should be used to pay for American obligations in the country involved or to finance international education and cultural exchanges. For overaged or surplus ships, receiving countries should be required to pay at least 25 percent of their acquisition cost plus the cost of rehabilitating and refitting them.

Interest rates for military credit sales should be set at the Export-Import Bank interest rate for comparable commercial programs. This would reduce but not end the subsidy.

The funds spent for international military headquarters, military-assistance missions, and military advisory groups should be authorized by the Foreign Affairs and Foreign Relations Committees and administered by the Department of State.

Finally, we should prohibit the use of Food for Peace funds for military purposes. This is proposed in a Proxmire-Mansfield-McGovern-Humphrey bill.

Taken together, these reforms should help to bring the chaotic military-aid programs under control. By doing these things we can serve our real national interest, save the taxpayers billions of dollars, and help bring peace to a very unpeaceful world.

Whether we will always make wise decisions is not the issue. These reforms would provide the facts by which wise decisions could be made. They would clearly place the power, responsibility, and accountability for the programs in one place. These are the first and fundamental steps in reordering foreign military-aid priorities.

Reorder Economic-Aid Priorities

Meanwhile the priorities for economic aid should also be reordered. We should return to the Truman principle that aid should "help the free people of the world, through their own efforts, to produce more food, more clothing, more materials for housing, and more mechanical power to lighten their burdens."

The major emphasis should be placed on population programs, humanitarian relief, self-help technical assistance, and the Peace Corps.

The big-project development programs should be reduced.

The success of the program should be measured by the proportions that go for schools, housing, job training, health, and co-operative farm programs. The fundamental test should be: Do the programs actually help those who need help the most? Does the aid get to the people of the country?

The military-training and public-safety programs should be stopped.

Direct, bilateral aid should be reduced, while aid through multinational institutions should be stressed. But this principle should not merely transfer bad aid programs from bilateral to multilateral institutions and from unfriendly national bureaucracies to unfriendly international bureaucracies.

Methods must be found to target multilateral aid programs to the poor, to shift big-project funds to self-help programs, to transform the thrust of international banking institutions from hard loans to humanitarian aid, to make certain that enormous windfall profits are not made by intermediary financial institutions because of high interest-rate margins, and to see that member nations contribute some fair proportion of the total amounts to international programs instead of the United States providing a disproportionate share of the total.

In their totality the foreign military and economic-aid programs should be drastically reduced, priorities shifted, and responsibility lodged in one department. We can do a much better job for far less by bringing the programs under control.

6 · Something in It for Everybody

It was one of those important occasions in the Senate when members were actually in their seats and the aides and attachés lined the chamber's walls below the marble busts of former Vice-Presidents which, according to the standing rules of the Senate, "shall be placed in the Senate wing of the Capitol from time to time."

The occasion was not the ratification of the Nuclear Test Ban Treaty, the advice and consent to the controversial appointment of Clement F. Haynsworth to the Supreme Court, or a vote on civil rights or the SST. It was the day when the annual public-works, navigation, and flood-control bill was before the Senate.

While the Senate floor was buzzing with Senators anticipating the passage of the annual largess which greases the political skids with civic groups and local chambers of commerce, the galleries were empty. The public-works pork-barrel bill is an internal occasion of great importance to Senators but of scant moment to the rest of the world.

Managing the bill was Senator Dennis Chavez, chairman of the Public Works Committee and senior Senator from New Mexico. The recipient of unctuous praise and even fawning thanks from fellow Senators whose aides had already composed the telegrams that would notify local constituents when the bill was passed, Chavez blanched with amazement when Paul Douglas, then Senator from Illinois, rose to chastise the bill and most of its works.

For a Senator to question the public-works bill was an act not unlike Cardinal Spellman criticizing the Pope. Chavez could not comprehend how any Senator in his right mind could oppose the bill. This was especially true of Douglas, whose state got tens of millions in money for dams on the Mississippi and Illinois Rivers and tens of millions more for the Cal Sag project, so important to the railroads and the steel, cement, and farm-machinery industries which rimmed the lower end of Lake Michigan. Finally, in exasperation, Chavez shouted, "Why is the Senator fighting this bill? There's something in it for everybody."

At a later date when a small navigation project was justified on the grounds that it would keep the motorboats in an East Coast river from "roiling the crabs," Douglas commented that while he believed in the welfare state he balked at extending it to crustacean life.

Welfare for the Crabs

Figuratively, public spending has been extended to a vast variety of forms of "crustacean life," namely federal spending that is wasteful, inefficient, and unnecessary. Billions are spent for public goods and services produced at greater cost than the private economy can make them. Alternative programs in either the public or the private sector would accomplish the goals of many existing programs more efficiently.

The clear analysis by former Budget Director and Brookings Institution economist Charles Schultze is ominous. Existing programs, even at a low 4 percent unemployment, will eat up every additional revenue dollar for several years into the future. The only meaningful way to get the enormous revenues for America's desperate needs, short of raising taxes, is by cutting back on wasteful programs. This fact is reinforced by the discipline of the full-employment-budget concept which provides for spending up to the full-employment-revenue level in times of recession. This means that federal spending is as high with 6 percent unemployment as with 4 percent unemployment. Recovery provides massive new resources for the economy as a whole, but provides no additional funds for federal spending. Federal spending, financed by large deficits, is at the full-employment level even when there is no full employment.

Cutting back the fat and the waste is therefore not only good in itself but imperative. It is necessary as a source of income, and as a means to guarantee that the private sector provides the abundance of resources upon which the government is dependent for revenues. The argument is clear and simple. It goes like this: With no new funds available unless we cut back on existing inefficiencies, new programs for health, education, welfare, antipollution, housing, and others, even in prosperous times, can be provided only through immense budget deficits.

This is highly inflationary. The federal government would become a vast engine of inflation. Excessive inflation, in turn, defeats the very goals society is trying to achieve, in at least two ways. First, if there is runaway inflation unacceptable costs are imposed on the aged, the poor, the saver, the salaried worker, and others with modest savings and fixed incomes. They are hit and hit hard. Second, if vast complex laws and regulations are erected to put a lid on inflation by controlling prices, wages, interest, and profits, then the frictions and inefficiencies forced on the private sector will reduce its ability to perform, impair its genius, and abrogate its function and purpose.

These are unsatisfactory choices.

What the term "reordering priorities" should really mean is not only the foresight to advocate spending for unmet needs but also the guts to cut back the frills and wastes as well. But, as in sandlot football, everybody wants to be a hero and carry the ball but no one wants the dirty, grubby, unpopular job of blocking for the ball carrier in the offensive line.

Public-Works Boondoggles

There are numerous examples where billions in savings can be made. Consider these.

The federal government will spend more than $1 billion on the Trinity River project. This is a public-works white elephant of monstrous proportions. It would result in a ship canal from the Gulf of Mexico to the Dallas–Fort Worth area. Some have said that it would be cheaper to move Dallas and Fort Worth to the Gulf of Mexico.

The government spent $70 million dredging the Delaware River from Philadelphia to Trenton to a depth of forty feet. The purpose was to make it possible for ore boats to sail up to the U. S. Steel's Fairless works. The project was designed to serve a single company. The taxpayers of the country contributed the bulk of the funds. The company thus shifted a substantial part of its transportation costs from itself to the public. Ironically, the heavily subsidized barge traffic took business away from the railroads, which were fighting for their economic life. More ironic, the ore barges for whom the forty-foot dredging was performed were built in Japan. When urged by Senators to make their private opposition public and to organize an open fight against the project, the railroads most directly involved refused to do so on the grounds that the steel company might retaliate. Thus, while the powerful economic interests benefiting from this boondoggle were not shy in lobbying and pressuring for the funds, the chief economic losers were unwilling to fight. This explains why many bad projects prevail.

Since completion, the Delaware River project has cost a great deal to maintain and in some years has been little used by vessels with forty-foot drafts. In the two most recent years, maintenance of the Philadelphia–Trenton stretch of the river has cost between $1.25 and $1.4 million annually. In one year only ten vessels with forty-foot drafts, carrying only seventy thousand tons, made the trip.

The $1.5 billion spent annually and the tens of billions mortgaged in the future for the public-works pork barrel are determined by a formula that promotes waste. Called a benefit-cost ratio, a public-works project becomes feasible when its benefits equal its costs. That ratio is expressed as one to one. It is a sad commentary on Uncle Sam, the last of the bigtime spenders, that with all our waste, public works is one of the few government spending programs which requires the objectivity of a benefit-cost ratio. The benefit-cost ratio isn't much, but it is something. Traditionally, the original estimates are far wide of the final mark. One major study showed that because of planning alterations and change orders, public-works projects routinely cost twice as much as their original estimates. In addition, benefits are routinely exaggerated. They amount in reality to about half those listed.

In the case of the Burns Ditch harbor project at the lower end of Lake Michigan, for example, conservationists who opposed the project because it and the new steel mills projected for the site would ruin the unique Indiana Dunes area established that the Corps of Engineers had double-counted the shipping benefits. The nearby Calumet Sag project was justified on grounds of increased shipping benefits. The Corps used many of the same benefits to justify the Burns Ditch project. Obviously the two were competing rather than complementary projects.

Every economist of any note who has testified before the Joint Economic Committee has questioned the economic merit of these programs. Their costs are high and their benefits are low. While unemployment is concentrated in the central cities and among teenagers and women, these and other water projects are built in relatively remote areas. The "something in it for everybody" philosophy determines that. Senators from rural, mountain, and border states have more votes than those from the populous industrial regions. Mutual back-scratching is necessary to get projects through. Three or four bad ones are included for every one justified on its economic merits.

More and more the environmentalists question these projects too. But the projects can and should be fought first of all on their lack of economic merit. One key issue concerns the discount rate and the opportunity costs of capital.

The Need for a Proper Discount Rate

The investment of private capital in the United States brings in a return of more than 12 percent. It follows that for the government to tax funds from the private sector to spend for public works or other economic investments, a return of 10 percent or more should be made. Otherwise it is an inefficient use of resources.

For years the discount rate or cost of the public funds invested in public works was calculated at 3⅛ percent. That has now risen to 5⅜ percent, and the Office of Management and Budget is correctly pressing for a higher, but still uneconomic, rate of 5⅞.

It is clear that, with the low discount rate applied as well as the traditional exaggeration of benefits and the underestimate of costs, a project should have a benefit–cost ratio of more than two to one to be justified on economic grounds. If that were required, and it should be required except where some great social subsidy can be justified on other than economic grounds, at least half the projects would be killed.

This is precisely why the President's proposal to spend almost $700 million more in 1973 than in 1972 for Corps of Engineers and Bureau of Reclamation projects was unjustified. Priorities for schools, antipollution, and housing gave way to the pork barrel. It was a dramatic reordering of priorities.

What the country needs are programs to build up the health and education of our children rather than programs that build dams in the desert. As the studies of men like Theodore Schultz at the University of Chicago have shown, the investment in human capital has a measurable return equal to or in excess of investment in private capital. Educated and trained people visibly raise the productivity of the economy. The shift in investment from wasteful public works to productive education not only is desirable now on social grounds but brings a greater return when measured by hard, tough economic standards.

At least $1 billion could be cut from the $2.5 billion annual expenditures for public-works, reclamation, and other water projects.

Spectacular Space Spending

Another prime candidate for cuts is the space program. The National Aeronautical and Space Administration's proposed space shuttle and station, if approved, would push NASA's annual budget to the $7-billion range in the late 1970s. No less an authority than Dr. J. A. Van Allen, for whom the Van Allen Radiation Belt was named, has challenged that expenditure. In a letter to Senator Mondale he wrote: "I estimate that the proper objectives of the national space program can be met in a vigorous and effective way by unmanned techniques at the annual level of some $2 billion."

The culprit is the space shuttle, whose supporters claim it can provide savings in costs to accomplish future space-program missions. But Dr. Van Allen has written that these claims are based on two mistaken calculations: (1) "gross over-estimation of the volume of space traffic (i.e., tons of payload into orbit per year) that can be reasonably anticipated"; (2) "substantial under-estimation of the developmental and operational costs of the shuttle program." One study estimated that the only thing the shuttle would "save" over a twenty-year period would be its own development and initial procurement costs.

These "savings" would have to come about from a vast increase in the space program itself. Under one of NASA's projections for the use of the shuttle, on which the "savings" are based, there would be 970 missions in the twelve-year period from 1978 to 1990, or 74 missions a year. In the peak year the payload would be over six million pounds, or three thousand tons. But, as Senator Mondale pointed out,

During the decade of the 1960s, NASA exceeded 30 launches a year only once—36 in 1966. And in terms of the weight of cumulative payloads launched, 1969 was NASA's biggest year, with 442,348 pounds—221 tons—over 97 percent of which was attributed to the four Apollo flights.

The significance is clear. For the space shuttle to pay out or, more accurately, even to break even, there must be an enormous increase in the space program itself. The obvious original purpose of NASA was a continuation of the highly expensive manned space flights. The "savings" can come only by spending billions of added funds. The Rand study for the Air Force found that we would have to spend $141 billion on space between now and 1990 to make the original proposal pay out. As Dr. Thomas Gold, a member of the President's Science Advisory Committee and director of Cornell University's Center for Radiophysics and Space Research, has also testified on the space shuttle, "It seems impossible to justify it economically except if a great increase in the weight to be sent into orbit, and in the NASA budget, could be foreseen, and even then only after very many years of usage."

To oppose the space shuttle is not to be against all space programs. Dr. Van Allen argues that a space program should have two fundamental objectives. He names them as the utilitarian use of space technology and scientific exploration. According to Dr. Van Allen, "The first of these objectives should be dominant. A well-designed program of space applications can be closely matched to human needs and desires and can be essentially self-justifying, i.e., it can 'pay its own way.'" He explains that program:

I am thinking here primarily of the areas of efficient radio communication with all of its immense potential for advancing the educational and cultural levels of many millions of persons throughout the world as well as for routine technical purposes, and of reconnaissance in its broadest sense.

He notes the small costs by which such a desired program can be accomplished:

> Both of these applications can be well served by a relatively small number (say 50) of long-lived, unmanned satellites in the 1,000 to 10,000 lb. class. Updating and replacement of elements of such world wide operational systems are envisoned as requiring no more than 10 launches per year.

The contrast is clear. By unmanned rather than manned flight stunts, the important space objectives can be accomplished with ten launches rather than seventy, with far smaller tonnage, and at a $2-billion annual level rather than one which is three or more times that high. In my personal view, it could be done for even less, namely about $1.5 billion.

And Dr. Brian O'Leary, an astronomer and a former scientist wrote to Senator Mondale and others of us opposing the space-shuttle program in 1971: ". . . it is a plain fact that nearly all tasks in space sciences and application can be done as effectively with existing unmanned spacecraft at one to ten percent the cost of existing manned aircraft."

Manned space flight and the space shuttle are two key frills that must be pruned from the U. S. budget. We can accomplish every important scientific and practical space objective for billions less than the National Aeronautical and Space Agency proposes.

Big Farm Subsidies: Candidate for Reform

The farm subsidy program is another candidate for reform. Farmers suffer from unique economic problems. They also suffer the consequences of their greatest virtues.

Since the introduction of the tractor, hybrid seeds, modern fertilizers, and mechanization, American farm productivity has increased many fold. It is a modern miracle envied the world over.

In the 1910–14 period a farmer worked 106 hours to produce 100 bushels of wheat, 135 hours to produce 100 bushels of corn and 276 hours to produce a bale of cotton. In the 1960s he worked only eight hours to produce 100 bushels of corn, eleven hours to produce 100 bushels of wheat, and thirty-two hours per bale of cotton. Those are phenomenal increases.

Mechanization and better breeding have brought the same phenomenal results in dairy and livestock production as well as in crops. In 1910–14 a dairy cow produced thirty-eight hundredweight of milk a year; now she produces eighty-five. And that production is produced with one-third fewer man-hours by the dairy farmer.

Nonetheless, the individual farmer is caught in a squeeze. As the United States becomes more affluent and incomes grow, food consumption declines relatively. A 10 percent increase in income in the United States results in less than a one percent increase in the demand for food. As farmers grow more productive, people spend relatively less on food. Surpluses pile up.

As the farmer produces more, he finds that prices fall disastrously as the demand for food goes up minutely.

Unlike the producers of many industrial goods, and unlike organized labor, farmers are unable to band together effectively with their fellow farmers to limit production. The only way an individual farmer can hope to get some reasonable return is to produce more and more and more. In the old days the only way an individual farmer could help himself was to pray for rain on his farm and drought for all his neighbors. This is at the root of the farm problem and the rationale behind the farm programs. The programs have a strong basis in the economic facts of life. Only the government can step in to limit total farm production effectively.

There are tremendous costs to the program. Estimates are that they now amount to about $10 billion a year. Over $5 billion of this cost is in direct farm payments and price supports. About $4.5 billion is in higher prices paid by consumers.

Even at these costs, consumers in the United States get a terrific deal, due to both the fantastic spurt in farm output and the quirk in the nature of farm prices under which small increases in farm production bring large decreases in farm prices. The economists call this phenomenon by the technical term "inelasticity of demand." It is the reason the consumer gets a great buy. Meanwhile the individual farmer gets it in the neck. A measure of this productivity is seen in the fact that the percentage of income that the American family spends for food, including the cost of the farm programs, is less than it has ever been before in the history of the United States and less than in any other country of the world.

The basic purpose in limiting the output of farm products through government payments and price supports is to increase farm income. Including the imputed income of rent and food grown on the farm, average farm income is only about two-thirds the amount of average nonfarm income. The average nonfarm family in the United States earns $10,000, but the average farm family earns only $6,700 per year.

Upside-Down Rewards

But who benefits from the farm program? Is the $10 billion per year in government payments and higher food prices redistributed from wealthy urban dwellers to the poor farmer? Do the programs serve the social purpose of preserving and enhancing the family farm as a means of promoting democracy and social stability? Do farm programs reward farmers fairly for the vast increase in their efficiency and productivity? If these goals were met, most people would support farm programs. This is especially true since, even with the costs, food prices are such great bargains for the consumer.

Unfortunately, farm programs reward farmers in inverse proportion to their needs. In the mid-1960s, the largest one percent of American farms had total cash receipts which were 50 percent higher than the total cash receipts of half the farms in the country. The figures are: one percent of the farms got 18 percent of the total cash receipts, while half the farms in the country got 12 percent of the farm receipts; the biggest 20 percent of farms got 50 percent of the cash receipts, while the smallest 20 percent got only 1.8 percent of all farm cash receipts.

When one looks at particular programs, the problem is even more intense. The top 5 percent of farms by size got 63 percent of sugarcane program benefits, 41 percent of the cotton program benefits, 35 percent for rice, 30.5 percent for wheat, 24 percent for feed grains, and 28.5 percent for peanuts. In each of these cases, the benefits going to the top 5 percent of the producers measured by farm size got a bigger share of the program benefits than did the lower 60 percent of the producers.

That the distribution of benefits is clearly in inverse proportion to the need for income can be further illustrated by a table from the Department of Agriculture's publication *Farm Income Situation, July 1970*. The department classifies farms in six classes based on the amount of their farm sales receipts. These are given in the table below for 1970.

Economic Class	Value of Sales (thousands of dollars)	Percent of Total Farm Sales, 1969	Percent of Total Number of Farms, 1969
I	40 and over	51.3	7.1
II	20-40	21.3	12.0
III	10-20	16.0	17.0
IV	5-10	6.3	13.1
V	2.5-5	2.4	9.6
VI	Less than 2.5	2.7	41.2

Based on these six categories, the Department of Agriculture has compiled a table on the distribution of farm program benefits for 1969 (1) in billions of dollars, (2) by the percent of the total, and (3) for certain income and benefits per farm in thousands of dollars. See the table below.

Distribution of Farm Program Benefits
and Income by Economic Class, 1969

Item	I	II	III	IV	V	VI	I & II	V & VI
				Economic Class				
Aggregate benefits				*(billions of dollars)*				
Price supports	1.90	0.76	0.55	0.22	0.08	0.09	2.66	0.17
Direct payments	1.08	0.90	0.88	0.43	0.20	0.30	1.98	0.50
Total	2.98	1.66	1.43	0.65	0.28	0.39	4.64	0.67
Distribution of benefits				*(percent of total)*				
Price supports	52.9	21.0	15.4	6.1	2.2	2.4	73.9	4.6
Direct payments	28.5	23.7	23.2	11.3	5.3	7.9	53.6	13.2
Total	40.3	22.5	19.4	8.8	3.8	5.3	62.8	9.1
Income and benefits per farm				*(thousands of dollars)*				
Farmer's net income	33.0	13.7	9.6	8.1	7.0	8.1	20.9	7.9
Net income from farming	27.5	10.5	6.5	3.6	2.1	1.1	16.8	1.3
Price supports	9.0	2.1	1.1	0.6	0.3	0.1	4.7	0.1
Direct payments	5.1	2.5	1.7	1.1	0.7	0.2	3.6	0.3
Total	14.1	4.6	2.8	1.7	1.0	0.3	8.3	0.4
Net income from farming under free market conditions	13.4	5.9	3.7	1.9	1.1	0.8	8.5	0.9

Farms in Classes I and II, which averaged $20,900 in net income per year, got 62.8 percent ($4.64 billion) of the total of all direct payments and price supports. Farmers in Classes V and VI, averaging only $7,900 per year, of which only $1,300 was from farming, received only 9.1 percent ($670 million) of the total benefits.

Payments to Big Producers

Some of the figures about payments to individual farmers are even more revealing. In 1971 the Senate Appropriations Committee published a county-by-county list for the entire United States, giving the name and amount of payments over $5,000 received by individual producers.

Five producers got price support, conservation, and other payments of more than $1 million in calendar year 1969. Some 362 producers got $100,000 or more. Sixty-eight thousand producers received $7,500 or more in payments. This is more money in payments alone for each of these 68,000 producers than the average farmer earned in that year. In fact, the 129,000 producers who received $5,000 or more in payments in 1969 got more in payments than the actual value of sales for more than half the farms in the United States. Of the $3,795,000,000 in payments in 1969 (exclusive of price-support loans and Wool and Sugar Act payments), $1,458,000,000, or 38 percent, went to producers who got $5,000 or more.

There is a great need for a farm program. But one which dis⁻ tributes income from average consumers to big farmers does not meet the purposes for which any reasonable and effective farm program can be justified.

A proper program should do several things. It should place a strict ceiling on the size of payments to any one farm or farmer. It should limit production. It should raise farm income for those farm families earning below-average annual incomes. It should promote the family-sized farm for social, political, and economic reasons. These latter are not incompatible goals. Numerous studies of farm efficiency indicate that the optimum unit is not the giant farm but one which can be operated essentially by a farmer and his son, or by a farmer and one hired man.

About $2 billion a year could be saved if payments were limited to those which had the effect of raising low farm income to the average level, and if they were reduced progressively for operators with above-average incomes.

Controlling the Uncontrollables

The biggest savings in the federal budget could be made by "controlling the uncontrollables." It is candidate number one for pruning waste.

Of the $246.3 billion that President Nixon requested for 1973, the Office of Management and Budget lists $175 billion as spending which is "relatively uncontrollable under present law." Included are $68 billion in spending for Social Security, Medicare, unemployment compensation, and civil-service retirement. The $21 billion of interest on the national debt is on the list. Veterans' benefits, Medicaid, Commodity Credit Corporation programs, military retired pay, and other trust funds costing $40 billion are itemized as "uncontrollable." Defense and civilian contracts and pay raises are in for another $46 billion. The budget experts argue that, short of major legislative change, very little can be done to control this spending.

I deny that the uncontrollables in the budget are uncontrollable. We could save billions in the $19.7 billion listed as an "uncontrollable" item under military procurement alone.

A prime candidate for cuts is the $14-billion item for Medicaid and Medicare. These cuts can be made administratively. They can be made within a year. They can be made without hurting the program in any way. Here's why: Medicare and Medicaid are needed and necessary programs, but their costs have gone through the roof.

In 1965, when Medicare was enacted, the costs for 1975 were projected at $4.3 billion, a conservative actuarial estimate; now the estimate is $11.5 billion. The 1965 conservative actuarial estimate for the cost of benefits by 1990, or twenty-five years down the road, was $8.8 billion; now that estimate has grown almost fourfold and stands at $32.8 billion. In 1965 the total federal-state medical-assistance spending was $1.3 billion; by 1970 it had grown to $5.5 billion. The federal share had increased from $555 million to $2.8 billion. This is a fivefold increase for Medicaid. By official estimates, the Medicare deficit over the next twenty-five years will be an astronomical $242 billion.

We must halt Medicare and Medicaid overruns just as we must stop weapons systems overruns. Some of the increase is due to a greater use of the programs than originally estimated. But the bulk of it is due to soaring costs. These can be stopped or slowed down. The Senate Finance Committee took a long look at the problem and came up with some answers. First of all, it found in a detailed staff study that there were grave abuses and some cases of corruption in the program. The staff report found that

many physicians are resorting to "gang visits" and unnecessarily frequent visits to nursing home and hospital patients in order to up their Medicare payments.

Under this practice a physician may see as many as 30, 40, and 50 patients a day in the same facility—regardless of whether the visit is medically necessary or whether any service is actually furnished.

The physician in many cases charges his full fee for each patient, billing Medicare for as much as $300 or $400 for one sweep through a nursing home.

Proof of the widespread abuse was further shown when the committee published a list of doctors who were paid $25,000 or more from Medicare or Medicaid in a single year. The list, which was partial and incomplete, included sixty-eight solo medical practitioners who got more than $100,000 under the program. Some 4,300 individual practitioners and 900 physician groups each received at least $25,000 from Medicare alone.

The study found numerous practitioners who were paid $15,000 to $20,000 for laboratory services. It reported "large payments being made for what appear to be inordinate numbers of injections. In many cases, we found what is apparently overvisiting and gang-visiting of patients in hospitals and nursing homes."

Further Medicare Findings

Among other reasons for the runaway costs, the study found that the Medicare payment structure encouraged high fees.

It found that because providers of medical services (hospitals and nursing homes) select the "intermediaries" (the insurance companies), many intermediaries "have been reluctant to apply positive administrative requirements with respect to costs . . . for fear of losing the provider's nomination." To put it simply, if the insurance companies don't pay up, they lose the business. The study charged that some intermediaries solicited business with implicit promises of special or preferential treatment and that some intermediaries also sell insurance to providers they serve, "creating an implicit conflict of interest."

The study found that "carrier performance under Medicare has, in the majority of instances, been erratic, inefficient, costly and inconsistent with Congressional intent." No one weeded out the inefficient carrier.

The study found fault with the Social Security Administration for lax administration. It charged the Bureau of Health Insurance with putting out instructions which were not issued timely, were often too voluminous and detailed, and were not written in clear and concise fashion with appropriate examples.

The staff found that a number of the nursing-home chains made a practice of selling stock to local physicians to make certain that the new facility got paying patients. The committee cross-checked the list of physicians receiving $25,000 or more in payments with those who had financial interests in proprietary hospitals or nursing homes. It found that a number of these physicians

showed unusual amounts and patterns of charges. In particular the frequency of visits to institutionalized patients and the aggregate amounts billed for such visits as well as for injections and laboratory services indicate an obvious need for thorough follow-up.

One abuse the study dug up was a trend toward changing the status of a proprietary hospital or nursing home to that of a "nonprofit" institution. For example, a group of physicians who own a proprietary hospital with a depreciated value of $2 million claim a "fair market value" of $4 million, including good will, etc. They sell it for that amount to a nonprofit organization which they control. The purchase price is paid from the excess of cash flow over expenses. Previously the net income, say of $200,000 a year, was subject to taxation. But it now becomes tax-free and can be applied to the inflated $4-million purchase price which goes to the group of physicians who own it. They in turn pay a capital-gains tax on the amount instead of ordinary income tax rates. This is an obvious abuse of the tax-exempt status and prompted the Finance Committee to ask the Treasury Department to submit remedial legislation.

These practices help to explain what a New York physician told me during a conversation with him in Antigua in the Caribbean. He was making so much money from Medicare, he said, that he worked only three to four days a week, owned a private jet, and spent several days a week in Jamaica in the winter and several days a week in Canada in the summer.

While legislation was needed to correct the abuse noted above, the Finance Committee staff study recommended a lengthy list of reforms which could be put into effect administratively. There was no need to wait. Legislation was not needed.

The plain fact is that under Medicare and Medicaid "uncontrollable" abuses can be brought under control. The same is true of the frills, fat, and waste which exist in the remaining $161 billion of "uncontrollable" spending. The cry that a big item of waste is uncontrollable and hence nothing can be done about it is a shibboleth devised to aid the bureaucrat in crossing the fords of public irresponsibility.

Who Regulates the Regulators?

Another major area of waste and inefficiency which must be brought under control is that fostered by the regulatory agencies. The economic inefficiencies spawned by the so-called independent regulatory agencies like the Interstate Commerce

Commission, the Federal Power Commission, the Federal Communications Commission, and others are not subjected to intensive review by either the Budget Bureau or Congress. But billions in higher costs to both the government and private industry results from their practices. Vast windfall earnings flow from their decisions. Billions in subsidies are ladled out under their auspices.

The point can best be illustrated by looking at one regulatory agency, the Interstate Commerce Commission.

The ICC was established by the political protest of the Populist movement, which objected to the monopoly practices of the railroads in the late nineteenth century. As the only form of transportation that millions of farmers could use to ship their goods to market, railroads held life-and-death sway over the economic livelihood of the American people.

To the producers' and consumers' great disadvantages, railroads practiced cutthroat competition until their rivals were driven out of business. Once established as a monopoly, they followed these abuses with unfair practices, including refusing adequate service and charging excessive prices, and insufficient financing and speculative dealings.

As the railroads were then a natural monopoly, the obvious policy to follow was to regulate them in the public interest. The ICC was established to do that.

With the advent of trucks, airlines, automobiles, and modern water competition, transportation policy has faced a dilemma. One solution was to let the various forms of transportation actually compete with one another. Regulation would be limited largely to safety conditions and the enforcement of competition through the Sherman, Clayton, and other antitrust acts. The other solution was to monopolize or cartelize the entire industry and then regulate it. This latter policy was followed. It was the wrong choice.

Motor trucking monopolies were established because the railroads were regulated as monopolies. Trucking firms were refused the right to carry goods on backhauls at rates covering the incremental costs of the service. Instead they travel back empty. The ICC prohibited truckers from carrying both regulated and exempt commodities in the same truck. Certificates for service were given for only limited numbers of towns and cities. Truckers were prohibited from serving intermediate points. As many as 40 percent of the regulated motor carriers were limited to carrying one commodity.

Regional and area trucking monopolies were established by the direct act of the ICC. The result was vast idleness in potential trucking resources. One study estimates that only about 50 percent of the physical capacity of the trucking industry is used.

The same conditions prevail with the railroads. The miles and miles of space that rail yards occupy in places like the center of Chicago are an economic waste. Most branch-line operations are uneconomic. Boxcars average somewhat under three hours' movement a day and stand idle in yards or sidings an average of twenty-one hours a day. They average only one and a half revenue round trips a month. Many cattle-loading pens, urban yards, and transit sheds are obsolete facilities which cost railroads excessive amounts.

The traditional resistance of the ICC, first to carload rates, then to multi-carload rates, and to unit trains or trainload rates for one commodity like coal, has inhibited over the years the development of more efficient technology.

Under the "rule of three" in barge operations, the bulk exemption is lost with tows of over three different commodities. Under the "mixing rule," exempt commodities lose their exemption if mixed with cargoes subject to regulation. These two rules result in barges carrying smaller loads than they would otherwise, and in empty movements to prevent violations.

Umbrella Ratemaking

The policy of the ICC is to universalize inefficient endeavors. The charge to "foster sound economic conditions in transportation" has led the ICC to protect each kind of service—rail, barge, truck—against the other. The result has been "umbrella ratemaking" which keeps rates high for one class of carrier for the express purpose of protecting another class. This raises costs.

Various estimates have been made as to the size of these costs. In a study done for the Joint Economic Committee by Professor George Hilton of the Economics Department of the University of California at Los Angeles some were cited.

When the movement of chickens by truck was removed from regulation, the truck rates on both fresh and frozen chickens fell by one third or more. Much of the fall was due to the new ability to provide multiple destinations.

Professor Robert Harbeson estimated that the use of trucks rather than carload rail transportation because of regulation results in an annual economic loss of $1 to $2.8 billion or an average of about $2 billion.

The economic loss from the ICC's refusal to allow rates for unit trains of coal was estimated by Paul McAvoy and James Sloss at $9 million a year.

The ruling by the Supreme Court banning barges from filling out tows with bulk commodities carried at special towing rates added between $207 to $287 million to the cost of moving freight, according to a *Transportation Journal* study by Karl Ruppenthal.

In a Brookings Institution study by Thomas Moore which attempted to give a comprehensive cost of rail, barge, truck, pipeline, and other ICC regulation, the conclusion was that the existence of the Interstate Commerce Commission entailed an implicit tax on the economy in the order of $5 billion or more.

In his study for the Joint Economic Committee where these facts were cited, Professor Hilton says: "One cannot avoid the conclusion that the present organization of the transportation industry is in the nature of a major tax on the economy which results mainly in waste, rather than in a subsidy which has major benefits for society or for many individuals." He reaches this conclusion on the basis that "the cartelization attracts unspecialized resources from other activities and wastes them in idleness, underutilization and inappropriate use." The estimate by Professor Moore is that about one fourth of the $27-billion income generated in transportation in 1968 may simply be waste.

The answer to all of this is to abolish the ICC and subject the carriers to the Sherman Act's provision against monopoly practices.

The example of the ICC is proof enough that vast waste exists in the regulatory agencies. Their purposes and functions should be brought under explicit annual Congressional review. The resources wasted in transportation, due in large part to the regulation of the industry by the ICC, are urgently needed elsewhere.

Gold in Them Thar Hills

The list of frills, fat, and waste in domestic programs is an almost endless one. Even minor attempts to ferret them out can be tremendously productive. Beyond the inefficiencies found in public-works, space, price-support, Medicare-Medicaid, and transportation programs, consider these additional ones.

The Buy America Act and the tied-loan program under foreign aid result in hundreds of millions of dollars of extra costs. These are promoted by public policy. It is probably impossible and unrealistic to attempt to remedy these abuses during periods of high unemployment. If we move again to a fully employed economy, changes in these programs can be made.

After paying out billions of dollars to produce the military cargo fleet, including the C-5A which is used only three to four hours a day, the government spends tens of millions in purchasing cargo space from commercial airlines. This is a form of double payment. It is like the commuter who routinely calls a taxi to take him to work while leaving his paid-up car at home.

The Aid to Impacted Schools program's original purpose has been corrupted and results in a cruel charge on the taxpayer. Designed to help educate children when the government built a new Army base or a big federal installation, it has now degenerated into a program which subsidizes some of the richest suburbs in the United States. It should be cut and cut hard. Funds should be provided only for those districts with demonstrated need.

In 1970 private government contractors held almost $14 billion in federal property at their plants. This included special tools, test equipment, industrial equipment, industrial real property and other materials. International Telephone and Telegraph held $1.3 billion of government-owned property, General Dynamics held $836 million, General Electric had $532 million, to name only a few cases.

In a General Accounting Office report on the use of the equipment great abuses were found. The report was shocking. In a random check of twenty-three contractors all but one were found to be using government equipment for commercial work in direct violation of the laws and regulations covering such use. This costs taxpayers millions which should be paid for by private companies and investors.

Shipping subsidies, subsidized second- and third-class postal rates, discrimination against American goods subjected to ocean freight rates, subsidies to private and commercial airplanes, the stockpiling of strategic minerals, interest-free government funds in demand deposits at commercial banks, the subsidies for waste treatment plants, the helium conservation program, and the failure of the highway program to rely on specific user charges for big trucks, all are forms of inefficiencies, subsidies, and costs which are borne by the American taxpayer rather than those who benefit from them.

As we work to reorder American priorities it is as important to cut back on them as it is to initiate needed programs. This is true not only because of the waste involved in the old programs but because we cannot possibly pay the cost of meeting our vast unmet needs unless we do so.

The time has come to cut back on the many forms of "welfare programs for crustacean life" which plague the economy.

7 · Loopholes, Truckholes, Bonanzas, and Other Tax Handouts

The emissary from the Senate Campaign Committee arrived in the arid Western state and approached the candidate a few days before election.

"I'm here with ten thousand dollars for your campaign. Can you use it?" he asked.

"Can I use it?" the candidate replied. "I've got a good chance to win. The campaign is picking up. But I'm almost broke. You bet I can use it."

"Great. But there's one condition. What are your views on the oil depletion allowance?"

"My views on oil depletion? I don't have a position. I've heard arguments for it and arguments against it. But I haven't studied it in detail. If you put a condition on the ten thousand that I have to support the oil depletion allowance to get it, I'll have to turn the money down. Sorry! I can't make that commitment."

A short time later the emissary, his conscience bothering him, called a wealthy party supporter in the East. He described the incident. "My God," he said on the phone. "We've got an honest man. He turned down the money. Could you help him with no strings attached?"

A few days later the money arrived, this time with no strings. The candidate was elected and still serves in the United States Senate.

The offer occurs dozens of times in each election year. But the outcome is not always as favorable to the public interest.

Some Senators More Equal than Others

It illustrates one way the oil depletion and other tax privileges are protected. After election, Senators and Congressmen with ties to the oil industry are favored for membership on the tax-writing committees. In the past they and their allies have also dominated the campaign committees of both political parties. Through direct contributions or the purchase of $5,000 tables to the annual campaign dinners, the party coffers are filled with funds from those whose power and privilege are protected. The funds are used to elect friendly candidates, especially from the small, one-party mountain or border states where campaigns can be won or lost for a few thousand dollars. These men are given key seats early in their careers on the most powerful committees, especially the Senate Finance Committee. There they protect the oil depletion allowance and other tax loopholes.

The process has the rhythm and flow of a nursery rhyme:

The favored industry contributes heavily to the campaign committees who contribute to the candidates who favor the industry's position who when elected are chosen for the key committees where they protect the interests of the powerful industry who contributes to the campaign committees who, etc., etc., etc.

This is the farmer who sowed the corn, that heard the cock that crowed in the morn, that waked the priest all shaven and shorn, that married the man all tattered and torn, that kissed the maiden all forlorn, that milked the cow with the crumpled horn, that tossed the dog, that chased the cat, that killed the rat, that ate the malt, that lay in the House that Jack built.

In my own case I was passed over for five years for membership to the Senate Finance Committee, during which time both Vance Hartke (D.-Ind.) and Eugene McCarthy (D.-Minn.), who were junior to me, were appointed on their election to the Senate. In addition, J. William Fulbright (D.-Ark.), who comes from an oil-producing state and who cosponsored the famous 1956 gas bill with Senator A. S. (Mike) Monroney of Oklahoma, exercised his seniority, left the Banking Committee, where he was the ranking Democrat, and took a seat on Finance.

Paul Douglas, who led the fight against the depletion allowance, was kept off the committee for seven years. Robert Kerr (D.–Okla.), chief defender of depletion, was put on the committee early in his Senate career although he and Douglas came to the Senate together. George Smathers (D.–Fla.), Douglas' junior by two years, and pro-depletion, was third in seniority on the committee when Douglas was seventh. During three vacancies Douglas was kept off when Lyndon Johnson (D.–Tex.), from an oil state, exercised the rights of the Majority Leader and got himself appointed, when Clinton Anderson (D.–N.M.), from another oil and gas state, was appointed over Douglas because his name came earlier in the alphabet in the 1949 class of Senators, and when Douglas was asked to step aside for Alben W. Barkley (D.–Ken.), who returned to the Senate in 1955 after a term as Vice-President.

Those who oppose the special tax bonanzas are relegated to minor committees or one where their views do not endanger the powerful interests. If they are tenacious and continue to apply, they find that after five or seven years in the Senate when they are finally chosen they are both greatly outnumbered by the protectors of the loopholes and very junior on the committees to Senators who were elected long after they were. While seniority is alleged to be an ironclad rule, when it comes to protecting tax loopholes some Senators are more senior than others.

Favors to Gas and Oil

The oil industry is the most favored of the powerful economic interests who pay little or no taxes. The laundry list of its privileges, loopholes, tax breaks, and special favors is legion. The most important are these:

Dry Holes. If an oil operator drills a dry hole, he can write off the amount as a business loss. This is proper.

Percentage Depletion. If an oil operator invests $10,000 for drilling rights to an oil well, strikes oil, and sells the oil at a rate of $100,000 a year for ten years, each year he can write off 22 percent, or $22,000, of the selling price of the oil. In most businesses he would write off $1,000 a year, or a total of $10,000 in ten years, but as an oil operator he not only can write off twenty-two times his $10,000 investment in ten years but can write off more than double the amount of his investment in the first year.

Oil producers, on the average, write off nineteen times their investment in the oil land itself, not merely the actual capital investment to produce the oil. This bonanza costs other taxpayers $1.3 billion a year.

Intangible Drilling and Development Costs. In addition to recovering the cost of the oil in place in the ground, the oil operator can also recover the money he invests in most machinery and other capital items. But unlike other businesses where the machinery is depreciated over the life of the asset, under the "intangible drilling and development cost" provision in the tax laws, the oil operator can "expense" most costs in the first year of the investment. He writes them off immediately. This increases the oil operator's "expenses," reduces his net income, and can produce a "paper loss" in the first year. Result? He pays no taxes. In the second, third, and additional years, he shelters the income from his new well by drilling additional wells and by using the depletion allowance against which to offset his income. Result? He pays little or no taxes again.

These special benefits, ostensibly justified on the grounds that they are needed to induce exploration for gas and oil in the United States, benefit the producers whether they drill at home or in the farthest reaches of Africa or Asia, and most of the drilling is abroad. It is a $300-million annual charge on the Treasury.

Foreign Royalties Masked as Tax Payments. Oil producers ordinarily pay the owner of the land on which they drill a royalty of one eighth of the selling price of the oil produced. This payment is properly deducted from the total income of the producer. When American companies ventured abroad they also paid the royalty to the owners of the land. But as time went on, many of the owners, who were in fact the governments of the countries involved, raised the royalty payments for the right of the American firms to recover the oil and sell it at home and abroad.

In order to save billions for themselves, the American firms prevailed upon Saudi Arabia first of all, and other countries later, to treat the royalty payments as a tax rather than a royalty. Saudi Arabia adopted an income tax, which, it is alleged, was drafted in New York by oil company lawyers, that converted the oil royalties into taxes but excluded almost all other incomes from the provision of the law. Now, instead of deducting these "royalty" costs from their income and paying U. S. taxes on the remainder, U. S. oil companies treat the royalties as "taxes paid" and offset them as a credit against the actual taxes owed to Uncle Sam. This saves billions.

Take a simplified example. A U. S. oil company produces $1 billion worth of oil in a Middle Eastern country. It pays the foreign government half that amount, or $500 million, as a royalty payment. In that case the $500 million is deducted as a cost from the $1 billion. The company then has $500 million in profits, on which the U. S. corporation tax is roughly 50 percent. Other things being equal, it owes Uncle Sam $250 million in taxes on its $500 million profit.

But if the royalty payment is treated as "taxes paid" to the Middle Eastern government, the American company has $1 billion in profit on which a tax of $500 million has already been paid. It thereby owes no further tax on the foreign income, and saves $250 million. The company is $250 million richer. The U. S. Treasury is $250 million poorer. The average American who pays his taxes must make up the difference. The American taxpayer has subsidized the oil company by a direct payment of $250 million.

This handout costs the Treasury $2 billion to $2.5 billion a year. In this case, Congress did not commit the dastardly offense. It was accomplished administratively through Internal Revenue Service Ruling IT4038, which was put into effect in 1950.

After spending these vast amounts to induce oil production not only at home but also abroad on grounds of national security, we have imposed an oil import quota system which has the effect of keeping oil out of the country. This raises the price of oil to the American consumer by about a dollar a barrel. According to one estimate, this costs the consumer 5.7 cents a gallon for gasoline. As a consequence the consumer pays first through vast tax subsidies to promote the drilling and exploration of oil, and once that oil is drilled and explored he pays for it again through the "Drain America First" program, which keeps the foreign oil out and raises prices about $1 a barrel.

The program does not thereby serve either the security of the country or the interests of its citizens. It produces windfall profits at taxpayers' expense for a giant industry. Meanwhile it helps corrupt the political process of the country.

Tax System in Shambles

The purpose of the income tax is to raise money to pay for needed government programs. If this were done directly with no deductions, exclusions, deferrals, credits, or preferential rates, the same amount of money could be raised with income tax rates almost half those now in the law. The minimum rate could be reduced from 14 to 8 percent, the maximum rate from 70 to 40 percent.

But the tax system is in shambles. It is scandalous. Consider these items.

At latest count some 112 American citizens with incomes in excess of $200,000 a year paid no federal income tax at all. Three individuals with income in excess of $1 million paid not one red cent in federal income taxes.

If you are an American citizen but a bona-fide resident of the

Riviera, Rio de Janeiro, Acapulco, or any of a number of famous spas throughout the world, you can exclude entirely from your taxable income the first $25,000 you earn abroad. If you live abroad for seventeen out of eighteen months but are *not* a bona-fide resident, you can exclude the first $20,000. But if you work forty hours a week, fifty weeks a year at the A. O. Smith plant in Milwaukee or the Ford plant in Dearborn, Michigan, or run a small business in Portland, Oregon, you pay the full statutory rate on the income you earn, which is probably a good deal less than $20,000 or $25,000 a year.

If you own a corporation in the United States, you pay a corporate income tax of 48 percent on income over $25,000. But if you operate a U. S. corporation elsewhere in the Western Hemisphere, your corporate income tax is fourteen points lower, or only 34 percent.

If you drive your car fifty miles to work every day you cannot deduct the expense from your income tax. But if you are a lawyer who flies to an American Bar Association convention in London, you can deduct the cost as a business expense.

If you earn $10,000 a year by the sweat of your brow, you pay a tax calculated at the full statutory rates. But if you earn $10,000 on the stock market and hold the stock for six months or longer, you pay half the income tax rate of the industrial worker.

If your father invested $10,000 in stock in 1945 which was worth $100,000 when he died and left it to you, neither he nor you paid any tax whatsoever on the $90,000 gain. If the stock increases in value to $200,000 and you leave it to your son when you die, he pays no tax on either the $90,000 gain your father made or the $100,000 gain you made. If the value of the stock rises to $300,000 and your son finally sells it, he pays a tax not on the $290,000 gain in value, but on only $50,000, or half the $100,000 gain in price since he owned the stock. Of the $290,000 gain, $240,000 escapes taxation entirely.

The estimate is that some $10 billion in capital gains passes tax-free every year.

Equal Incomes Not Equally Taxed

These examples illustrate how the tax system offends against a fundamental principle, namely that two people equally situated with equal incomes should pay the same amount in taxes.

Under the present system, income from wages and salaries is taxed at a higher rate than income from dividends and stock speculation. Coupon clipping is favored over physical or mental effort. This is a great anamoly in a society which prides itself on hard work and individual effort.

This was not always true. Before World War II there was an "earned income credit" in the tax law. Now unearned income is favored. If you get your income from interest on state and local bonds, live in Puerto Rico, cash in on a stock option, or receive dividends from a real-estate investment trust, you pay a much smaller tax than the man who earns the same amount of money by factory labor or government employment.

If you spend your money to buy a house, to rehabilitate real-estate property for sale or rent, for a self-employed pension plan, or as a contribution to a nonprofit organization, you pay a smaller tax than the man with exactly the same income who rents a house, contributes to his employer's pension plan, or pays tuition to a private school.

As a fundamental principle of taxation, a fair tax system should not differentiate as to where the income comes from or what it is spent for. Two men each with a wife and two children who receive $15,000 a year should not pay different amounts in federal income tax. There should be no distinction because A receives his income from the oil business, is buying his home, and makes contributions to a private foundation while B gets a salary from his company, rents his house and pays through the nose to send his child to a parochial school.

Universalizing Sin

Because the system has been riddled with loopholes, basic equality is now sought by means of universalizing sin. Instead of reducing the exclusions, exemptions, deductions, credits, preferences, and deferrals, we give a tax break to almost everybody for almost everything. As a result we have special tax provisions for political-campaign contributions, to promote exports, for gifts to charity, for job training, child care, retirement income, medical expenses, vacation and beach cottages, stock and bond purchases, rehab housing and railroad rolling stock.

But universalizing the loopholes does not bring equality. Poor people who pay no taxes get no tax breaks. Middle-income people with little "unearned" income get few tax breaks, and those they get are worth very small amounts to them. High-income people with vast quantities of "unearned" income on which they would otherwise pay very high rates pay little or no taxes at all. As a result, the bulk of federal taxation is on earned income spent for needed consumption items—food, rent, clothing, and getting to and from work. It favors to a fantastic degree "unearned" income which is invested—income from stocks, bonds, and capital gains, and investments in real estate, gas and oil, and farm tax shelters.

Erosion of Progressive Tax System

The present tax system also offends more and more against another basic principle of taxation. That principle is that a just individual tax system should be a progressive tax system. Those with high incomes should pay a higher proportion of their income in taxes than those with low incomes.

The state and local tax systems are highly regressive. They tax a higher proportion of the income of those with low incomes than of those with high incomes. The main villains are the sales tax and the property tax, through which the bulk of state and local revenues are raised.

Sales taxes are regressive because they fall heavily on needed consumption items—food, clothing, and retail purchases. The poor pay a big proportion of their income for these necessities of life. They make up a small proportion of total expenditures by the wealthy. Hence the tax falls disproportionately on low-income families and is highly regressive.

The property tax is even worse. The nation's number-one expert on property taxes, Professor Dick Netzer, head of the all-university Department of Economics at New York University, did a study for the Douglas Commission entitled "The Impact of the Property Tax," based on data in the 1960s. He found that property taxes amounted to 19 percent of the $34.9-billion cash outlays by homeowners and rental payments by renters detailed in census data. This amounts to 24 percent of housing expenditures *excluding* the tax payment. Because of the rising rates and increased incidence of property taxes in recent years, Netzer's figures no doubt underestimate the present impact of the property tax.

No one in his right mind would, if starting over, advocate a 24 percent "sales tax" on such a fundamental need as housing. But that is the impact of the property tax.

The regressive nature of the state and local tax system makes a "progressive" federal tax system imperative merely to offset the injustice of the state and local system. When the tax incidence of all levels is combined, the overall tax system in the United States is roughly proportional. Citizens at every income level pay about the same proportion of their income in taxes. There are, of course, enormous individual exceptions to this general rule, and those at very high levels actually pay a decreasing proportion of their total income in taxes.

The federal tax system is getting less and less progressive from year to year. This is due to two fundamental factors: (1) the loopholes, truckholes, bonanzas, and erosions in the federal tax system, and (2) the tremendous growth in Social Security and other social-insurance taxes over the last decade.

Since 1960 the percentage of budget receipts derived from social-insurance taxes has almost doubled—from 16 percent to 29 percent of total budget receipts (see chart). Because they are imposed at a flat rate and are limited to the first several thousand dollars of income, they are regressive. The income above $9,000 is not even subject to the Social Security tax.

Where the Tax Dollar Comes From: Percentage of Budget Receipts Derived by Source

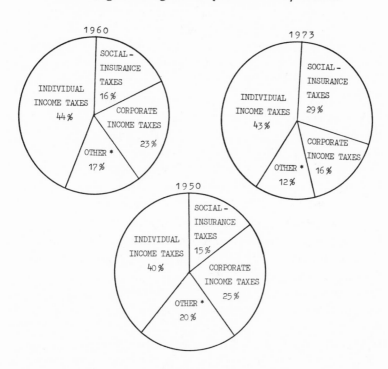

*Includes excise taxes, estate and gift taxes, customs duties, and miscellaneous receipts.

Of the federal taxes now raised from individuals—the individual income tax, social-insurance taxes, excise taxes, custom duties, etc.—only half are raised through the progressive income tax. The remainder is gathered through some form of regressive or, at best, proportional tax.

Value-added Tax

The erosion of the progressive nature of the federal tax system is a compelling reason why a searching and critical public examination must be made of the value-added tax (VAT). (One wag has said that if Mr. Nixon had proposed it when he first came to office, it could be called VAT '69.)

Even more important than its revenue implications is the consideration of how VAT might change the economy and the society.

The value-added tax, a tax widely used in Europe, is assessed at each stage of production. If a company pays $100 for the components to manufacture a product and then sells the finished product for $125 after its manufacture, a flat percentage tax is assessed against the $25 increase in value and is added to the total. At each new stage in the process, from manufacturer to wholesaler to retailer to the ultimate consumer, the value-added tax is imposed on the incremental increase in value.

It is a regressive tax. It is in effect a federal sales tax. But it is a sales tax levied not only at the final or retail stage, but at several stages in the production process. Its proponents argue that with administrative exclusions for such necessities as food or housing it could become a "proportional" rather than a regressive tax. That argument fails on at least two counts. Even if it were proportional, it would have the effect of reducing the total progressive nature of the federal tax system; an even smaller part of federal revenues would be raised through the progressive income tax. In addition, the exclusions and exemptions would soon be discarded, just as the sales tax exclusions and exemptions for necessities have been repealed in state after state as revenue demands mount in intensity.

VAT is a hidden tax. It is therefore an open invitation to higher and higher levels. Once imposed, it will continue to be raised. In fact, it will be the first to be raised when government officials are pressed for funds. Raising direct taxes or cutting pet projects are highly unpopular acts. But a hidden tax about which the consumer is unaware is an open invitation to abuse.

What is most likely to happen is this. When economic conditions or political pressures force a reduction in taxes, it will be the progressive income tax which will be cut. That tax is out in the open where people see it, feel its effects, and complain about it. But when public officials need to increase taxes, the increase will come by raising the value-added tax, because it is hidden and its effects are not obvious.

If the value-added tax is ever adopted, it means an even greater shift than is now the case from the use of progressive taxes to pay for needed services to reliance on taxes that take an enormous bite from ordinary people. In fact, its proponents argue for it as a tax which can be raised easily when revenues are needed.

VAT is an inflationary tax. It adds a new tax and a new cost at each new stage of production. Taxes are a price increase like any other price increase. But this form of taxation is even worse. It means a pyramiding of price increases as manufacturers' and merchants' percentage markups are made on a larger base. Apart from its basic unfairness, an era of rampaging inflationary pressure is hardly the time to impose an inflationary, price-busting tax.

Cutting wasteful spending, closing the tax loopholes, providing incentives to states to impose progressive income taxes in lieu of regressive sales and property taxes, and increasing revenues through a fully employed economy, all have a clear priority over VAT as a means of producing needed revenues and providing a just tax system.

Tax Subsidies

While the loopholes, truckholes, and other tax handouts are a disgrace, the most scandalous aspect of the tax system is the tax subsidies it provides.

The federal income tax is not merely a structure by which the government collects the individual and corporate income taxes owed under the authority of the Sixteenth Amendment, which authorized Congress to levy taxes on "incomes, from whatever source derived." In addition it is a vast system of tax expenditures and tax subsidies which give financial assistance to a variety of groups and programs. These two prongs of the tax system have little or nothing to do with each other.

The tax subsidies amount to at least $38 billion a year, or more than 15 percent of the entire federal budget. They are merely the other side of the coin of budget expenditures. If the government wants to encourage housing for the poor, develop minerals, help savings institutions, or promote a particular purpose like rehab housing, it can do so either by an actual budget expenditure or by a tax incentive. The former is often ill-advised or badly carried out. The latter is almost always a disaster. It is probably the least efficient way of meeting the goal of a federal program.

In recent years the Joint Economic Committee has held detailed hearings on tax expenditures and has published voluminous accounts of tax subsidies. The testimony of Stanley Surrey, formerly Assistant Secretary of the Treasury for Tax Policy, and of Philip Stern, author of *The Great Treasury Raid,* the superb technical work of Joseph Pechman and Benjamin Okner of the Brookings Institution, and the fine Joint Economic Committee staff study on subsidies by Jerry Jasinowski and Dr. Carl Shoup, have developed massive evidence on the scope of tax expenditures and tax subsidies.

Welfare Payments to the Rich

The tax expenditures are not only large but badly distributed. Philip Stern calls them "welfare payments to the super-rich." Surrey points out that once in the law they are "undisturbed and unexamined."

What are they and how do they work? Compare these two circumstances. A small contractor incorporated in most states pays a federal income tax of 48 percent of his income on earnings in excess of $25,000. Suppose the government decides that it wants to promote the rehabilitation of housing, especially for the poor in the central cities. Instead of paying the contractor directly from the Treasury, it gives him a tax incentive. The money earned on rehab housing for the poor becomes tax-free. The contractor is allowed to keep it without paying the corporate income tax on it. But suppose another man owns and runs a steel foundry employing five hundred persons and clears $125,000 a year. On the $100,00 earned after the first $25,000, he pays $48,000 in tax and keeps $52,000 as a profit for his shareholders. But if he is in rehab housing, he keeps the entire $100,000. The result is the same as if the Treasury paid him $48,000 directly from appropriated funds.

The same tax benefits are worth different amounts to different people. After the first $25,000 in corporate profits, they are worth 48 cents of each additional dollar earned. If the benefits accrue to an individual, they are worth whatever the marginal tax rate happens to be: $70 per $100 for the 70-percent-bracket taxpayer, $14 per $100 for the lowest-bracket taxpayer, but nothing at all for the person who earns too little to pay a federal income tax.

Most tax expenditures either are designed for wealthy citizens or mean so much more to the 70 percent taxpayer as against the 20 percent taxpayer that the former goes out of his way to shelter his income. But the latter does not have the resources, time, or expertise to hire a high-priced lawyer or to draw up the technical contracts to achieve the tax purpose.

Take a specific example. Everyone agrees that promoting housing is a good idea. There is a special reason to promote housing for those with incomes below $10,000. At present housing costs, a family with an income much below that amount cannot afford to buy a house. A great social purpose is served by providing decent, safe, and sanitary housing for the American people.

We can do this in one of several ways. One is for the Treasury to pay a direct subsidy to the renter or homeowner. Another is to provide a tax subsidy. The latter is done in the tax code by providing that homeowners can deduct on their federal income tax return the interest on their mortgage and the property taxes paid on the home. "Good idea! Promotes a social purpose. Helps house the country. Fine!"

In fiscal year 1971 that program cost almost $6 billion. For each $100 paid out in interest and property taxes, the 70-percent-bracket taxpayer got $70 and the 14 percent taxpayer got $14, but the family with no taxable income got no deduction at all. Of the almost $6 billion paid out in that year, 70 percent went to families with incomes over $10,000. There is no limit whatsoever to the amount the wealthy can deduct.

The question is this: If you were Secretary of Housing and Urban Development and proposed a $6-billion housing program, what would both the public and Congressional reaction be to a program which gave no help to the poor, provided only 30 percent of the funds to 50 percent of the families in the United States with incomes below $10,000, and gave 70 percent, or almost $4 billion, of the $6 billion to families who can afford to buy and pay for their own homes? But that is the principal program by which housing is promoted in the United States.

Loopholes Lead to No Tax Payments

Consider also the charitable-deduction provision in the tax code. It was through that provision, the capital-gains provisions, the gas and oil loopholes, and the tax-free provisions for interest on state and local bonds that 122 Americans with incomes in excess of $200,000 a year paid no taxes at all.

If a man in the 70 percent bracket earns an additional $10,000, he keeps $3,000 and pays the government $7,000 in taxes. But by giving away the $3,000 he, rather than the President or Congress, determines what happens to the $7,000. Stanley Surrey gave this example in testimony before the Joint Economic Committee. Suppose that instead of a tax subsidy for charitable giving, the Secretary of HEW proposed a direct-expenditures program which achieved precisely the same results. Here, Surrey said, is what the HEW Secretary would propose.

We propose to establish a Division of Charitable and Educational Assistance which will distribute its funds as follows:

Suppose a person calls and says: "I am too poor to pay an income tax, but I am contributing $15 to my favorite charity. Will the Government also help it?" The answer here will be: "We appreciate your sacrifice, but we cannot use our funds in this situation."

Suppose a person calls and says: "I am quite well off and want to send a check for $3,000 to one of my favorite charities. Will the Government also aid it?" The answer here will be: "We are delighted to be of assistance and are at once sending a Government check for $7,000 to that charity."

Take the case of the tax-free interest on state and local bonds. This not only benefits the high-income taxpayer but extracts a fantastic price to achieve its goal of providing a market for state and local bonds. As Stanley Surrey rightly points out, ". . . generous commissions paid by the Treasury are not unusual in this tax-subsidy world. The Treasury . . . pays $1 in tax benefits to a top-bracket taxpayer who buys a tax-exempt bond, so that he will pass along seventy-five cents in interest-rate benefits to the state or city issuing the bond—a 133 percent commission." This is an excessive price to achieve a desirable goal.

Under a bill I have proposed, state and local governments would have the choice of continuing the present practice of issuing tax-free bonds or of issuing them at the market rate for taxable bonds with the Treasury subsidizing one third of the interest cost. If *fully used,* this would save an average of $1.2 billion a year for the Treasury and $600 million a year for municipalities over the next ten years. My plan would therefore provide more funds to the states and cities at less cost to the Treasury.

The Tax-Subsidy Welfare Payment

Philip Stern outlined the consequences of the "tax-subsidy welfare payment" program as it applied to J. Paul Getty, reputed to be one of the richest men in the world.

As Stern testified before the Joint Economic Committee, if Congress were to apply to Mr. Getty the standards of the Sixteenth Amendment and tax his income, "from whatever source derived," at the current tax rates, Mr. Getty would write out a check to Uncle Sam each year for about $70 million. Actually he paid no more than a few thousand dollars in the early 1960s, according to what President Kennedy told two U. S. Senators. The annual savings to Mr. Getty are $70 million.

How does this differ in effect from a program in which Congress voted him a $70-million annual welfare payment from the Treasury? Here is Stern's comparison:

Consequences of a $70-Million Direct Welfare Payment to Mr. Getty	Consequences of a $70-Million Tax Forgiveness to Mr. Getty
1. Mr. Getty is $70 million richer.	1. Mr. Getty is $70 million richer.*
2. The U.S. Treasury is $70 million poorer.	2. The U.S. Treasury is $70 million poorer.†
3. The rest of the U.S. taxpayers have to pay $70 million more taxes to make up the difference.	3. The rest of the U.S. taxpayers have to pay $70 million more taxes to make up the difference.

*Than if he had paid the full tax at the statutory rates provided by law under authority of the 16th Amendment.
†Than it would have been had Mr. Getty paid the full tax.

As Stern sums up, "The fact is there is no real difference, and so all the special gimmicks and escape hatches that Congress has been writing into the tax laws over the years—for the lowly as well as for the mighty—amount to welfare payments for the lucky recipient of tax favors."

There is one further distinction. Unlike the welfare laws applied to the poor and the blacks and the welfare mothers, the law does not require Mr. Getty to work to qualify for this welfare payment.

The Fortunate Few

But who gets the tax expenditures? Who are the fortunate recipients of these "tax welfare payments"? Who, in fact, gets the gravy?

Based on the original work of Pechman and Okner, Philip Stern calculated how some $73 billion in what he defined as tax-expenditure welfare payments was distributed. The six million families whose annual income is $3,000 or less got $92 million, or about one tenth of one percent of the total. By contrast, the three thousand families with an income in excess of $1 million a year got $2.2 billion.

Families with incomes under $15,000, who comprise over 70 percent of the population, got less than 25 percent of the "tax welfare" benefits. The three tenths of one percent of the population with incomes over $100,000 a year got 15 percent of the tax expenditures.

Stern illustrated the distribution of the tax-expenditure program for 1972 in a revealing table based on what a typical family in each class of income groups receives under the present tax-expenditure system.

If You Make:	Your Average Yearly Family Income Is:	Your Average Yearly Tax Welfare Payment Will Be:	Your Average Increase in Weekly "Take-Home Pay" Will Be:
Over $1 million	$2,316,872	$720,448	$13,854.78
$500,000-$1 million	673,040	202,752	3,899.07
$100-500,000	165,992	41,480	787.21
$50-100,000	65,885	11,911	229.07
$25-50,000	32,028	3,897	74.94
$20-25,000	22,181	1,931	37.13
$15-20,000	17,198	1,181	20.79
$10-15,000	12,346	651	12.52
$5-10,000	7,481	340	6.54
$3-5,000	4,017	148	2.85
Under $3,000	1,345	16	.31

The distributional effects from the special capital-gains provisions in the tax laws are even more regressive. One reason is that eleven out of twelve people have no capital gains at all.

If You Make	Your Yearly Tax "Welfare" From Capital Gains Will Be:
Over $1 million	$640,667
$500,000-$1 million	165,000
$100-500,000	22,630
$50-100,000	3,795
$25-50,000	534
$20-25,000	120
$15-20,000	55
$10-15,000	24
$5-10,000	9
$3-5,000	1
Under $3,000	—

The distributional effects from the tax provisions exempting the income from state and local bonds may be the most regressive of any of the tax expenditures in the laws. It is of no value at all to half the American people whose incomes are below $10,000. Taken together, the capital-gains and the tax-free-interest provisions for state and local bonds account for $15 billion of the tax expenditures calculated in the Pechman-Okner study. The distributional effects as noted by Philip Stern are given in the table below.

If You Make:	Your Yearly "Welfare" From Tax-Free Bonds Is:
Over $1 million	$36,333
$500,000-$1 million	19,167
$100-500,000	3,630
$50-100,000	205
$25-50,000	24
$20-25,000	4
$15-20,000	1
$10-15,000	1
$5-10,000	—
$3-5,000	—
Under $3,000	—

No Way to Run a Railroad—or a Tax System

Apart from their outrageous distributional effects, Stanley Surrey makes these points about them:

No agency studies or controls them. The Budget Bureau neglects them, for the items are not in its Budget. The executive departments likewise are not concerned, for the items are not in their program. The Treasury is apparently not evaluating them, but rather is adding new and indefensible items.

He concludes: "This is clearly no way to run a tax system and no way to run a budget policy."

As Surrey correctly points out, "Once we see that we are not evaluating technical tax provisions but rather expenditure programs, we are able to ask the traditional questions and use the analytical tools that make up the intellectual apparatus of expenditure experts." Among those questions are: Who gets the benefits? What are the costs? What are its objectives? Does the program accomplish them? Would a direct expenditure or some other way of doing it provide more benefits for the cost involved?

But those questions are never asked. As tax expenditures do not appear in the annual budget, the Budget Bureau does not question them. As they are not a part of the annual appropriations bill, Congress does not review them. And even when the tax-writing committees legislate about them, the tax-expenditure consequences are not prepared by the Treasury, presented to the committees, or provided to the House and the Senate. Tax expenditures are a mindless way by which the federal government shovels out at least $38 billion a year.

Beyond the talk of tax-base broadening, loopholes, and truck-holes, there is this vast wasteland of tax expenditures. What they involve is a double standard for government subsidies and government handouts. While those with great economic power and wealth, wrapped in all their virtue, complain bitterly about welfare payments for the poor which are accomplished through direct expenditures or more or less open or obvious programs, the powerful get vast subsidies and welfare payments surreptitiously through hidden and complex provisions of the law. This makes it possible for them to sup at the public trough while retaining their superior attitude that welfare payments and government subsidies destroy character and sap the nation's moral fiber.

Presidential Leadership

What's the outlook for tax reform?

Without powerful and persuasive Presidential leadership there is little hope. After fifteen years in the Senate I'm not overly bullish. One very personal experience will explain why.

To get from my office in the New Senate Office Building to Hearing Room S-407 in the Capitol of the United States was not an easy task. From my office I scampered down three flights of stairs to the basement, took the subway trolley under the East Mall of the Capitol, and climbed up one flight of stairs to the Senate wing.

Then I zipped up one floor in the Senators' private elevator and took a right turn and a left turn down the hallway leading from the Senate to the House, until I reached a cavernous ground-floor crypt directly under the Great Rotunda of the Capitol itself.

On the left in this damp and echoing chamber sits Adelaide Johnson's sculpture of the three woman's suffrage leaders, Elizabeth Cady Stanton, Susan B. Anthony, and Lucretia Mott, which everyone calls the three ladies in the bathtub. When tourists ask —as they invariably do—why it's unfinished, the Capitol guides trot out their little joke that the sculptress deliberately made it appear that way because "woman's work is never done." That draws laughter from the women and groans from the men.

Also on the left, hidden in the corner, is an express elevator— the only way to the hearing room. I entered it and zoomed up to the attic floor of the extended east front of the Capitol. Back under a low-ceilinged hallway is the Atomic Energy Committee hearing room, where on this morning the Joint Economic Committee was to hear from Joseph W. Barr, the Secretary of the Treasury.

Barr, whom we had all known first as a Congressman from Indiana and then as the Treasury Department's chief legislative liaison, was now serving as the head of the Treasury for a few waning days in the Johnson Administration. As he testified I rose out of my chair to listen. There was a fire in his belly that day that I had never seen in a Secretary of the Treasury before.

"I think the greatest unfinished agenda item we have is tax reform. I will hazard a guess that there is going to be a taxpayer revolt over the income taxes in this country unless we move in this area," Joe testified. "Now, the revolt is not going to come from the poor. The revolt is going to come from the middle class. It is going to come from those people with incomes from $7,000 to $20,000 who pay every nickel of taxes at the going rate. They do not have the loopholes and the gimmicks to resort to."

Barr was testifying in January 1969, not during the Presidential primaries of 1972. He preceded George Wallace's and George McGovern's message by almost four years. And his testimony helped create the "taxpayers' revolt" he talked about. That morning he told the Joint Economic Committee, "There were 155 tax returns in this country with incomes of over $200,000 a year and twenty-one returns with incomes of over $1,000,000 for the year in which the 'taxpayers' [sic] paid the U. S. government not one cent of income taxes."

That set it off. The AP and the UPI reported the testimony. TV and editorial writers deplored the loopholes. The mail poured in to Senatorial and Congressional offices. By the time federal taxes were due in April the taxpayers' revolt was in full swing.

Meantime *The Progressive* magazine asked me to write an article on tax loopholes for its April issue. I agreed. I quoted Barr's testimony, detailed the most glaring loopholes, but concluded that at most we would make only modest changes in the tax code.

The editors called me and my staff, argued vehemently that the article was too pessimistic, and urged me to be far more optimistic than I was. They wanted me to beef up the conclusions.

I resisted. I knew that the new Nixon Administration wouldn't lift a finger to help close the big loopholes. It represented the very economic forces who get the gravy from them. And without strong Presidential leadership there is no way to mold that unwieldy group of 535 members of Congress into concerted action, especially to close tax loopholes.

I knew, too, that the House Ways and Means Committee was packed with supporters of the depletion allowance. They would slow-ball tax reform with weeks of hearings until the taxpayers' revolt simmered down. Then when they finally voted out a modest bill—which might open more loopholes than it closed—it would go to the House floor under a "closed" rule so that no amendments could be made.

I knew that next it would go to the Senate Finance Committee

—the graveyard for tax reform. Republicans on that committee are more conservative than the Republicans in the Senate, and almost all come from states with minute populations—frontier areas like Arizona, Idaho, Utah, Nebraska, and Wyoming—where concern for consumers and industrial workers is still dormant. It's also loaded with Democrats from the South and the Southwest. Tax reform in the Finance Committee has about as much chance as civil rights in Mississippi or free speech at the entrance to Moscow's subway.

I knew that even if we improved the bill on the Senate floor it would go to that third body of Congress, the conference committee between the House and the Senate, where the most conservative senior members of the Senate and House tax-writing committees would meet behind closed doors in one of the secret hideaways of the Capitol to do in even the most modest reforms. And I knew that standing outside those doors would be the lobbyists and the big campaign contributors who benefit from the loopholes. While the average taxpayer might write a hot letter to his Congressman, the lobbyists would spend night and day for months pressuring, cajoling, and wheedling over the details of that bill. And they'd have receptive Senators and Congressmen from those committees for their views.

Having watched this process for over eleven years, I was not about to make a fool of myself by predicting instant tax reform. I agreed to give a little. I agreed to tone down my pessimism. But I refused to perjure myself by predicting great results.

Unhappily I was right. We made a few modest gains but opened up as many new loopholes as we closed. Over the years I've had to restrain myself in talking with my editorial friends from *The Progressive* and gulp down the words "I told you so."

But the moral of the story is that only strong, effective, dynamic Presidential leadership, even with an aroused electorate, can insure significant closing of loopholes in the tax laws. That's what it takes. That's what we need.

Let the Sunshine In

In addition to Presidential leadership, knowledge is the key to action. Several things need to be done to bring the tax-expenditure program under control. It is as important to make intelligent judgments about them as it is to examine the military budget, space programs, Lockheed loans, public-works projects, and direct spending for housing, health, and schools. In fact immense tax expenditures are made for housing, education, and city services through the tax-expenditure budget, although it is almost always done inefficiently. Information is the key to intelligent analysis. We should take the following action.

The Treasury Department should be required to provide for publication in the tax-writing committees' reports on tax bills detailed information concerning the consequences of a proposed tax provision. This should include not only its total annual cost but what its objective is, whether that objective is actually carried out by the "tax expenditure," what income groups benefit, what income groups do not benefit, the alternative means of achieving the objectives, and the costs of the alternative means.

The same analysis should be provided annually by the Treasury and the Bureau of the Budget for "tax expenditures" already in the law.

The budget itself should include, under the proposals for spending by individual departments and agencies of the government, a line item for each tax expenditure. As a consequence, the Housing and Urban Development Department budget would include not only line items for public housing and model cities but items entitled "interest on homeowners' mortgages, $2.8 billion," and "property tax deductions by homeowners, $2.9 billion," etc.

The tax-expenditure items should be reviewed and passed on annually by the Congress as a part of its appropriations, rather than tax-writing, process. The tax expenditures should be raised, lowered, or cut out entirely, just as direct expenditures are passed upon. That is what they are. That is how they should be examined.

Meanwhile, the same information as to the distributional effects, costs, benefits, and alternative programs should also be provided for the direct-expenditure programs, a reform which is now carried out more in the breach than in practice.

Tax expenditures have the same consequences as direct expenditures. They distort public priorities. Their reform is a prerequisite for reordering priorities and meeting the vital needs of the nation.

8 · Housing Priorities: A Case Study

The National Commission on Urban Problems was holding its first public hearings in New Haven, Connecticut, the showcase for urban renewal. More than $800 per person had been spent on slum clearance, urban renewal, and housing projects in that city. New Haven and its leaders were the winners of dozens of prizes and adulations from architects, builders, and planners for their contribution to the rebuilding of the American city.

Mayor Richard Lee, the most experienced urban-renewal expert in the United States, was the first witness. As he finished speaking, up rose a turbaned black man from the audience and shouted, "You people have listened to the mayor. How about listening to us? How are you people helping us when you listen to people like that, that decide what happens to our lives, and we are never given a chance to speak up and say what we think should help our neighborhood? It's a lot of jive, a public hearing, man. We have to go through this. We have to live through this."

The showcase city was seething with tension. The Oak Street slum, made famous by a Sinclair Lewis short story, was bulldozed. But it was not replaced by housing for the poor. Instead the city built a highway, expanded a hospital, built a parking area, housed the telephone company and erected a commercial building. In other areas pleasant townhouses for Yale University faculty replaced the hated slums. But the poor blacks were removed to the Hill section of New Haven.

Pouring out his soul, Fred Harris, the black spokesman, continued in a moving speech:

Most people think we're rabble-rousers because they never come down in our neighborhoods with open minds and see what is happening. All we want is a decent place to live and decent schools for our children, and to give us rents we can afford so that we can become desirable citizens.

You can't take a guy with a white shirt and a tie, with a college degree, that doesn't understand the functioning of these people's minds, and comes down looking down his nose on us, when he lives in Woodbridge or he lives in a better neighborhood and doesn't have the same problems that we have, and he's going to tell us, "Clean yourself up. Pull yourself up by your bootstraps."

After Mr. Harris finished his speech, the former director of New Haven's antipoverty program, later New York City's Human Resources Administrator, and a vice-president of the Ford Foundation, Mitchell Sviridoff, testified. He replied to Mr. Harris' charges. Then, after Mr. Harris interjected that Mayor Lee "controls the whole town. The people don't have no voice here," Mr. Sviridoff rather haughtily replied, "I see no point in conducting a debate on this level." Mr. Harris shot back, "You live in Woodbridge. That's why."

That exchange symbolized the problem. At that moment you knew why New Haven was in trouble.

By the end of that day it was clear that a lot was wrong with the urban-renewal showcase of America. In the hot summer that followed, those who were removed from the Oak Streets to the Hill sections, and who were preached at by the planners from the Woodbridges of America, led the riots and civil disorders that descended on New Haven and her sister cities of the nation. And you are taxed to provide this urban renewal which destroys housing for the poor.

The 1949 Housing Pledge

Almost twenty years before, the Housing Act of 1949 pledged the United States to provide a decent home in a suitable living environment for every American family.

To carry out that pledge it instituted a program of slum clearance and public housing. Like the animals embarking on Noah's Ark, the intent of the Congressional movers and shakers was that the two programs should move together, clearing the slums on the one hand and providing public housing for those whose dilapidated, substandard, or overcrowded housing was removed, on the other.

But two decades after that Magna Charta for housing was passed, these conditions prevailed:

As in New Haven, the slums were torn down. Huge vacant spaces were left in the center of our cities, notably in Detroit, Cleveland, and St. Louis. But the public housing did not get built.

Urban renewal destroyed some 400,000 housing units. These units, by definition, housed the poor, however badly. But only about 20,000 public-housing units, or 5 percent of the number destroyed, were built on the urban-renewal sites during the first twenty years of the program.

Of the 810,000 public-housing units proposed to be built under the 1949 act, only two thirds, or 540,000, including the 20,000 on urban-renewal sites, had been completed at the end of the twenty years.

And one could say, with complete assurance, that virtually none of the public-housing units built at the end of the two decades housed the large poor family in the central cities of the United States where the need was greatest. Because of administrative ceilings on public-housing-unit costs, almost half the units in recent years were efficiency or one-bedroom apartments, and virtually none were units with three or more bedrooms for the poor families.

Negro Removal

Meanwhile, urban renewal, highway programs, equivalent demolition, demolitions for public-housing sites, code enforcement, and other public actions destroyed more than a million housing units. Most of these were housing for the poor. Thus, more housing for the poor was destroyed by public action than was built by public action.

While some $10 billion had been spent on urban renewal, the projects took an interminable amount of time to finish. Over one third of them took from nine to fifteen years to complete. Many called it "Negro removal." Downtown commercial renewal became a major goal of the program. The concept, the cost, and the thrust of urban renewal came under attack from many quarters, including the original sponsors of the program.

For almost the entire two decades following passage of the 1949 act, the Federal Housing Administration refused to guarantee loans in the ghettos of the central cities of the United States. FHA policy thus not only failed to help the poor. It was not merely neutral. It was actively hostile to the housing needs of the poor. The policy was called "red lining" for the real or mythical red lines drawn on maps around certain geographical areas of the central cities where FHA refused to insure and banks and savings-and-loan companies then refused to make loans.

In addition, under federal housing-code laws and regulations, no funds could be spent to upgrade blighted areas or to prevent their further deterioration. The funds to the cities for housing-code enforcement and the grants and loans to the occupants could be spent only in "declining" or "gray areas." They could not be spent in the slums or areas designated for future urban renewal. If the area had hit rock bottom, there was no money for it.

Under the public-housing policy of HUD, the loan programs of FHA, and urban renewal, the poor and the homes of the poor were essentially abandoned in the blighted areas of the central cities for the first two decades under the Housing Act of 1949.

The moderate-income housing program—the below-market interest-rate program named after Section 221-d-3 of the 1949 Housing Act—was supposed to add 45,000 new units a year to the subsidized-housing supply. But it was not until the end of the sixth year of its existence that it had built a total of 45,000 units which it was supposed to supply in a single year.

Corruption of Intent

There was nothing intrinsically wrong with the Housing Act of 1949. But the Federal Housing Administration and the Urban Renewal Administration corrupted its intent.

To this day, leading officials of Urban Renewal insist that it was never meant to house people or that the public-housing provisions of the 1949 act were an integral part of the whole. As time went on and upper-class housing and downtown renewal became the central focus of the program, there was even greater loss of the act's original intent.

Until 1952 the FHA retained in its individual housing contracts a written restrictive covenant against blacks and other minorities, and in spirit long after that. The "workable program," adopted later, which insisted that cities have a zoning, land use, and housing-code ordinance before they could qualify for public housing was an open invitation to the white affluent suburbs to exclude the poor. As the suburbs were opposed to public housing in any case, they merely failed to pass a workable program. Instead of public housing being tied to the things suburbia wanted —water and sewer grants, for example—it was tied to the things the more affluent suburbs did not want.

For all of these reasons the intent of the Housing Act of 1949 was negated. The major villains were the FHA, HUD, and the Urban Renewal Administration bureaucracies, the real-estate lobby, and the ungenerous spirit of white upper-middle-class suburbia which was intent on excluding the poor and the blacks from its neighborhoods.

At the end of the two decades there were at least seven million substandard housing units which were so bad, so dilapidated or lacking in elementary plumbing, that they were unfit to live in and needed to be destroyed or replaced. There were an additional four million units which were so overcrowded that for each of them an additional new housing unit was needed. There was therefore a need for at least eleven million units merely to replace the existing dilapidated units and to house those living in overcrowded units.

Needs Underestimated

This estimate of housing needs at the end of the second decade after passage of the 1949 Housing Act was very conservatively stated.

The estimate was based on census data. A housing unit with no kitchen, with plumbing in the basement although the unit was on the second floor, with inadequate total space or sleeping space, with an absence of light or ventilation, or with low ceilings, to use several examples, would not necessarily be called a "substandard" unit.

Tens of thousands of so-called "standard" units were provided during the mass migration from rural to urban areas by carving up the old central-city brownstones and other multistoried single-family houses into multifamily units. Within a mile of the White House there are hundreds of such units which routinely pass the District of Columbia's "housing code" inspection but which most Americans would refuse to live in.

The above estimate of housing needs also grossly underestimates those needs because it is based solely on the condition of the house and makes no judgment about the environment in which it exists. This is true despite the fact that the 1949 act calls not only for a "decent home" but also for one located in a "suitable living environment." A house would not be classified as substandard if its physical condition met certain minimum standards and had a minimum amount of indoor plumbing, even though it is unfit to live in because it is surrounded by freeways or railroad tracks, noxious fumes pour down on it from nearby factories, the lot next door is littered with garbage, there are no street lights, there is an absence of police or fire protection, a liquor store is on the corner in a residential neighborhood (a condition found almost universally in the black ghettos of the nation), there is a rendering works in the block, the noise level is excessive, the streets are not paved or there are potholes in the blacktop, or the house or the neighborhood is infested by rats.

As a result, the housing needs of the nation based on census standards are grossly underestimated.

Subsidies to the Well-to-Do

This record of failure to house those who need housing the most was made while billions in housing subsidies were provided annually to help solve the problem.

The estimate for 1966 is that about $8 billion in housing subsidies of all kinds, measured by the actual benefits received in that year, was provided. In 1972, it was $11 billion. About $10 billion of the total was provided through the tax code, while another $1 billion plus was the value of the annual benefits from public housing, rent supplements, Farmers Home Administration, subsidies under Sections 235 and 236 of the 1968 Housing Act, and other subsidy programs.

The reason there is such a shortage of housing for the poor is that the bulk of the housing subsidies are provided to the well-to-do. This may surprise many who believe that housing subsidies go to the poor and that the well-to-do are somehow self-sufficient.

Alvin Shorr, formerly of the Department of Health, Education and Welfare and one of the nation's foremost experts on welfare and housing, made some interesting calculations for the early years of the 1960 decade. He found that the value of the housing subsidies for those with middle incomes or higher was three and a half times as great as the value of housing subsidies for the poor.

Mr. Shorr estimated that the poor received $820 million a year in all forms of housing subsidies. He included in this amount the public-housing subsidy, 25 percent of welfare payments as an estimate of the portion of the payment spent for rent, and the actual dollar savings from income tax deductions for interest and property taxes paid.

Middle- and upper-income groups received $2.9 billion when their subsidies were measured by the actual dollar savings in the federal-income-tax deductions they received for mortgage interest paid and for personal property taxes. Mr. Shorr did not count the total deduction, but only the actual tax savings. He also did not count the imputed value of rental income to the homeowner.

Even more shocking was his calculation that the upper 20 percent of income groups—the wealthiest one fifth of the population—received $1.7 billion a year in housing subsidies, or twice as much as the $820 million received by the lowest 20 percent of income groups. This is due to the incidence of tax deductions for mortgage interest and property taxes paid on various incomes. As Stanley Surrey testified before the Joint Economic Committee:

If cast in direct-expenditure language, the present assistance for owner-occupied homes under the tax deductions for mortgage interest and property taxes would look as follows, envisioned as a HUD program:

For a married couple with income of $10,000, HUD would pay the for each $100 of mortgage interest on the couple's home, pay $70 to the bank holding the mortgage, leaving the couple to pay $30. It would also pay a similiar portion of the couple's property tax to the state or city levying the tax.

For a married couple with income of $10,000, HUD would pay the bank on the couple's mortgage $19 per each $100 interest unit, with the couple paying $81. It would also pay a similar portion of the couple's property tax to the state or city levying the tax.

For a married couple too poor to pay an income tax, HUD would pay nothing to the bank, leaving the couple to pay the entire interest cost. The couple would also have to pay the entire property tax.

He added, "One can assume that no HUD Secretary would ever have presented to Congress a direct housing program with this upside-down effect."

The tax incentive in the 1969 tax law to promote rehabilitated housing, which gave a quick five-year write-off of capital expenditures, also had an upside-down-subsidy effect. For the 70 percent bracket it was the equivalent of a 19 percent investment credit; in terms of an interest subsidy on a rehab loan, it was equivalent to reducing an 8 percent interest charge to a 3 percent interest charge. But for the 20-percent-bracket taxpayer, it was the equivalent of only a 5 percent investment credit and of reducing an 8 percent interest charge by only one point to 7 percent.

Surrey charged that "the rehabilitation incentive is probably a waste of government money all around. It is not likely to increase the amount of rehabilitated housing over what would be accomplished through the existing HUD direct subsidy alone, so that the tax incentive will just make some wealthy people more wealthy."

Trickle-Down System

In a study prepared for the Joint Economic Committee entitled "Federal Housing Subsidies," Henry Aaron of the Brookings Institution reached a number of stunning conclusions:

The favorable tax treatment of homeowners leaves them with about $10 billion more in disposable income than they would have if they were treated like other property owners. The figure excludes tax savings arising from accelerated depreciation, but includes the imputed value of rent in owner-occupied dwellings.

Income tax savings to homeowners are more than ten times as

large as benefits under the next largest program, low-rent public housing.

Only 8 percent of the tax subsidy goes to those with incomes below $5,000, while 84 percent of all benefits goes to taxpayers with incomes of $7,000 per year or more, 64 percent to those with $10,000 or more, and 36 percent to households with incomes of $15,000 or more.

Yearly tax savings to households with incomes of $50,000 per year or more are nearly as great as annual benefits under low-rent public housing and are larger than annual benefits under any other housing program.

All housing programs intended for low-income and lower-middle-income households provide large amounts of help to a small fraction of eligible households and no direct help at all to all the rest.

Under the Farmers Home Administration housing program, "fewer than one loan in ten is made to farmers."

Those are startling conclusions as to the effects of a national housing program.

Some Success Too

The fact that the present system of housing subsidies is a filter-down, trickle-down, excessively costly system does not make it all bad. It is true that it helps only a small minority of lower-middle income families, and almost none of the really poor. But the combination of FHA insurance and income tax subsidies has provided tens of millions of new houses in the United States for middle- and upper-income groups. The progressive Congressional policies of smaller and smaller down payments and longer and longer mortgage periods for FHA and Veterans Administration housing guarantees have made home ownership a reality for millions of middle-income and upper-middle-income American families who could never have afforded a home under the conventional terms of twenty or thirty years ago which required enormous down payments for short-term mortgages.

In spite of its shortcomings, the conventional public-housing program has been a success. More than one million public-housing units are now provided for needy Americans. There are very, very low vacancy rates and very, very long waiting lists. This indicates that those in need consider public housing much more desirable than the housing they can rent or buy on the open market.

While there have been some public-housing abominations, such as the Pruit-Igoe project in St. Louis, generally speaking public housing provides needed housing services and increases the real incomes of the tenants. On the whole, the projects are well built. The shift away from massive high-rise projects to scattered-site and smaller units in the last decade has brought great improvements to the program.

The problem with public housing is that there has not been enough of it. It suffers from the fact that in the North it has been rigidly confined to the central cities while suburbia has refused to take its share of the housing poor. It has thus suffered from the white noose around the black cities. But the fact remains that it is a great housing buy, subsidized through an amazingly successful formula, which has provided relatively high-quality housing to needy Americans.

Growth in Subsidized Housing

Since the passage of the Housing Act of 1963 and the establishment of a ten-year housing goal under the Proxmire amendment to the law, there has been a two-and-a-half-fold increase in the number of subsidized housing starts.

The increase is due mainly to the spurt in housing starts under the subsidized-interest-rate programs named for Sections 235 and 236 of the 1968 act. Simply stated, what these sections require is that the homeowner (235) or renter (236) pay 20 or 25 percent respectively of his adjusted income for housing. If mortgage interest rates are 7 percent, as they were in 1968, and if the 20 or 25 percent payment by the buyer (235) or renter (236) covers the monthly payment of principle on a thirty-year mortgage and one percent or more of the interest rate, the government makes up the difference.

For example, if the 235 homeowner's income was sufficient to pay the monthly principle plus 3 percent interest, HUD would make a payment for the remaining interest charge up to the market rate of 7 percent.

The program has a number of advantages. First, the annual charge on the federal budget is much smaller than is the case with most other forms of housing subsidies. For a charge of about $600 per unit per year on the budget, the government can house one family.

Second, the funds are drawn mainly from the private sector. The mortgage money is supplied from conventional sources. As far as the lender is concerned, he gets a monthly payment of principle plus the market interest rate. It matters little to him whether his 7, 8, or 9 percent comes entirely from a home buyer, or from a low-income home buyer plus an additional sum from the federal government. Since the government guarantees the 235 or 236 project, the lender is in fact better off than if he held a conventional mortgage from a similarly situated low-income family.

Third, since the housing is essentially conventional housing, it can be built quickly, located in almost any area, and bought and sold like conventional housing. This has speeded up the process, made it possible for the poor to live in areas where they were previously excluded, and produced a vast number of new subsidized housing starts.

Weaknesses and Scandals

But there are great weaknesses in the program. Since the government can borrow long-term money at almost two percentage points lower than the cost of market mortgage funds, a high cost is extracted by paying private market interest rates for the funds. In 1970, for example, while FHA new-home mortgage yields averaged 9.05 percent, long-term government bonds yielded 6.58 percent, or almost 2.5 percentage points less. Costs could be greatly lowered if the government used its borrowing power to provide the funds at government borrowing rates.

In addition, the program has come under considerable criticism because of the low quality of the 235-236 housing, the concentration of it in poor communities, and in some areas outright scandals. As one local housing official testified before Congress, "Most of the stuff we are getting is garbage." In Detroit alone the FHA faced a potential loss of $200 million because the mortgages on 18,000 to 23,000 houses, or 20 to 25 percent of the total, were in default.

Moreover, as interest rates rose to 9 percent, a higher average income was required of the renter or buyer. The programs housed lower-middle-income groups rather than the poor. This created great friction between those who were subsidized and those with equal incomes who were not. Critics complained that Section 235 home buyers got wall-to-wall carpeting and central air conditioning which their neighbors with equal incomes could not afford, yet the latter subsidized the former through the federal income tax.

The 235-236 programs are also criticized because investment in them provides a tax shelter for high-income investors. For this reason as well as the point that the cost of money is much higher than if borrowed by the government, the ultimate costs of the program are very great even if the initial annual budget expenditure per unit purchased is small.

Finally, as the programs have developed, conventional public-housing starts dropped by a third (from 99,000 in 1970 to 68,000 in 1971) and the below-market interest rate (BMIR) program under Section 221-d-3 was reduced to negligible proportions, from 45,000 new starts in 1968 down to 5,660 new units in 1971.

Thus, while the traditional programs were being abandoned their successors were subjected to charges of scandal, speculation, and poor quality. This may prevent the housing-act goal of 600,000 units a year for ten years of housing for low-income families from being met.

The Need to Atone for the Past

Nevertheless, the American society has a moral obligation to meet those housing goals. The moral dimension of the statistics on housing needs arises from the deliberately imposed policies of the past—red lining, the failures of urban renewal, the FHA-imposed restrictive covenants, the excessive proportion of public housing for the elderly and the denial of housing to families with children, the providing of the overwhelming proportion of subsidies to those who needed them least, the design of the workable program which enabled white affluent suburbs to refuse to house the poor and especially the black poor, and the destruction of far more housing units for the poor through public action than were built through public action.

There is one further consequence of public policy which creates an obligation on society to provide an abundance of housing, especially for the needy. Monetary policy as carried out by the Federal Reserve Board has had a disproportionately adverse effect on housing. Sherman Maisel, former governor of the Federal Reserve Board, who is also an economist and a specialist in housing economics, made a computerized study of the 1966 credit crunch that showed the effects of Federal Reserve monetary restraint on housing. His findings: 60 to 70 percent of the cutback was absorbed by housing. This burden was imposed on the housing sector even though it composed only about 3 percent of the gross national product. Housing is extraordinarily sensitive to the higher interest rates that are the prime instruments of restraining inflation by restraining credit.

Those in charge of public policy therefore not only have a duty to mitigate the sacrifices imposed on the housing sector of the economy through tight money policy but have an affirmative obligation to atone for the past.

How to Meet Housing Goals

What are the means by which the housing goals established by the 1968 Housing Act can be met? How can we provide six million housing units over a ten-year period for low- and moderate-income American families and assure the 26-million-unit goal established by the act?

The existing FHA and VA loan guarantee programs should be continued and expanded. These programs, which promote the purchase of single-family housing, have been responsible for building about 25 percent of all new housing units since the end of World War II. This has been done substantially without a federal subsidy, by insuring lenders against losses should the borrower default on his payments.

These programs have been a singular success and have revolutionized home ownership in the United States. Down payments have fallen from an average one third to one half before World War II, to 25 percent twenty years ago, to 7 percent or less today. Since 1950, the length of mortgage loans has increased by 50 percent, from twenty to thirty years. This has placed conventional home ownership within the reach of millions of Americans. These practices in government programs brought institutional changes to conventional mortgage lending as well.

The small one-half-of-one-percent charge for the FHA insurance fund actually redistributes income from higher- to lower-income groups. Because all borrowers pay the same premium, the effect is for upper-income borrowers to subsidize lower-income borrowers, since the risk of foreclosure is greater for the latter.

In any event, the continuation and expansion of the FHA and VA loan guarantee programs, along with even greater liberalization of terms over time, is the single most important contribution that public policy can make to housing programs.

Conventional public-housing programs should also be stressed. Their decline in the early 1970s is distressing, as they provide more housing and better housing for lower-income people at a smaller subsidy cost than any other program.

Extension and promotion of cooperative housing as a form of housing ownership could also bring a great reduction in housing costs and a vast expansion of housing for lower-middle-income families. The savings available to cooperative housing members are not necessarily unique. But what can be said is that it takes the cooperative form of housing for many of the advantages of home ownership, especially the deduction of property taxes and mortgage interest payments, to become available to middle- and lower-income citizens. In addition, as the Douglas Commission pointed out, savings accrue to members from the initial production of a large number of units and from lower closing costs or legal fees which the cooperative receives by acting on behalf of a large number of people. Thus the cooperative form of organization can provide housing at less cost to those who take part in it than would otherwise be available to them.

But the HUD record on cooperative housing is an indifferent one. In some regions, such as Detroit, it has had spectacular success, due in large part to the efforts of the Foundation for Cooperative Housing. Cooperative housing has also flourished in New York City under the Amalgamated Clothing Workers' United Housing Federation, and has had reasonable success elsewhere when undertaken by similarly knowledgeable and dedicated groups. But there are regions where HUD officials have either ignored or disparaged this means of providing a decent home in a suitable living environment to individuals whose income level is such that they could not otherwise acquire it.

The Need for a Capital Budget

If a means could be found for the federal government to substitute its superior power to borrow funds for subsidized programs in lieu of borrowing those funds on the private market, immense amounts of additional housing could be provided to those who cannot now afford it—and at lower costs to the government.

For example, on a $25,000 thirty-year mortgage at 7 percent interest, the monthly payment for principal and interest is approximately $165. On a $25,000 thirty-year mortgage at 5 percent interest the monthly payment for principal and interest is approximately $132 or $33 per month, or almost $400 per year, less. Over the thirty-year life of the mortgage, the difference in carrying charges is almost $12,000.

If, instead of borrowing from the private market at the 7 percent rate to finance Section 235 and 236 housing, the government got the funds through the long-term-government-bond market at 5 percent, billions of dollars could be saved in providing a large share of the six million subsidized housing units called for by the Housing Act of 1968. But because the federal government has no capital budget, it is reluctant to provide housing or housing subsidies through direct means—the most effective and least costly way of doing it. It does not do so because capital expenditures by the federal government are charged as an immediate cost in the year expended instead of amortized over the reasonable life of the asset, as every private business does. And every President and every Congress fight to hold down the budget in the least painful way. Loan programs, especially housing-loan programs, are the most vulnerable areas.

An expenditure by the government for a house returns both principal and interest, is secured by real property, and would be treated by a private company as a blue-chip asset. But the federal government, in its budgetary process, treats it as a liability and enters the entire amount as an expenditure for the year in which the liability or asset is incurred. It is to avoid this consequence that the government has devised complicated, tricky, and excessively costly means of subsidizing numerous forms of housing. On any modern balance sheet the transaction would be entered on one side of the balance sheet as an asset, on the other side as a liability, and only the subsidy would be charged against the operating budget as an expenditure. This accurately reflects the transaction.

The use of such accounting methods alone could save the federal government and the taxpayers tens of billions of dollars in meeting the 1968 Housing Act goals.

Feast or Famine

One of the most costly aspects of housing production is the feast-or-famine nature of the industry. Neither the private builder nor the public agencies can maintain efficient programs if the number of units fluctuates widely from year to year. One of the simplest means to reduce the cost of housing programs is to foster a climate which promotes continuity of production.

It is more important to fund federal programs at a stable and adequate rate than it is to pump in large sums of money one year followed by a drought in the next. It is also important at the national level to avoid tight-money policies one year and easy-money policies the next. A private builder's costs skyrocket if he builds 750 units one year and only 400 the next. He finds it impossible to organize his work force efficiently, to make savings by buying in quantity, to use his capital equipment effectively, or to provide equilibrium in his inventory.

In this respect economic policies which provide relatively

full employment and stable prices can do more to provide an abundance of housing than any other single factor. In addition, the Federal Reserve Board must devise policies which will insulate housing from the full brunt of credit crunches and tight-money policies that have devastated the industry in the past. Far too little thought has been given by the monetary experts to this devastating economic consequence of their policies.

Restrictive Practices

Restrictive building practices are another facet of the problem. They stem not only from the efforts and interests of unions but from those of contractors and producers as well. Among the more common issues are the refusal to use or restrictions on plastic pipe in drainage systems, prefabricated products, nonmetallic-sheathed electrical cables, and two-by-four-inch studs twenty-four inches on center in non-load-bearing interiors, as well as numerous safety and job-security provisions in union contracts which employers complain about.

Some restrictions are more common in construction in general than in home building in particular. The reason is that home building is about 80 percent nonunion. Nonetheless there are restrictions written into construction contracts or practices followed in the industry which prevent the most efficient use of time and labor.

Among the more important means of reducing restrictive practices are through project agreements negotiated prior to construction, the adoption of area or state building codes, the use of the federal government's leverage as the consumer of about one third of all construction put in place annually to reduce restrictive practices and provide uniform standards, and the trade-off of steadier work, guaranteed annual earnings, and job security for a reduction through negotiation of alleged restrictions.

In one form or another each of these proposals—continuity in building, reduction in restrictive practices, better ways to subsidize, emphasis on cooperative housing, a return to the public-housing formula, and an expansion of the FHA guarantee-program—is a means of reducing housing costs in order to meet the housing-act goals.

Industrialized Housing

There is another major proposal to reduce housing costs. That is through industrialized housing. Here is why it is important:

At the present time, housing costs too much to build to meet these goals without massive subsidies. As median family income is $9,000 to $10,000 per year, and as the rule of thumb is that a family can afford a house roughly two and a half times its family income, the average family can afford a house costing $22,500 to $25,000.

But $22,500 to $25,000 is the rock-bottom price at which housing can be built. In fact, with the price of money at 6 percent or more, 50 percent of the families in the country cannot afford to buy a house at that price or higher. Therefore, in order to meet our housing goals at present housing prices, the upper half of income groups would have to subsidize the lower half.

That is too much. That is impossible. It is possible for the upper 80 percent to subsidize the lower 20 percent, but for the upper 50 percent or upper 40 percent of income groups to subsidize the lower 50 to 60 percent of income groups is both undesirable and impossible, at least on the massive scale needed to meet our housing needs.

In theory at least, considerable savings can be made through mass-produced or industrialized housing. Among the theoretical cost reductions are year-round production, substitution of machines for labor, substitution of industrialized labor for craft labor, fewer hours to produce, quantity purchases of materials, lower interim financing costs due to speedier erection at the site, lower building fees because of lower risks, lower professional fees for architects, planners, and lawyers because they spread their talents over a larger number of units and are hired by a company as employees rather than as independent professionals, savings on vandalism, and lower maintenance costs

These savings may be offset by higher costs for the transportation of the unit to the site and for original outlays for capital and machinery. Over the years dozens of factory-built, prefabricated housing units have been built, but virtually none of them has reduced costs. If they do not reduce costs, there is no reason to build housing in the factory rather than conventionally.

The Lustron house was excellent, but it floundered because of high costs and corruption. The Koppers Company builds a great house, but it has found marketing problems difficult to overcome. U. S. Steel has had an industrialized house on the market for a number of years, but without great success. At the Expo world's fair in Canada there was a marvelous exhibition of industrialized housing, Habitat, but the costs exceeded $80,000 per unit, scarcely useful for mass-produced housing for low-income, subsidized housing.

When the Douglas Commission examined industrialized housing in some twenty-two cities in the U. S., the builders either said they did not know their costs or produced cost figures which were two to three times greater than useful for a national housing program. In every case the industrial builder claimed that he had insufficient volume to prove that the costs could be reduced below conventional housing. Time after time the industrial producer replied that he needed at least 1,000 units of volume production per year to cover his heavy capital overhead and to lower costs.

Must Lower Costs

As of today no producer of industrialized housing has been able to prove that his costs are lower than the most efficiently built conventional housing. The highly successful Levitt house, for example, is a conventional house built by taking the assembly line to the site rather than building the house on an assembly line and shipping it to the site.

In Section 108 of the Housing Act of 1968, the Proxmire amendment provided an opportunity to answer the question, Can industrialized housing be built at significant reductions in cost? Modeled on a recommendation of the Douglas Commission, it provided that 1,000 units each of at least five industrialized housing prototypes be built each year for five years (25,000 units) under HUD auspices to prove whether or not industrialized housing could pay.

Financing for the 25,000 units was provided for under existing programs of public housing, 221-d-3 and the 235-236 programs among others. There was no problem in funding the Section 108 experiments.

Such a program could have proved once and for all whether industrialized housing could cut costs significantly.

"Operation Breakthrough" the Wrong Concept

Instead of proceeding with Section 108, HUD devised "Operation Breakthrough." Instead of proving whether housing costs could be cut, its basic purpose was to develop new technology, to provide for innovative demonstration housing projects, and to develop experimental housing systems. Its concept was wrong for the following reasons.

1. It was just another HUD demonstration project, such as "In-Cities" and hundreds of individual housing demonstration

projects that HUD has sponsored over the last thirty years without significant success. In fact, most of them have been outright failures.

2. Housing does not suffer from a lack of new techniques, new materials, new ideas, new technologies and systems. These are available in abundance. The problem is to produce in such significant volume as to reduce costs.

3. It was not designed to reduce costs.

Here is what HUD did: In Phase I, it sent out a request for proposal (RFP) for two types of innovations—Type A, complete housing systems, and Type B, new innovative ideas (toilets, furnaces, heating systems, etc.) for individual housing items.

HUD received about 915 responses, of which 550 were for Type A and 365 for Type B.

The Type-A number was reduced to twenty-two housing systems. An examination of them indicates there is not a single new industrial housing technique proposed in the system. In almost every case they are built of materials or by methods which have been available for considerable periods of time. They consist of existing factory panels or modules made from plastic, concrete, wood, metal, fiberglass, stressed-skin plywood, and cellulose. None of this is new in any way.

To pay for the program, HUD got an increase in its research and development funds from $10 million to $45 million, of which about half ($25 million) is for Breakthrough.

In Phase II the twenty-two systems were allocated to eleven sites around the country. But instead of 1,000 units of each of five prototypes, there are twenty-two systems and a total of only 2,500 to 3,000 units. Some of these are apartment-type units (four or five of them) of 250 to 300 units each. That leaves fewer than 100 units on the average for the remaining seventeen or eighteen prototypes. In some cases it is far less than that. In some cases, the "innovative" feature is not the unit but the marketing method or the means of aggregating markets.

Phase II, therefore, proves nothing about reducing housing

costs. It is just another housing demonstration project of new techniques or new marketing methods which will prove nothing that the housing industry has not known for years. It fails to come to grips with the fundamental issue of whether or how housing costs can be reduced by industrialized methods. As Secretary Romney said, Breakthrough is "not a program designed to see just how cheaply we can build a house, but a way to break through to total new systems of housing production, financing, marketing, management and land use." Breakthrough is irrelevant to the problem of reducing housing costs.

In Phase III, which is to follow, the units put up on the eleven sites will be tested for such things as "consumer acceptance" and livability and can then be marketed by the individual companies on the commercial market. But at the end of Operation Breakthrough, HUD and the housing industry will know little more about the illusory question of industrialized housing costs than they know now.

Breakthrough misses the point. It is another demonstration project for new techniques, not a test of housing costs. It duplicates methods, designs, and techniques which have been known for up to thirty years.

It is time to return to fundamentals and to carry out the legislative mandate of Section 108. The vast empty spaces in the central cities created through urban renewal and other demolitions can provide ideal sites on which industrialized housing can be tested. If costs can be cut, then the industrialized units can be used to provide a large part of the 1968 act's goal of six million subsidized housing units. It can mean the difference between success and failure. It is a way both to meet the goals and to reorder housing priorities.

Operation Breakthrough will not help solve the fundamental housing problem—how to lower the costs of housing to such a level that we can meet the 1968 Housing Act goals. It does not answer the question, Can industrialized housing reduce costs sufficiently that 80 percent of the American public can afford housing without direct government subsidies? Four years after Breakthrough was announced, there were no concrete results as to how industrialized housing can reduce costs.

Breakthrough is a colossal failure. It fails on all counts.

The housing goals in the 1949 and 1968 acts can be met. The United States has the manpower, the materials, and the resources to do it. The $11-billion annual housing subsidies through direct appropriations and tax-subsidy expenditures are more than sufficient to pay for the housing, provided only that the funds are distributed more equitably. In addition, vigorous and more intelligent efforts must be made to reduce housing costs so that most people can afford to pay for their own homes and the subsidies can be directed toward those whose needs are most demanding.

These are the ways to provide a decent home in a suitable living environment which more than two decades of indifferent public actions have denied to every American family.

9 · The Executive Branch— How Power Is Usurped and Priorities Are Distorted

On February 13, 1969, Henry Kearns, highly successful business man, developer of domestic and international ventures, former Assistant Secretary of Commerce, and long-time ardent political backer of President Nixon, appeared before the Senate Banking Committee. Mr. Kearns had been nominated to be president and chairman of the Export-Import Bank of the United States.

The problem was that Mr. Kearns owned 100,000 shares of stock, worth as much as $1 million, in the Siam Kraft Paper Company in Thailand. The company was founded three years earlier with a $14-million loan from the Export-Import Bank. Because he was unable to sell the stock, Mr. Kearns proposed that he keep it and place it in trust, and that any matters or decisions with respect to the Siam Kraft Paper Company be insulated from him. Decisions about Siam Kraft by the Export-Import Bank would be made by Mr. Kearn's subordinates, particularly Walter Sauer, first vice-president and vice-chairman of the Export-Import Bank.

I objected to this procedure. At Mr. Kearn's confirmation hearings I said:

What concerns me about this kind of arrangement is that you're the boss. You're the president of the corporation. Mr. Sauer is your subordinate, and the other members of the Export-Import Bank work with you and under your direction. . . .

It's hard for me to really see how this effectively protects the public interest where you do have a very clear degree of authority over the people who in turn are going to determine whether or not this loan is repaid on time and so forth.

Because of this apparent conflict of interest, I opposed Mr. Kearn's confirmation. I was the only member of the Senate to vote against him.

After Mr. Kearns took office he kept his word and remained insulated from decisions affecting Siam Kraft Paper Company. But the Export-Import Bank took some exceptional steps. The bank rescheduled Siam Kraft's debt. It extended the loan, which was due in 1976, to 1992, one of the longest extensions in the history of the Export-Import Bank.

The Export-Import Bank recruited a man who was subsequently hired by Siam Kraft Paper Company as manager. The Export-Import Bank loaned Siam Kraft $80,000 at 6 percent interest, somewhat less than market interest rates and considerably below the amount a foundering company would pay, to insure the U.S. dollar cost of the manager's salary for two years. The Export-Import Bank postponed repayment of that loan until December 1, 1973, when it would be repaid in six equal semiannual installments. The effect of the postponement was to provide the money interest free for about a two-year period.

On three occasions the Export-Import Bank sent individuals or teams to Thailand to survey the company's activities. In addition, the bank's Hong Kong representative visited Bangkok to consult with Siam Kraft officials.

It may be argued that the presence of Mr. Kearns as president and chairman of the Export-Import Bank did not influence his subordinates in making an exceptionally long extension of Siam Kraft's loan and in providing services and the funds, interest free for two years, to hire a new manager. But it should be said that apparently his presence did not hurt the company in which he retained 100,000 shares. It can be said, too, without fear of contradiction, that the U.S. government seldom lends $80,000 interest-free to the weak and the poor, or extends the repayment period of a government loan for sixteen years unless the individual or company has massive economic or political power.

FDA Abuse of Power

A considerably greater abuse of power and position occurred in another agency a few years earlier.

The Annual Symposium on Antibiotics took place in Washington, D.C., sponsored jointly by the Food and Drug Administration and M.D. Publications, Inc., the publisher of two scientific journals, *Antibiotics and Chemotherapy* and *Antibiotic Medicine and Clinical Therapy*. The head of the Food and Drug Administration's Division of Antibiotics, Dr. Henry Welch, gave the opening address. His job at FDA was to supervise the certification of antibiotic drugs as required by law.

Antibiotics were highly controversial. Charges had been made in public sources that there was overpromotion and overuse of them. Physicians were said to prescribe antibiotics instead of making thorough diagnoses. Manufacturers were accused of failing to advise doctors of untoward reactions to their drugs as well as of excessive zeal in advertising them.

One of the main controversies was over the "synergistic" effects of combining two or more antibiotics instead of using only one. The argument revolved around whether using drugs in combination produced a total effect greater than the sum of the individual effects of each drug. Millions of dollars in drug sales as well as the recoupment of drug-development costs were at stake. In addition, the health and safety of millions of patients in all parts of the world were involved. The way the head of the Food and Drug Administration's Antibiotics Division, the chief traffic-cop agency, viewed this issue was the key to the drug companies' problem.

Happily from their point of view, Dr. Welch agreed with their position. That was a major point in his opening remarks at the symposium. But there was far more to it than that. Dr. Henry Welch also edited the two ostensibly scientific journals dedicated to antibiotics which were the co-sponsors of the symposium. He and his wife also held a half-interest in a corporation called Medical Encyclopedia, Inc., which published *Antibiotics Annual*. The speech Dr. Welch gave that day would be reprinted by the companies in which he had a financial interest and which were co-sponsors of the symposium, would be purchased in bulk quantities by the drug companies he was charged with regulating, and would be distributed to doctors to promote drugs he certified.

During the period of his editorship of the two journals, eleven major drug companies purchased almost $310,000 in advertising in them. Dr. Welch approved all advertising for the journals. Fourteen major drug companies paid $685,000 to the journals for reprints of their articles. The articles were edited and approved for publication by Dr. Welch. Drug companies also paid almost $70,000 to M.D. Publications, the parent company of the journals, for extra pages.

Over a seven-year period while he was head of the Division of Antibiotics, Dr. Welch received from M.D. Publications $20,-294.43 which was 7½ percent of the net advertising revenues, $173,293.02 which was 50 percent of the net profit on the sales of reprints, $9,726.91 which was 25 percent of the net profits for extra pages, $18,972.89 for his share of the returns from a British edition of one of the journals, and $1,729.45 as commission on bulk sales. In addition, he got $36,750.00 in salary from Medical Encyclopedia, Inc., and $26,375.70 for his and his wife's half-interest in it.

Conflicts Approved by FDA

Dr. Welch's earnings from M.D. Publications, Inc., and from Medical Encyclopedia, Inc., was $287,142.40. All of it was received while he was head of the FDA's Antibiotics Division. His editorships and ownership were specifically approved by the FDA. While a full-time government employee and head of the Division of Antibiotics, Dr. Welch also applied for and received six patents for work on antibiotics and received payment for their foreign rights.

Dr. Welch avoided an appearance before the Kefauver Investigating Committee to go into these matters when his doctor claimed that his life would be endangered from the effect of the appearance on his heart condition. FDA allowed him to resign quietly. No prosecution of the direct conflicts of interest were ever undertaken. He was allowed to leave with a tap on the wrist.

During the controversy the head of one of the major drug companies complained to the FDA that articles concerning Dr. Welch in *Saturday Review* and the St. Louis *Post-Dispatch* were based on "half-truths, false innuendoes, and outright distortions." The drug company had purchased more than $256,000 in advertising, reprints, and extra pages from M.D. Publications over the years. They were the single largest source of income for M.D. Publications and Dr. Welch. To add insult to injury, the head of the firm requested FDA to provide him with the names of the concerned people who had written to FDA as a result of the exposé, so that his company could reply to them.

The Agencies Represent the Powerful

The FDA-Welch episode was only one of the worst and most flagrant conflicts of interest which abound in government agencies. It is a truism, supported by hundreds of examples, that the great departments of the government routinely act on behalf of the major economic interests under their jurisdiction rather than in the public interest. The Treasury represents banks. The Defense Department promotes the military-industrial complex. The Agriculture Department puts the interests of big farmers ahead of the public interest. These great agencies of government, designed to protect and promote the interests of all citizens of the country, end up promoting the interests of the few and promoting them against the public interest when the two conflict.

The politically appointed Secretaries, Undersecretaries, and Assistant Secretaries come from the political and economic-interest groups with a stake in the agency's activities. At the end of their term they return to work for these same groups.

There are many examples. When he left office in 1969, the Assistant Secretary of Housing and head of the FHA, Philip N. Brownstein, went into law practice in Washington, D.C. He and his firm represent the National Council of Housing Producers, which includes the biggest housing firms in the country—Boise-Cascade, Larwin, Levitt, National Homes Construction Company, ALCAN Design Homes, Ltd., Centrex, Luwers and Cooke, Inc., and other giants. As head of the FHA, Mr. Brownstein had the last word over FHA mortgage guarantees, co-op loans, and the moderate-income-housing subsidy program. As counsel for the Housing Producers, he represents those seeking vast privileges from the agency he just headed.

Melvin R. Laird, when he was still a Congressman and before he became Secretary of Defense, initiated a survey which showed that 83 of 813, or more than 10 percent, of scientific, medical, and technical employees who left the Food and Drug Administration in a five-year period went to work for FDA-regulated companies.

The 2,100 former high-ranking Pentagon brass who were working for the 100 biggest members of the military-industrial complex in 1969 which I publicized, were joined by almost 1,000 of their brethren in the following three years, according to the results of a Pentagon survey required by my amendment to the 1969 Military Authorization Act.

Department advisory committees are stacked with agents of powerful private economic-interest groups. Regulations and proposed actions are routinely cleared with them before they go into effect. The heads of major government departments have an open-door policy for the presidents of giant industrial firms or economic-interest groups. Ordinary citizens either have no access to them at all or cool their heels in the waiting rooms.

This is important not only because of the conflicts of interest and the effect that private economic-interest groups have on government policy. It is chiefly important because until the system of influence is ended it will be virtually impossible to apply objective analysis to government programs, to make intelligent public-interest judgments about government policies, and to reorder the national priorities.

Abuses abound. The FDA does not only routinely act in the interests of the big drug companies, while routinely harrassing small firms or individual innovators through the police power the FDA exercises, but it protects the economic interests of the food giants as well. Take some examples.

Too Good for Bread

Modern American bread is a disgrace. Most of the nutrients have been removed from the flour from which the bread is made.

Traditionally bread was made from wheat flour which contained wheat germ. But the grinding of the wheat on modern rolling machines crushed the wheat germ, which made the flour rancid. As a consequence, milling firms removed the wheat germ, the most nutritious part of the flour, and sold it to farmers to use to slop their pigs. Meanwhile, with the wheat germ removed, the remaining white flour contained little but carbohydrates. This makes it necessary to add artificial nutrients for it to be sold at all. While the pigs got the nutrients, people got lousy flour. Some believe that the absence of wheat germ in the American diet is partially responsible for the epidemic of heart disease from which this country suffers.

When Cornell University devised a bread containing the whole wheat germ, soya beans, and other highly nutritious ingredients, the FDA banned it. It could not be sold as bread. FDA claimed that the Cornell formula was too good for bread, and that there was an upper limit as well as a floor on how much nutrition there could be in bread.

Dangerous DES

Another area of FDA laxity was found with respect to diethylstilbestrol (DES), an artificial hormone used to fatten livestock, which is produced and marketed by more than half a dozen major drug firms.

Under the Food and Drug Act, no new animal drugs may be certified and used if they induce cancer in man or animals, unless no residue of such drugs is found in any edible portion of the animals. DES caused cancer in mice at 6.25 parts per billion, a high incidence. Tests of DES at smaller levels to induce cancer in mice were never made. Residues of DES were found in the livers of cattle fed the hormone. Nevertheless, FDA not only approved the use of DES in livestock but in 1971 increased the allowed rate from ten to twenty milligrams per day.

At a time when Commissioner Charles Edwards of the FDA was still defending this practice, which seemed clearly against the law, he was in possession of a memorandum condemning the practice. The memorandum was a blockbuster. Adrian Gross of the Office of Pharmaceutical Research and Testing of the FDA wrote to Commissioner Edwards that the testing method for detecting DES residues in slaughtered livestock "does not constitute sufficient protection that carcinogenic levels may not be present." He went on to say that "it is extremely unlikely, if not well-nigh impossible, that under the best of circumstances and with the best of fortunes, the sensitivity of the analytic procedure would approach anything of what is needed here."

In simple language, the tests were inadequate. They were insufficient as proof that DES was harmless.

Residues of less than two parts per billion cannot even be detected in cattle or other animals fed DES. This led Mr. Gross to state that the ability of DES to elicit malignant tumors in female mice is so marked that an estimated safe level of the agent is a minuscule fraction of one part per billion. And Dr. Nathan Mantel of the National Cancer Institute, writing to Congressman L. H. Fountain (D.–N.C.), who was holding hearings on DES, said: "I understand that detection levels for DES are not sensitive below 2ppb [parts per billion], so that no direct measurements of DES in slaughtered animals could give assurance that the level was low enough."

Thus, long after it was known that DES could not meet the requirements for certification, it was still approved by the FDA.

On October 28, 1971 a public-interest consumers' group filed a court case against the Secretary of HEW, the FDA Commissioner, and the Department of Agriculture to enjoin the last-named from continuing to allow DES to pass into commerce and thus into the human food supply, and to enjoin HEW from granting any new animal drug applications for DES until the law was compiled with. In his memo to Commissioner Edwards, Mr. Gross wrote that because of the insensitivity of the tests for DES to determine the levels of it below two parts per billion, "it would seem . . . that neither the USDA nor the FDA are likely to have a strong case at the forthcoming trial."

Such are the ways of the FDA, established originally by a strong reform movement to protect the public against harmful food and drugs.

The Fight over the SST

The way in which priorities are distorted by the action of the government itself in support of private interests was never clearer than in the fight over the SST.

The SST was an economic lemon. In addition, it was not a military plane built to enhance national security. It was a strictly commercial, profit-making venture. There was no justification to use public money to subsidize it. Nevertheless it was approved, but President Kennedy promised that the total development costs would not exceed $750 million, 90 percent of which was to be borne by the U. S. government and the taxpayer. But by the time we stopped it, the government had put up $864 million, and the new $1.3-billion total estimate was still open-ended.

After the huge research and development investment for the prototypes, it was clear that the project was not economically sound. If it had been, private industry would have jumped in to take it over. The government heavily subsidized SST research and the building of the prototypes. From the studies made by a domestic U. S. airline of the operating costs of the British Concorde, there was every indication that a subsidy would be required for the operation of the SST as well. Yet the SST was a commercial plane to be used on commercial flights to get a relatively few high-income travelers from New York to London and other points at a few hours' saving in time.

In addition, there were great environmental problems still unsolved. Sonic booms, sideline and takeoff noise, and the possible environmental disturbance of the upper atmosphere were foremost among them.

But the chief lobbyist for the SST was the government itself— the White House, the Department of Transportation, and the aviation regulatory agencies. The White House lobbied Senators. The DOT spent tens of thousands of dollars on propaganda, brochures, and testimony. At one stage they used their muscle to keep me from appearing on the Dick Cavett Show so that William Magruder, the Administration's chief lobbyist, could make the SST case unchallenged.

Internal adverse reports on the effect of the SST on the environment were suppressed. A children's comic book entitled *The Super-Sonic Pussy Cat*, lauding the project, was produced. Madison Avenue moved into the government in an unseemly display of public-relations muscle.

But not everyone was persuaded, especially not those with special analytical knowledge. Professor Milton Friedman, University of Chicago economist and the leading conservative economic intellectual in the nation, was among them. He said, "The economic selections of Mr. Magruder's testimony are special pleading of the most blatant kind. They display a willingness to drag in any argument however disreputable, so long as it appears to support a preordained conclusion." Professor Friedman called Magruder's balance-of-payment arguments "simple-minded protectionism," his employment-effects argument "a fallacy of composition," and continued: "I find it disgraceful that knowledgeable government officials should use arguments—such as the Balance of Payments argument, the job arguments, and the claim of additional taxes from jobs—that are demonstrable fallacies and have been so demonstrated."

Walter Heller, chairman of the President's Council of Economic Advisers under Presidents Kennedy and Johnson, testified that "on strictly economic grounds the SST is an enormously costly way to create jobs." He testified that the SST could not "begin to match the job-creating power of a public-service-jobs program, or a housing program, or even a carefully selected program of consumer stimulus that could be mounted with the same funds that are involved in the SST."

The SST failed on every count. As Heller said, "If private industry can't take it from here [after $864 million] . . . one can only conclude that the SST dismally fails the fundamental test of the marketplace."

Paul Samuelson, Nobel Prize winner in economics, called the SST "a colossal economic folly." "In this day," he said, "there is no excuse for pyramid building to make work and add to a nation's spurious glory....Government subsidy of the SST or similar supersonic aircraft is at this stage of technology and economic development both an economic and a human disaster."

And as Arthur Okun, also a former chairman of the Council of Economic Advisers and a fellow at Brookings Institution, summed up on the SST and priorities, "A limited volume of federal funds has to be carefully allocated among high-priority programs that serve vital national interests. SST is not one of those high-priority programs."

As the vote neared, the battle took on classic proportions. Could the diffused but overwhelming public opinion against spending billions of dollars on the SST be organized to defeat the concentrated power of the aerospace industry, big labor, and the major departments of the government itself, including the political muscle of the White House? Our count showed us even or slightly ahead, but we believed that the power of the President, with all of his political persuasion and the political loyalty he had at his command, could change enough votes to beat us.

We learned a day or so before the vote that the President was calling and meeting with some of the GOP Senators thought to be soft in their opposition to the SST. One of these was said to be the late Winston L. Prouty (R.–Vt.). To firm up his vote on our side, Dick Wegman of my staff suggested that we call one of the Vermont papers and have them phone Prouty and double check on how he would cast his vote. We called the Rutland paper. The reporter followed through with a call to Prouty. Prouty said yes, he hadn't changed his mind, he still opposed the SST. Subsequently, when the President did call Prouty (and we were told he did), Prouty was locked in and told the President he couldn't switch his vote. Prouty voted with us.

We weren't so lucky with Senator Marlow W. Cook (R.–Ky.). Cook was evidently another of the Senators the President called down to the White House. Still, up until the day of the vote we assumed he was a firm vote on our side—mainly because Cook not only had voted with us in December but also was one of the four co-sponsors of our amendment to kill the SST.

We did not find out about the change until 3 p.m. on the day of the vote, which took place an hour later. The SST debate had been proceeding since about noon. I was in charge of scheduling Senators to speak against the SST; Senator Alan Bible (D.–Nev.) was doing the same thing for the pro-SST Senators. At about three, one of our men had just finished speaking and I went up to Bible and asked, "Whom have you got on tap next?"

Bible pointed to the other side of the aisle and said, "Cook wants to speak."

"Cook!? On *your* side?"

"Sure, does that surprise you?" Bible said, looking as if he had just swallowed a canary.

"Surprise" was hardly the word for it. I was stunned—because our vote tally at that point showed us one vote up, and this would put us one vote down.

What made it so difficult to take was that when Cook spoke he used the we've-come-this-far-so-we-may-as-well-finish argument for the SST—and this was precisely the argument that had been rejected during the floor debate in December when Cook spoke against the SST.

Fortunately, the White House badly bungled its handling of Senator Margaret Chase Smith (R.–Maine). Mrs. Smith's vote was in doubt right up until the day of the vote—it almost always is, on controversial issues, because she keeps her own counsel.

One of the projects that Mrs. Smith had always regarded as very important to her was the naval shipyard at Portsmith, New Hampshire, bordering on Maine. It had always provided a substantial source of employment and revenue for the Maine communities near the New Hampshire border. In the later years of President Johnson's term in office, the shipyard was closed down in one of the Pentagon's rare efforts to save costs. Mrs. Smith was furious. From the moment Richard Nixon came to office in January 1969 she pressed him to reopen the shipyard. Nixon responded with vague promises but no action, waiting until the right moment to grant her request. He found it.

On the day of the SST vote, Nixon sent a hand-carried letter to Mrs. Smith announcing that he was granting her request and that the shipyard would be reopened. I found out about it about noon of that day. A little later I heard that the press had a copy of the Nixon letter to Mrs. Smith, which Mrs. Smith had released. It was clear to us that if Mrs. Smith was releasing this letter, it could only be because she resented this transparent attempt to buy off a completely honest Senator and intended to show her independence by voting against the White House on the SST—which is what she did.

Finally four o'clock arrived. The Senate gallery was full to overflowing. It was one of those great moments in the Senate, with the eyes of the country watching its every move.

As the clerk began to call the roll silence fell over the chamber. My list showed us slightly ahead, but I was waiting for the full force of the President's lobbying to produce some additional surprises. There were ten or more Senators whom I believed to be with us but whose votes I refused to count until they had actually been cast. That group would make the difference.

Several of them came early in the alphabet—Clinton Anderson (D.-N.M.), Lloyd M. Bentsen, Jr. (D.-Tex.), John Sherman Cooper (R.-Ky.), Lawton Chiles (D.-Fla.), David H. Gambrell (D.-Ga.), Vance Hartke (D.-Ind.), and Hubert Humphrey (D.-Minn.). I knew the unions had put great pressure on Hubert Humphrey. There was a real question whether Hartke, who was with us, would be there. Lockheed Aircraft's big plant was located in Gambrell's state. The aerospace industry was very powerful in both Florida and Texas. Clint Anderson was chairman of the Space Committee itself. And after Cook switched, I feared his fellow Kentuckian John Cooper might follow suit.

Technically the vote was on an Appropriations Committee amendment to add $134 million for continued development of the civil supersonic transport during the period from March 30 to June 30, 1971. A yea vote was for the SST. A nay vote was against it.

One by one the votes were called. Anderson? Nay. Bentsen? Nay. Chiles? Nay. Cooper? Nay. Gambrell? Nay. Hartke? He was present and voted nay. Humphrey? Nay.

At this point I knew we had won. The grin on Dick Wegman's face could not be suppressed. Up in the press gallery the AP wire service man was already phoning in word of the victory. Both NBC's Robert McCormack and CBS's Roger Mudd were on their feet and leaving at the exit next to the radio-TV gallery.

The remainder of the roll call was perfunctory. We kept all the other doubtfuls as well—Montoya, Jordan of Idaho, Prouty, and Mrs. Smith. The *coup de grâce* to the SST was the final announcement by the Senate clerk, "On this vote the yeas are forty-six, the nays fifty-one. The amendment is rejected."

It was clearly a victory for an aroused public opinion against a coalition of very powerful interest groups, including the White House itself. But the problem of government lobbying and the full force of federal power being thrown into the breach on behalf of narrow private economic interests goes on.

Interest-free Deposits

The Treasury Department is a conspicuous example of how the clout of a government department is routinely used to distort priorities and aid the most powerful economic interests in the country.

During the calendar year 1970 the Treasury maintained interest-free deposits of over $1 billion in ten of the nation's largest banks. By investing these free Treasury deposits in the federal-funds market, the ten big banks could have earned over $77 million in interest in 1970 alone.

The value of the privilege can be seen if it is turned into personal terms. Suppose the Treasury were to leave $1 million for an entire year with your next-door neighbor. By using it to invest in government or municipal bonds, in certificates of deposit, or in second mortgages, your neighbor could earn about $70,000 on the money. Public opinion would never stand for such action, especially if the funds were left with a welfare mother, a poor farmer, or a migrant worker. You can hear the screams now if it went to Caesar Chavez' farm labor union for them to invest and keep the proceeds. But that is precisely what the Treasury does for the banks.

The banks claim they deserve the funds for the services they perform on behalf of the Treasury, such as cashing war bonds. But a study by the General Accounting Office concluded that banks received benefits from interest-free Treasury deposits far in excess of the services they supposedly provide the Treasury. In any case, services provided to the government should be charged for directly, not taken out in kind or in unofficial barter.

Either one of two actions should be taken. Either the money should be placed in interest-earning accounts or it should be set aside to be used for some important public purpose. It could be loaned to individuals and small businesses in urban or rural poverty areas, for example.

At the state and local levels, the nefarious practice of interest-free deposits of public funds has been one of the most corrupting influences in government. Money was disbursed to pet banks and political favorites. While no question of corruption has been attached to the federal policy, there is no reason why Chase Manhattan, First National City Bank, Bank of America, Continental Illinois, and the other ten biggest banks in the United States should hold average Treasury balances that make up 27 percent of all Treasury funds deposited annually in the nation's banking system. If this squalid practice is to continue, at least the smaller banks and the ghetto banks should be allowed to get their noses into the public trough. The correct answer, however, is to stop it. Any private business official who failed to get a return on his company's idle balances would be cashiered in a week. No less should be expected from public officials when they are dealing with public funds.

Some may say that $77 million is not a lot of money. But it would pay for the expenses of the Peace Corps for a full year.

The Lockheed Bail-out

There are other ways in which the Treasury distorts the goals and priorities in the economy.

The Treasury Department was the prime mover and shaker behind the notorious Lockheed $250-million loan guarantee. Some felt it should be called "A Bill for the Relief of the Lockheed Aircraft Corporation." There is no better example of government action which distorted priorities.

The Treasury threw its full weight, resources, and political muscle behind the loan. Treasury officials provided the major arguments. They lined up the votes. When the going got really tough, they called on the President to use his personal influence to switch enough votes to carry the day for Lockheed in the Senate. But it was not the salvation of Lockheed's fortunes alone which was behind the Treasury Department's move. It acted on behalf of the twenty-six-member big-bank consortium to guarantee the $250 million the banks were putting out to save this highly inefficient firm.

Spurious arguments were used. At times the Treasury argued it both ways. On the one hand it argued that the outlook was so good for Lockheed's Tri-Star Air Bus business that there was no danger the government would be left holding the bag. On the other it argued that the outlook was so precarious that banks would not make the loan without the guarantee.

Lockheed's Missile and Space Division alone has more than $300 million in outstanding stock which could have been pledged as collateral for the loan. That was not done.

It was argued that 60,000 jobs were at stake. That was not true. If the company went bankrupt, all of Lockheed's defense jobs, making up 85 percent of its total business, would continue. Trustees would be appointed, as in the Penn Central case, and production would go on. If the Tri-Star production itself were truly viable, as both the Treasury and Lockheed maintained, the trustees would continue to operate it as they would any other profitable part of the business.

But the 60,000-jobs argument—the key to the loan—was grossly exaggerated. First of all, it was double the actual 30,000 people who worked on Lockheed's civilian-aircraft business. It included indirect as well as direct jobs. Second, 14,000 employees had already been laid off. That left only 16,000 direct jobs, 10,000 at Lockheed and 6,000 at major suppliers. But it turned out, from company work records, that only 6,583 of the alleged 10,000 jobs at Lockheed itself were jobs on the air bus.

An even stronger point against the argument was that the government guarantee of the loan to Lockheed meant fewer jobs for Lockheed's competitor, McDonnell-Douglas, which builds the DC-10. As the total air-bus business is limited, what Lockheed gains, McDonnell-Douglas loses, and vice versa. But as McDonnell-Douglas' DC-10 is equipped with an American-built General Electric engine while Lockheed uses the British Rolls-Royce engine, the backing of Lockheed by the Treasury actually reduced the number of American jobs.

The job argument was phony, spurious, and unbecoming to an Administration whose policies had caused two million more Americans to be unemployed at the time the Lockheed loan passed than when it came into office. Despite the rhetoric about saving jobs, the Treasury's real concern was to bail out Lockheed's creditors, the twenty-six banks, not the 6,583 direct Lockheed jobs.

The Lockheed loan was wrong on every count. The risk of a $250-million loss was shifted from Lockheed shareholders and creditors to the American people. It violated every tenet of competitive business philosophy by rewarding inefficient management. It was unfair to the 10,000 business failures each year who are not bailed out. It was an example of socialism for big business and free enterprise for the Mom and Pop stores.

It also distorted the allocation of credit. Credit in this case was based on political clout, not economic merit. It was also unfair to Lockheed's competitors, who could not get credit at a price below the private market rate, which was the effect of the government guarantee.

It also put the government in an untenable conflict of interest. Because of its financial stake in the solvency of Lockheed, the pressures will be on the Defense Department to throw "sweetheart contracts" to Lockheed, on the Civil Aeronautics Board to grant favorable routes to the airlines which fly the L-1011 air bus, and on the Security and Exchange Commission to look the other way when reviewing Lockheed's financial statements.

The Lockheed bail-out can only lead to greater government intervention in the functions of private business. The government is bound to intervene in Lockheed's business decisions to protect its guarantee.

The Arrogance of Power

The fight over the Lockheed loan was also a case study in the arrogance of power.

The Treasury withheld vital information on Lockheed's cash flow, and the Department of Defense refused us the details of its study on the economics of the L-1011 until the eleventh hour.

Administration supporters of the Lockheed loan vehemently opposed my proposal to call Ralph Nader as a witness. In the secret session of the Senate Banking Committee, Republican Senators called Nader "a publicity-seeking opportunist," charged that he was "speaking outside his field of competence of consumer activity," said that he was "partially motivated by hatred of the corporate structure in this country," and charged that he had demonstrated "no competence, no expertise, no knowledge in this field whatsoever." Interestingly enough, these statements were never repeated in the public session.

Although I sent letters to the heads of the top one hundred

corporations asking them to testify, the letters produced no witnesses and only one strongly critical statement, by John Connor, former Secretary of Commerce. This was true even though a *Wall Street Journal* story showed overwhelming opposition to the loan by top business leaders.

The committee refused to subpoena an internal McDonnell-Douglas study showing an increase in employment for them if their rival's L-1011 project was canceled. This was vital information, since the main argument revolved around unemployment in the industry.

From Treasury Secretary John B. Connally we got a soft-soap job. When we asked him how he, an alleged supporter of free enterprise and rugged individualism and a strong defender of Texas buccanneer operators, could support the bill, he replied, "We sometimes kid ourselves it is a free-enterprise system, but it is not all that free. Much of it lives under regulation. Much of it lives under subsidy."

The arrogance of the bankers was unsurpassed. They were disdainful of the committee and Congress. After failing to explain why the taxpayers should shoulder the risks for a loan to private enterprise which was too risky for the banks, C. J. Medbury, chairman of the board of the Bank of America, disdained to be questioned further, declaring, "I think we have said about what we can say. . . . I have already missed the last plane to the Coast, and I am willing to continue to discuss this with you gentlemen, but I think we have tried to get across our point, and I don't think that the discussion is going forward any further now." Imagine a small businessman or ordinary taxpayer telling a committee of Congress or the Internal Revenue Service that he had missed his last plane back to the Coast and there was no further purpose in discussing his loan or tax problem!

In the end the Administration was unable to provide a single independent, public-interest witness to support it. Everyone who testified for the loan had a financial stake in the guarantee.

Steamroller Tactics

Steamroller tactics were used to rush it through as well. In the executive session of the Banking Committee, it was proposed that we not debate amendments, since the pro-Lockheed forces had the votes. The executive session was held, the bill was reported to the Senate, and a full day's debate took place even before the hearing record was printed.

The big banks got to work, too. One business critic told me personally that his company was "ordered" by his bank not to intervene in the Lockheed matter. We got workers' petitions from Lockheed's plant in Georgia although the plane was made not there but in California.

A boycott against Wisconsin products was organized, ostensibly because of grass-roots sentiment by aerospace workers in Georgia and California. But when dozens of letters with the same wording began to appear in papers throughout Wisconsin and in the Congressional mail, we knew it was no grass-roots organization.

There were even threats on my life and that of Henry Durham, a brave and courageous Lockheed employee who had bucked the company's wasteful practices. We got the FBI to protect Durham around the clock, and I had the FBI and the Secret Service check out in detail the threats I received. One of them, a threat to come to Washington to kill me, was made by a Lockheed employee in Georgia before a group of his co-workers. When he was interviewed he claimed he had said it in jest, but several of those who had heard it reported it to me and to the authorities precisely because they thought the man meant it. In the end no harm came to us. I changed my jogging run-to-work route to avoid an easy sniper pickoff.

Aided by allies like Senators Lowell P. Weicker, Jr., and Robert Taft, Jr., we fought down to the wire. At one stage the managers for the bill reneged on their promise to vote when they were shocked to discover from their informal nose count that they didn't have the votes to win. At that point, while charging us with filibustering, they prevailed in postponing the vote.

As in the SST vote, the full force and weight of the White House was thrown into the breach. But this time in the end the President prevailed on Senators J. Caleb Boggs, William V. Roth, Jr., John Sherman Cooper, Paul J. Fannin, and Roman L. Hruska to change their votes. Senator Humphrey, alone among the Democratic Presidential contenders, voted for the Lockheed loan, and Senators Russell Long and Allen J. Ellender of Louisiana, Metcalf of Montana and Mike Gravel of Alaska succumbed to the jobs argument at the last minute and switched to the other side.

When the roll call was finished, it was a forty-eight to forty-eight tie, with Cook of Kentucky not voting. He then voted yea, despite a previous speech in Louisville in which he had announced opposition to the loan guarantee.

The Lockheed guarantee, like government funding of the SST, provided virtually no benefits for the public, but great disadvantages. It not only distorted public priorities but exempted a purely commercial business proposition from what Princeton economist William Baumol called "the merciless penalization of the inefficient and its reward to the efficient," which is the secret of the success of the free-market economy.

It is proper for government to act to ameliorate the harshness of business failures and to provide a safety net for those who fail in life. It is quite another thing for government to abet and abide incompetence, inefficiency, and waste itself.

Sugar Subsidies

It is not only the FDA and the Treasury, Agriculture, and Transportation Departments which use their clout on behalf of narrow vested interests. The State Department also distorts priorities and raises prices to the American consumer and tax-payer. Take sugar subsidies, probably the biggest bonanza and perhaps the most outrageous of all government programs.

In most parts of the United States, to grow sugar is an inefficient, wasteful, and unproductive operation. It is like growing bananas on Pike's Peak or cucumbers in hothouses in Maine. Sugar is grown efficiently in the Caribbean and other warm parts of the world. In order for it to be produced at all in most of the United States, a gigantic subsidy must be paid to the producers. This subsidy includes a quota which limits the total amount that can be produced domestically and imported from abroad. It includes an import tariff which raises the price and protects the domestic producer. An excise or processing tax is then levied on all sugar, whether produced domestically or imported. Finally production payments are made to domestic producers.

While the subsidies vary from time to time, depending on the price and volume of world production, over the history of the program the American consumer has been charged a subsidy of somewhat more than three cents a pound, or sixty dollars a ton, or $700 million a year. It costs the average family thirteen to fifteen dollars a year.

When Cuba went Communist, its annual quota of three million tons was up for grabs. It was not merely a question of sugar producers selling sugar to the American market at the world or a competitive price. It was a lush bonanza because of the artificially high American price brought about by the subsidies, quotas, gimmicks, and other devices used to raise it.

When, during the 1960s, the Senate adopted an amendment to purchase much of the old Cuban quota at world market prices and hence to give the American consumer and taxpayer some minor break, the skies over Washington were darkened with the planes flying in economic attachés from every part of the world to lobby against the action and to secure a slice of the lucrative former Cuban sugar quota for themselves.

The biggest lobbyist of them all was the State Department. Its representatives testified in Congress against the American consumer and on behalf of the foreign producers. Chief aides in charge of Latin-American and African affairs phoned key Senators, urging them to reverse the action. Quotas were demanded for possessions of both Britain and France, even though those two nations had their own subsidized-quota programs from which most non-British and non-French producers were excluded.

Under pressure from the State Department and the American beet and sugarcane interests, the Senate's attempt to protect the American consumer was massacred. The diffused and unorganized power of the American consumer was sacrificed to the intense and organized efforts of foreign and domestic producers. In this battle, the State Department threw its very considerable weight into the balance against the American consumer's interest in getting a cheap and abundant supply of sugar and for windfall prices for foreign producers.

Stacked Advisory Groups

One of the major ways economic-interest groups influence government policies is through the system of advisory groups and blue-ribbon panels established by virtually every department. Their influence on policy and priorities is pervasive.

In April 1970 the President established the National Industrial Pollution Control Council to advise the President and the chairman of the Council on Environmental Quality through the good offices of the Secretary of Commerce. These men really knew their job. The Council was composed of the top brass of the sixty-three biggest polluters in the United States, including steel, airlines, autos, private utilities, detergents, paper products, oil, chemicals, containers, and many others. Missing from the National Industrial Pollution Control Council was a single member from a university, a consumer organization, a conservation group, or any other public-interest organization. As Senator Lee Metcalf commented, "the Council must be placed in the category of the rabbit sent to fetch the lettuce."

When the Secretary of Defense wanted to examine the scandal created by cost overruns and to "restore public confidence and credibility in the Department of Defense," he appointed a Blue Ribbon Defense Panel. Unfortunately, nine of the fifteen members were from businesses or organizations which on the average had over $250 million apiece in either defense contracts or defense-industry holdings. The combined total for the nine was over $2.3 billion worth of interests in defense business or holdings. Secretary of Defense Laird urged the group to bring to the problems of the Defense Department "a fresh, objective and uninvolved perspective." In a joint announcement, the President and Mr. Laird expressed an urgent hope that the panel would "restore public confidence and credibility in the Department of Defense."

To insure that fact, the panel selected as its top staff man J. Fred Buzhardt, at that time a special assistant to the Assistant Secretary of Defense, a graduate of the U. S. Military Academy, and a former legislative assistant to Senator J. Strom Thurmond, Republican of South Carolina. Finally, the Blue Ribbon Panel negotiated a major research contract with the Stanford Research Institute, which received over $27 million in government contracts in the year immediately preceding its appointment, including a $2.5-million grant to study the feasibility of the ABM missile system.

Some of the 1,500 or more advisory committees to the federal government make no pretense of avoiding conflicts of interest or holding open meetings. As Vic Reinemer, executive secretary to Senator Lee Metcalf and a real expert on the subject, wrote in the November 1971 issue of *The Progressive:*

...consider how Chase Manhattan Bank (Rockefeller) associates dominate the Civil Aeronautics Board's Finance Advisory Committee, appointed last year. At its first meeting (in the bank's home office, under the chairmanship of one of Chase's 298 vice-presidents) this "Government" Committee decided to exclude the press and public, to make recommendations to the CAB on its "procedural and philosophical conduct" and to begin by recommending changes in the Board's method of compiling financial reports.

Then Reinemer asked the crucial question:

And who is the major creditor for five of the nine local service air carriers, as well as the principal stockholder in both the Eastern and Northwest Orient airlines? By coincidence, Chase Manhattan Bank.

Reinemer points out that this situation is almost universal. The Federal Power Commission calls on the American Gas Association for estimates of gas reserves. The members of the 119-man National Petroleum Council advise a dozen agency and Office of Management and Budget advisory committees, panels, and commissions. The Rail Passenger Service Act called for a fifteen-man panel to give financial advice, seven members of which were to represent the public, but except for two government employees all of those appointed were financiers or railroad officials. When the Interstate Commerce Commission created a Tariff Users Advisory Committee, it had seven industry and four carrier representatives, but not a single tariff-user member.

Business, industry, railroads, airlines, banks are all on the inside. Rarely does the consumer or the public interest get even token representation. This is the way public policy is made. This is how priorities are ordered.

These are the chief reasons why public priorities are what the executive branch of the government says they are. Powerful interest groups have an instinct for the seat of power. They smell it, search for it, seek it out, and dominate it. They work at it day in and day out. Ordinary citizens are aroused to action only fitfully and occasionally. It is a vastly uneven struggle.

LBJ, King of the Senate

To charge the executive branch with usurping power is not to be unaware of the weaknesses of Congress itself. We have failed, too. I learned that when I first came to the Senate.

Before then, I had had one brief legislative experience. That was as an assemblyman in the Wisconsin state legislature. The session lasted six months and was a revelation of how democracy can work and work well.

As a Wisconsin Democrat I had run in the 1950 election on a platform of specific legislative promises. I viewed this as a contract with the people of Wisconsin. If I were elected this platform was what I would try to put into effect. And I was impressed that that was just what the Democratic Party in the state Assembly tried to do. All of us elected Assembly Democrats met in caucus. We elected our leaders and drafted a bill to reflect every promise made in the platform. The bill was assigned to an assemblyman, and he introduced it. Every member of the party was made aware that this was a committee position. He could support or oppose it depending on his conscience, but it would be pushed in committee, if possible brought to the floor, and members of the Assembly would be called upon to stand up and be counted on it.

As the session progressed we would have regular weekly Democratic caucus meetings. At the meetings the members would debate and discuss the timing and tactics of the fight on the floor or in committee for our party platform legislation, and then vote on how to instruct our leadership to carry them out. As a new member I had as much voice as any other member of the caucus, including our elected leaders. Our elected leaders were, in fact, the instruments of the caucus membership.

This greatly appealed to me. Each of us had been elected. In most cases our position on legislation had been clearly understood by our constituents. They knew what they were voting for. In turn we had a full opportunity to make that pledge effective through our party caucus. We had party responsibility that meant something.

Now, how about the United States Senate? How did the "greatest deliberative body in the world" operate?

You may not believe this, but when I arrived in the United States Senate the situation was completely reversed. The democratic process was set right on its head.

The Democratic Party was the majority party in the Senate, as it has been in the fifteen years I have served in this body. The legislative responsibility was ours. How about party responsibility? Forget it.

First, the Democrats in the Senate had exactly one caucus a year. That's right. Just one.

And the caucus! It would begin with a forty-five-minute address by Majority Leader Lyndon Johnson. This was dubbed Lyndon's State of the Union address. The address *set forth what the program and policies of the party would be in the coming year.* Debate? None. Platform pledges? Wholly ignored.

Majority Leader Johnson finished and he would quickly move to a different subject. In 1959, for instance, Senator Hubert Humphrey had just returned from his marathon eight-hour talk with Russian Premier Khrushchev, so Johnson called on Humphrey, who spoke for half an hour and answered a few questions. And, believe it or not, that was it. We adjourned, finished. It was all over.

The next time the members of the Democratic Party would come together again in a caucus would be one year later, when the same fiasco would be repeated.

I was outraged. This meant that neither I nor any other Democratic United States Senator would have any voice in determining what our party policy would be in the Senate.

Now, of course, as a Senator I had my rights on the floor, I had my opportunity to vote and work in committee, but the *party* responsibility was nil. Except as an individual Senator would decide to introduce a pledge from the party platform, and that would happen only occasionally, the promises of our party were empty. As far as I could see, our platform was a plain, simple lie. The Democrats in the United States Senate had no intention of paying any attention to it.

Proxmire's Farewell Address

I decided to take the floor of the Senate and tell my colleagues and the country how devoid of power all United States Senators were except the Majority Leader, Lyndon Johnson. He had it all.

I picked Washington's Birthday for my first speech against the leader. (I gave three others within the next month.) The first action on the floor of the Senate on Washington's Birthday is a reading of Washington's Farewell Address. I immediately followed with my attack on our all-powerful leader. A wag in the press gallery observed that 1959 marked a precedent in Senate activity. He said, "For the first time there were two farewell addresses: Washington's and Proxmire's."

The reaction of my Senate colleagues was fascinating. Publicly almost all of them were diplomatically silent. But privately they were a great cheering section. Those cheers were about as private as they could get. Phone calls at home at night, almost always preceded by "Keep this under your hat." Or "If you tell anyone I will flatly deny it, but you are absolutely right. I'm with you all the way." Only a few, like Paul Douglas and Joseph S. Clark and Wayne Morse and others, spoke up publicly in support of my position.

After my second speech, Senator Richard L. Neuberger of Oregon counterattacked on the floor and told me I was an ingrate, biting the hand that was feeding me. After all, asked Neuberger, "Who gave you your committee assignments? Wasn't it the Leader?"

Neuberger made my point. John F. Kennedy, then the junior Senator from Massachusetts, made it better when he said, "Lyndon has the power, because he hands out the loaves and fishes."

Finally Majority Leader Johnson entered into debate with me and charged (a) that I needed to be wet-nursed, (b) that I was using the easiest publicity gimmick in the world, making a punching bag out of the Majority Leader, and (c) that I was frustrated because he had kept me off the tax-writing Finance Committee.

At any rate, the results were good, and Richard Strout, the able reporter from the *Christian Science Monitor*, told why. He pointed out that Proxmire was like the naive little boy who watched the mighty monarch ride by in the parade and had the simplicity to observe that the emperor wore no clothes.

But things were never the same between Johnson and me. When I came to the Senate eighteen months earlier, Johnson gave me the red-carpet treatment. He met me at the airport and sent me as a Senate representative to West Germany (which, incidentally, did far more harm than good with the folks back home; in the end I coughed up the dough out of my own pocket, and I haven't gone on a Congressional junket since). I got the royal welcome because my victory guaranteed that the Democrats would continue to control the Senate, which was then almost equally divided, and Johnson would remain the Majority Leader. My upset victory was also about the first good news for Democrats since Eisenhower's Republican landslide victory in 1956 and seemed a harbinger of things to come in the 1958 elections.

The fact that a Senator said the Majority Leader was using naked power was our first step. Caucuses began shortly. They have never served the party-responsibility function that they do in the Wisconsin legislature, but they began, and the overwhelming power of Majority Leader Johnson departed with him when he left the Senate the following year.

Congress Loses Control

But just as the Democrats in the Senate gave up their power to Lyndon Johnson, so Congress itself has lost control to the executive branch.

Congress is a coequal power in name only. This is due to many reasons. In some areas, especially foreign and defense policies, the Executive has usurped the prerogatives of the Congress. In other areas, Congress has deliberately delegated its power to the Executive or to an independent or outside group. In still others, power is exercised by the Executive because of the diffusion of power in the Congress among 435 Congressmen and 100 Senators and between the House and Senate. This gives a single-minded and determined Executive great tactical advantages in determining priorities. But it is also the result of the supine way in which the Congress, time and again, has fallen all over itself to rubber stamp mistaken policies. Examples abound.

Everyone now knows that overruns on military weapons have reached scandalous proportions. Yet the Congressional committees in charge of military procurement continue to be pushovers for the Pentagon. This weakens our military defense. Scarce resources which should be used to strengthen the country are wasted and thrown away.

The F-14 fighter plane, as we have seen, is one of the biggest lemons to be built in decades. Yet when the crucial vote came, the alleged supporters of military defense in the Senate voted for the F-14. Of the Republicans, all except four cast their votes for it, in deference to the fact that their party controlled the White House. Far too many liberal and progressive Democrats either were absent or went along with the Pentagon.

The rubber-stamping of the Lockheed loan is another example of Congressional culpability in wasting taxpayers' funds and undermining the competitive American economic system. Some of the loudest supporters of free enterprise and opponents of government interference switched their votes at the eleventh hour, caving in to Presidential pleadings and appeals to party loyalty.

In the field of wage-price guidelines, Congress gave the President an unwarranted grant of power largely for political reasons. It not only gave him the ball game but gave him the ball park as well. When the program came up for review, key members of Congress urged that the grant of power be extended without even taking a good tough look at it.

While Congress has complained of the excessive power wielded by the executive branch, it has been far too soft and weak-minded when the chips were down. Instead of sneering and whining at mistaken Presidential proposals while surrendering to White House and Cabinet blandishments, Congress should stand up on its own two feet and rebuff mistaken requests.

In doing that, Congress will not only have to exercise courage, it will also have to exercise great skill. The ways in which the intent of Congress is defeated, its views and directives overcome, or its delegated powers misused are legion. Here are some ways Congress has lost control.

Negotiated Interest Rates

The national debt is about $450 billion. Historically when the Treasury wanted to borrow money it had to come to Congress to get specific approval to do that. Congress would approve but, because of popular pressures, only after insuring that the bond issues would be floated at low interest rates.

In modern times it is clearly impossible for Congress to approve every bond issue. Today the average length of the debt is a little over three years. This means that $450 billion of new borrowing occurs in that period. Congress would do nothing else if it had to approve every government bond issue which is made. Because of this, Congress delegated general authority to issue bonds to the Treasury.

This has meant fewer popular pressures to keep interest rates down. When the Treasury intends to float a major bond issue, it calls in the movers and shakers of the financial community. It discusses the issue and the rate of interest with them. A "negotiated" interest rate is set. The bond issue is then opened to subscription by the banks and financial houses. Routinely, it is over-subscribed. This means that the demand is greater than the supply. In the circumstances, the price should go up and the interest rate should go down. Massive oversubscription means that the negotiated interest rate is too high.

In the delegating of this power to the Treasury, a highly public function was transformed into an essentially private and negotiated settlement, with the big banks and the financial community calling the tune. No competitive market exists initially for these issues in the way other commodities like corn, stock, and eggs are marketed. The result, most competent economists believe, are interest rates higher than they would otherwise be. Interest rates are the prices charged by the banking community for money, and the banks generally do not give advice to the Treasury against their own interests. This is one area where Congress, due to the complexities of the economy, has lost control. Because the government interest rates set the pattern for commercial rates, the effect is higher interest rates all along the line.

Delegation of the Money Power

A comparable example exists with respect to the money power. Article I, Section 8, of the Constitution states that "Congress shall have the power...to coin money and regulate the value thereof." Congress delegated that power to the Federal Reserve Board when it created that body.

The Federal Reserve makes a fetish of the fact that it is an "independent" agency. In theory it is "independent" of the executive branch but is an "agent" of the Congress. In practice, because of the diffusion of power among members of Congress, the Federal Reserve is independent of Congress as well.

While there has been a vast improvement in the general quality of its members since 1960, the Board and its Reserve Districts are still dominated by bankers. They tend to act like bankers, to think like bankers, and to be especially congenial to the interests of bankers.

This is a natural result of the Congressional delegation of power which was necessary because of the complexity of the economy. But its effects, like the delegation of the bond-issuing authority to the Treasury, has been to transfer a public function to a quasi-private (banks own the Federal Reserve System), largely independent agency which tends to exercise its power more on behalf of the dominant interests of the banking community than would be done if Congress were still capable of exercising its authority on a day-to-day basis.

While one should not exaggerate the situation, the marginal effects of these losses of Congressional power are seen in higher interest rates, a slower economic growth, a poorer distribution of income, and higher unemployment than would otherwise be the case. On the other hand, it may result in a smaller rate of inflation than would exist if Congress still exercised these Constitutional functions, because bankers are more apt to raise interest rates and tighten the money supply than Congress would be.

Lost Control of the Purse Strings

Congress has also lost power over spending. It does not control the purse strings. The President does that.

It is a routine practice for every Administration to charge that it is up against a big-spending, irresponsible Congress. One major *New York Times* reporter writes that story at least once a year, with appropriate quotations from White House or Budget Bureau spokesmen. But the fact is that Congress has reduced the President's requests for money every year for the last quarter of a century. It never votes more than the President asks for. It always appropriates less.

Yet the total amount the government spends remains essentially unaffected by the Congressional action in any one year. The most important reason for this is the backlog or pipeline of funds which the executive branch has squirreled away. Tens of billions in backlog balances remain in the pipeline. For fiscal year 1973 the unexpended balances of federal funds came to a whopping $155 billion. Another $134 billion was piled up in the trust funds. This made a grand total of $289 billion. The Pentagon alone held $40 billion of the total.

As Congress cuts the budget, agencies continue to draw on their unexpended balances. It is for this reason, among others, that budget outlays equal or exceed those proposed by the President even while Congress slashes the total amounts. The control lies with the executive branch. The President decides the actual level of spending. And that, in turn, determines priorities.

Backlogs, Re-programmings, and Long-Lead-Time Funds

There is a series of more subtle methods by which the Executive Branch exercises control over spending and priorities. One of these is "re-programming." This is power to take funds appropriated for one program and transfer them to another. Ordinarily the agency reports the action to the senior majority and minority Senate and House member of the Appropriations Committee or subcommittee with jurisdiction over its functions. All it requires is two-member approval or acquiescence. It was under re-programming that Congress lost control over spending for the F-14. Re-programming also revised the once dead Cheyenne helicopter project.

Another means is long-lead-time funds. The Navy requested $299 million for advance funding for the new attack carrier, CVN-70, before the carrier itself was approved. As this amounts to a third of the total cost for production of the carrier itself, if the long-lead-time money is approved the project is under way.

A variation of the long-lead-time means of committing the Congress to immense future expenditures for weapons systems is the building of prototypes.

Everyone now agrees, in theory at least, that whenever possible prototypes of the big weapons should be built before billions are committed to mass production. Get the bugs out first! But prototypes are built not only with research and development funds but with production funds. In the former case, production of the weapon must still be approved. In the latter case, the military service argues that, by getting the money for the prototypes, it already has won approval for the production run as well. It is one of the methods most often used to get a commitment for the ultimate development of the weapon before it has been tried and proven.

The Illustrative Budget

As chairman of the Foreign Operations Subcommittee of the Appropriations Committee, I handle the foreign-aid bill. Various devices are used by the executive branch to reduce Congressional control and to usurp the purse-string functions of Congress.

When the requests for economic and military aid come to Congress, the State and Defense Departments insist that the country-by-country lists and the amounts of aid proposed are merely an "illustrative program." Their position is that Congress votes the total which afterward the State and Defense Departments can use in any way they choose. They can cut Country A's grant and increase Country B's, or give it to Country C which was not even listed in their "illustrative budget." This has the advantage of giving great flexibility to the executive branch, but it removes from Congress virtually all control over what is spent, how it is spent, and where it is spent.

Furthermore, until I ended the practice, they stamped the illustrative program "Secret" and published the amounts only a year and a half after it was submitted to Congress. When I insisted that the "Secret" stamp be removed unless some clear national-security issue could be demonstrated, the State Department agreed to make all but a handful of the country amounts public. While the Tonkin Bay Resolution was the spectacular event by which Congress lost control of Vietnam spending, the "illustrative budget" was the less spectacular but day-to-day method by which funds were channeled into new areas, for new purposes, and for new commitments not only in Southeast Asia but elsewhere.

As chairman of the Foreign Operations Subcommittee of the Senate Appropriations Committee, it is my intention to cut the number of countries receiving military foreign aid from forty-six to no more than ten, to end the illustrative-budget fiction, and to appropriate specific amounts for specific countries. I also intend to end the secrecy about where the money goes. That could return some modicum of control to the Congress.

Impounded Funds, Direct Transfers, and the Idiot Treatment

Another method used by the executive departments to set priorities their way when Congress disagrees with them is to impound appropriated funds for progams that Congress favors. By dipping into the backlogs, they can simultaneously spend above the budget estimates for programs they favor. In fiscal year 1971, for example, Congress boosted housing funds and cut back on the military, but, in direct contradiction of this action, the Office of Management and Budget impounded almost a third of the money approved for housing and increased the Pentagon's spending $2 billion above the Pentagon's own estimates. The President reordered the reordered priorities.

The most blatant example of unauthorized spending by the executive branch was the more than $1 billion in military aid that the Pentagon shoveled out the back door to South Vietnam, Thailand, Laos, and Korea in fiscal years 1971 and 1972. As I pointed out earlier (Chapter 4), these funds were not appropriated under military-grant aid or funded under the Military Assistance Service Funded program. Nor were they declared "excess" under the regular procedure. When we asked for an accounting of the amounts, the military first gave us the "idiot treatment." That's the standard procedure by which they pretend not to know anything about the request, act stupid, and send you to one dead end after another. We persisted, but they waited until they got their military-aid funds, under a highly controversial continuing resolution, before they gave us the facts.

When we pressed them for the law under which such transfers were authorized and for the reason why no accounting was made, they could give no adequate reply. Simply stated, the military turned over the supplies and weapons on their own, and then claimed that no law required an accounting of it. Since the action was not authorized by law, obviously there was no law requiring accounting.

As J. Frank Crow of the Defense Comptroller's Office told Tim Ingram of the *Washington Monthly* when Ingram queried him about this massive transfer, "Hell, man, that's my job: to lose track of it."

Rigged Congressional Rules

Not all the blame for the way Congress has lost control of spending and priorities can be laid at the doorstep of a devious executive branch. The rules of the House of Representatives, for one thing, are rigged in such a way that issues like oil depletion, the SST, and the Mansfield resolution on the Vietnam pullout are prevented from coming to a direct vote. Oil depletion was reduced but has not been voted on directly in the House for years. The crucial votes on the Mansfield amendment and the SST were held on procedural matters like "instructing conferees" or "to recommit." Twenty to thirty votes were lost when members who were against the SST were unwilling to instruct House conferees as a matter of procedural principle. In fact, the SST was defeated in the House only after interminable maneuvering finally brought a direct vote on the issue.

Congress is also notorious for holding closed-door or executive hearings, for receiving only "ex-parte" or one-sided testimony from the agencies whose money or legislation is involved, and for totally inadequate staffing. The Senate Appropriations Subcommittee on Foreign Operations, which passes on more than $3 billion in military and economic aid, has only one majority staff man and one minority staff man who works with five other subcommittees assigned to it. It is thus impossible to compete with the dozens of bureaucracies and their directors, legislative-liaison, and budget officials assigned full time to lobby for their funds.

Even worse are some Congressional practices like the House Ways and Means Committee's "member bills," in which each member was assured that one of his bills would automatically be passed by the committee and by the House regardless of Treasury or other objections. After several decades of abuse, this procedure, under which numerous loopholes were added to the tax laws, was finally challenged by Congressmen Wright Patman and Leslie Aspin in 1972.

These are among the institutional ways by which the executive branch has usurped Congressional power over programs and priorities, and by which Congress either deliberately or by default has allowed it to happen.

There is no way the nation's priorities can be intelligently reordered until reforms in both branches take place.

10 · Reordering Priorities—
Institutional Reforms
Needed to Get the Job Done

The President's 1972 budget message was in the hands of reporters three or four days before its Monday noon release. Background briefings were held by the President's closest advisers and in the intimate surroundings of the White House. Reporters had ample time to review the document and advise their editors on key issues. The major papers not only played it two columns on page one above the fold but gave massive inside space to reprinting the pie charts, bar charts, tables, and texts from the document itself.

From the point of view of the White House and the President—any President—the imposing treament of the budget document, the economic report, and the State of the Union message flows from the power and prestige of the office of the President itself. Because the President has command of what Theodore Roosevelt called "a bully pulpit," the President's most mundane views generate massive publicity. They are examples of the active use of the President's prestige and high visibility to insure vast space for the positions presented on these institutionalized occasions.

Among the key tenets of the dogma proclaimed from the "bully pulpit" was that "priorities had been reordered." Under the rubric "Meeting Human Needs" President Nixon claimed, "My Administration has begun widespread reform and has sought to take new directions in Federal human resources programs. From 1969 to 1972, outlays for these purposes grew by 63 percent, while total budget outlays grew by only 28 percent."

The claim was made that "human resources spending will be

45 percent of the 1973 budget, while defense programs will be 32 percent.... This exactly reverses the priorities of the prior administration. In 1968, the defense share was 45 percent and the human resources share was 32 percent."

These assertions were picked up, printed, and repeated *ad nauseum*, not only by the press but especially by the President's partisan supporters.

No Change in Priorities

When the Joint Economic Committee of Congress examined this claim in detail in its annual report, appearance gave way to reality. Here's what it found:

First, there was not a single major decrease from the previous year's budget. As the JEC report pointed out, "Resource misallocations cannot be corrected unless we are willing to cut back as well as expand." The committee charged: "The failure to significantly reform any existing programs in this year's budget indicates a retreat." Sugar subsidies, the superhighway program, grandiose public works, aid to big farmers, military procurement, water and reclamation projects, urban renewal, military aid, and the space program—each and every one of them a highly contentious, controversial issue in the battle over priorities—were untouched. Not even the scalpel, let alone the meat axe, was applied to them.

Second, the actual claim for reordering priorities was highly misleading. The human-resource category, for example, did not include programs for housing and the environment. It did include, on the other hand, civil-service retirement funds. In addition, and even more important, 80 percent of the claimed shift was caused by Congressional programs previously enacted, particularly Social Security. It did not reflect a single new initiative or Administration change in programs. The proportions changed merely because the Social Security trust funds grew, not from a deliberate, conscious policy of reordering priorities. It was like taking credit for good weather.

Third, and most important of all, was what happened to the actual new funds generated by the annual growth in the economy. The total new obligational authority was estimated at $21 billion, an 8 percent increase over the previous year. As there were no major decreases in programs, this $21 billion represented every dime available to meet new pressing needs—schools, health, housing, antipollution, welfare, crime, drug control, poverty, hunger, small business, and mass transit, among others.

Where did it go? Military, space, and related spending got the lion's share—$7.2 billion, or 34 percent. Social Security and Medicare—programs funded by the trust funds and previously authorized by Congress—took $4 billion. Proposed general revenue sharing cost $5.3 billion. These items took 78 percent of all the new money, and the new money was all that was available to meet changing needs. Less than $5 billion—$4.6 billion, to be precise—of the estimated $100-billion increase in GNP over the previous year was available to meet the most urgent national needs funded by the federal government.

No new funds were generated by cutting back on the big subsidy programs. Not a dime was available from closing tax loopholes. No new money was forthcoming from cutting back on a major old program in order to fund a major new program. There was no reform in military aid, no cutback on subsidies to the big farmers, no decrease in the public-works pork barrel, no reduction or reform in military procurement, no reordering of the housing subsidies, no significant savings due to government efficiency or productivity.

Of the new resources generated by a growing economy, a disproportionate share was grabbed by the military. Four years after "reordering priorities" was raised to the level of a great national issue, priorities needed reordering more than ever before.

Unread Literature

Unlike the massive publicity which the President's claim to reordering priorities received in the national press, the careful analytical work of the Congressional experts was added to the great unread literature of the world. On the day the Joint Economic Committee's report was released, AFL-CIO president George Meany resigned from the Pay Board, the presidents of the television networks testified before Senator John O. Pastore's commerce subcommittee and dominated TV coverage, and the Ways and Means Committee finally completed action on the controversial revenue-sharing bill. As the Congress has no "bully pulpit" of its own, its critical interpretation of White House doctrine received no significant public attention, and the press denied any responsibility to offset White House preachments by printing these countervailing views.

The significance of this gigantic failure to reorder priorities goes beyond the issues of whether we choose defense instead of housing, public works over school lunches, or subsidies to Lockheed instead of programs to save the environment. These are the consequences of the present system, not their causes. Before we can make the right choices and reorder the nation's priorities in an intelligent way, we must break the grip of existing institutions over the budgetary process.

The President Proposes the Priorities

At the present time, priorities are what the President proposes in his budget. That budget reflects, in turn, the views of the powerful departments and agencies of the government. They, in turn, are largely dominated by existing economic and political forces. In many cases that domination is not one which the agency or department resents. In most cases the great departments of the government believe it is their function and their purpose to represent the dominant forces of business, labor, farmers, doctors, planners, builders, hospitals, commercial mail users, shipbuilders, exporters, bankers, savings institutions, defense contractors, water users, truckers and railroads rather than the consumer, the taxpayer, or the general public.

These are the forces which dominate the secret, behind-the-scenes struggle for government funds, government privileges, and government subsidies. It takes place long before the priorities document, the President's budget, is released to the public. And in the struggle no countervailing forces are present at the scene to contest the match.

Merely the most shameful manifestation of this rigid, anti–public-interest institutionalism is the fact that in a $246-billion budget not a single major program was cut. Somewhere in the 570-page Presidential budget, its 1,103-page phone-book-size detailed appendix, and the 309 pages of special analyses on nineteen separate general subjects from federal credit programs to aid to state and local governments, there must be at least one major, significant program which intelligent administrators could reduce. But the budget contains not a single one—none, zero, zilch!

As Charles Schultze has warned us, expansion of existing programs will eat up every dime of new revenues even at a 4 percent level of unemployment unless we have the fortitude to cut waste and inefficient and outmoded programs. If we fail to do that, our great national needs can be met only by enormous deficit spending. The deficit will act as an engine of inflation generating vast price increases. This in turn will lead inevitably to massive permanent economic controls over prices and wages. Then bureaucratic judgments will be substituted for the efficient judgment of the marketplace in the private competitive economic life of the nation. This in turn will reduce the productivity and efficiency of the society, strike a fatal blow at the economic genius of the country, and make it even less possible to meet the nation's desperate needs. It is a sure way to kill the goose who lays the golden egg.

Change the Priority Process

There is an alternative to the present budget process and the bleak future which failing to change it portends. That alternative, applied program by program, means this:

1. The precise objectives of every major government program must be stated explicitly and quantitatively. We can no longer afford, for example, the luxury of space programs based on political muscle where objectives are vaguely stated, estimates of the costs are worthless, and alleged gains are couched in general language.

2. The specific economic benefits of programs designed to improve the allocation of resources must be analyzed and stated.

3. The costs of these programs must be provided in systematic detail.

4. The economic costs of alternative programs must be measured to determine if there is not a method to achieve the goal either at smaller costs or with greater benefits.

Where the program involves the efficient allocation of resources, such as taxing the private economy for funds to invest in public projects, explicit, quantitative costs and benefits can be measured.

Where the government is involved in redistribution of income to provide greater fairness or equity, this is not always possible. In these cases, where the benefits cannot be measured precisely, the program, or alternative program, which can achieve the goal at the least possible cost is clearly the desirable choice.

If the program objective is to raise the income of low-income farmers, for example, the choice can be absolutely clear. It cannot be done by a program of tax incentives, because low-income farmers do not pay taxes and tax benefits go to individuals in proportion to their income and marginal tax rate. The higher the income, the greater the benefit. It probably cannot be done efficiently by production payments. Big farmers obviously produce more, have larger quotas, or can remove more acres from production than can poor, small farmers. Big farmers will therefore get more income from any program based on volume of production, previous production history, or landholdings than the small poor farmer for whom the program was ostensibly designed.

Some form of direct income payment to poor farmers, with a ceiling or graduated ceiling on income, is obviously a far more efficient means of raising the income of low-income farmers than either of the two alternatives. And even within an income-support program there are alternative means of achieving the goal, some of which are bound to be more efficient than others.

If the goal of the program is really to raise the income of poor farmers, and not merely an excuse to justify some other objective, such as shoveling out funds to wealthy farmers in a humanitarian guise, clearly these tough choices should be made. But no system now exists by which intelligent choices can be made, or it exists in such rudimentary or token form that it has no significant influence.

There are means by which intelligent judgments can be brought to bear on priorities and choices. This demands reform in both the executive and the legislative institutions. The solution flows naturally from the examination of the problem.

Criticism of the President's Procedures

The budget of the United States is *the* priority document. Most issues are settled when the President approves it. Congress, for all its oversight function and responsibility to control the purse strings, affects only a minute percentage of the total. At best, Congress nibbles at the edges. For every SST that Congress stops, a dozen lemons go through unscathed or uncontested. There is proper criticism of the way Congress does its job. But by comparison, the way Congress examines the budget in its institutionalized forms is vastly superior to the behavior of the executive branch. If Congress is criticized, properly, for its procedures, the way the President and the Budget Bureau put the priorities document together should be criticized in spades.

The President's budget—the priorities document—is put together entirely in secret. Public groups have no knowledge of what is going on. There are no adversary proceedings whatsoever. The entire advocacy is from the department or agency seeking the funds. While the Budget Bureau examiner acts as a judge or referee, there is no body or group detailed to present systematic criticism of any department's budget. In the case of the military budget, for years the Pentagon budget officers had equal billing with the Budget Bureau examiners. Proceedings were held at the Pentagon and joint budget amounts were agreed on.

Virtually no critical analysis of programs is generated at all. The minute proportion which is generated suffers from the fact that the analysis is produced by the agency requesting the funds and that it remains secret. If the budget office cuts, trims, or reorders an agency's funding request, the Cabinet official can take a personal appeal to the President against such action. In the fiscal year 1973 budget, for example, the Office of Management and Budget opposed some of the massive increases in Pentagon weapons programs—the vast increases which mortgage the future —but in every instance the Pentagon won its case and got the action overthrown by a direct appeal to the President.

Needed: A Public Process and Public Information

There are two general actions which must be taken to reform this process. First and foremost is to open the process to public scrutiny. It must be made a public process. The second is to vastly improve the volume of information, the quality of analysis, and the objectivity of the data.

Here is what I propose.

First of all, long before the final decisions are made in January, public hearings should be held in the executive branch on budget programs, agency by agency, department by department, before approval by the President. The budget program, department by department, should include not only the formal spending proposals but also tax expenditures and subsidies of all kinds, including direct cash, credit, benefit-in-kind, purchase, and regulatory subsidies.

Second, the agency requesting the funds should provide important information, including (a) a detailed, explicit statement of the objectives of each of the programs; (b) the costs of the program, including the discount rates, opportunity costs, and externalities upon which the cost of the project was determined; (c) the benefits of the program—in particular, the benefits as they apply to various income groups. It is not enough merely to show that a project will provide so much in benefits from added shipping tonnage, transportation time saved, or the number of persons served by a hospital grant. It is important wherever possible to show which income groups or what persons will receive the benefits. A forty-mile stretch of highway might be justified as a public project on the grounds that it creates $100,000 in benefits for each $50,000 of expenditures. But an entirely different light is thrown on the project if its location is such that its benefits go exclusively to one company. The costs of alternative programs to achieve the specific objective should also be required.

Third, there should be adversary proceedings in which the views and analyses of competent critics are brought to bear on the agency or department's request and evidence. A group of cost analysts, independent of the agency or department involved, should review the findings, program by program, and present those results for the public record. The views and analyses of both the agency and the critics should be public documents presented in public proceedings.

If such proceedings had been required in the past, the SST, the space shuttle, the C-5A, the F-14 and other billion-dollar public programs would either have been aborted in their early stages or vastly modified before approval.

For example, during the SST fight the Office of Science and Technology commissioned the Garwin study on economic and technological prospects of the SST. The study, which was negative, was stamped "Secret" and refused to the public throughout the debate. After a suit was brought by Congressman Henry S. Reuss (D.–Wis.) and Friends of the Earth, a court ordered that it be made public. But this happened after the SST was killed by Congress. The benefits of this study paid for by public funds was refused to the public until it was too late. The point is that such information should be routinely required and made public as a basis on which a rational public decision can be made.

Fourth, in the examination and analysis of the budget request, the entire program, not just the request for the incremental annual additions, should be reviewed. This is called "zero-based budgeting" and should be a routine procedure in the budget process.

Fifth, the budgetary procedures should encompass five-year budget projections of the cost for each major expenditure, tax expenditures, or subsidy program. The future implications of contemporary decisions should be required for ongoing programs as well as for new programs under Public Law 84-801.

Scrutinize the President

These are the means by which secret proceedings can be transformed into a public process, adversary hearings and objective analysis substituted for *ex-parte* proceedings, and the power and influence of government departments wrested from powerful private groups and returned to the public.

This process would provide a public record on which the Office of Management and Budget and the President of the

United States could make their judgments. The President would be free to propose actions and programs as he determined, but in doing so he would have to present a much more convincing case than he would if an objective public record had not been made.

The President must establish public procedures to scrutinize the budget. But the system can work no better than the man in charge of it. It is more important that the citizen scrutinize the President and the men presenting themselves to the electorate for the office of the President than that the President scrutinize the budget. He makes the decisions and determines the priorities.

The President should believe in the public process—of open decisions openly arrived at. He should cherish knowledge and information, so that as nearly as possible in an imperfect world the truth may prevail. He should clearly and overwhelmingly be the agent of the people of the United States and not the errand boy for powerful political and economic interest groups. He should be both tough and compassionate, experienced but open to new ideas, scrupulously upright and honest but equally understanding of the weaknesses and follies of ordinary people.

He must, above all, lead. Only the President can mount a national campaign to close the tax loopholes. Only he is powerful enough to win the fight to cut military fat and waste, curb space and public-works excesses, and knock bureaucratic heads together to get those jobs done.

He must possess great strength of personal character. When the chips are down, his integrity must instinctively tell him right from wrong and his courage must give him the will to act on that judgment.

Strengthen Proposals to Congress

The President's budget document to Congress should also include a detailed statement of the objectives of each major program. It should be organized by program and include each of the public actions (expenditure, tax, and subsidy) to achieve the proposed ends and goals. The cost–benefit analysis, alternative programs, and five-year projections should either be a part of the document or be included in the formal budget presentation by the departments to the Congressional committees. The budget document should also include specific proposals for administrative action or legislation to control the so-called "uncontrollable" budget items which compose almost half of the expenditure requests.

As a result of these reforms of the Presidential budget process, Congress would be fortified in its ability to do its job. Armed with the public hearings, the public justifications, and the detailed objective analysis, Congress would then be in a position to make an equally constructive critical examination of the budget.

Closed Congressional Meetings

For Congress to do its job successfully, however, its budgetary procedures must also be reformed.

Congressional-committee budgetary proceedings are too often closed to the public. At the present time the House Armed Services Committee operates almost entirely behind closed doors. The Senate Armed Services Committee is only somewhat less secret. These committees annually authorize about $20 billion of the military budget. With rare exceptions, their proceedings are secret or in "executive session."

The House Appropriations Committee and its subcommittees hold all their hearings in secret; this applies to scrutiny of the budgets of the Census Bureau, the Patent Office, and the Small Business Administration as well as hearings on strategic weapons or the CIA. The Senate Appropriations Committee, except for occasional hearings on classified subjects, holds its hearings in public. In this respect its procedures are vastly superior to those of the House. But the markup sessions, when the subcommittees and the full committee determine the amounts to be recommended, are held in secret. This is also true of the sessions of the conference committees between the House and the Senate to iron out differences between bills passed by the two Houses.

Other Congressional Failures

In addition to closed hearings, Congress can be criticized fairly for other failures, among them these:

Congress receives mostly superficial information. It gets last year's amounts and this year's request with the evidence largely aimed at justifying the incremental increase.

It gets no detailed cost analysis, benefit analysis, income distribution, cost of alternative programs, or five-year projections of ongoing programs.

It gets no analysis of tax expenditures. While requests for subsidies are often part of the expenditure budget, it gets no analysis of the income distribution of the benefits.

The testimony is almost entirely *ex parte* in nature. The agency requesting the funds is generally the only witness. Except on rare occasions there is no adversary proceeding, rebuttal evidence or testimony, or any challenge to the request.

Congress has an extremely small staff. They do amazing work under impossible conditions, but they are dependent on the agencies they review for basic information. Obviously few agencies voluntarily present to Congressional staffs or committees any information unfavorable to their views.

Zero-based budgeting is virtually never followed.

There is no formal process by which the $120 billion or more in uncontrollable budget spending is reviewed. This is left purely to chance.

A vast improvement in Congressional knowledge would follow

from the budget procedures proposed here for the reform in the executive branch. In addition, Congress should reform itself.

Stop Secret Hearings

Hearings should be open except where matters of the most secret national-security issues are involved. An even larger proportion of Armed Services and Defense Appropriation Subcommittee hearings in the Senate and almost all of the now closed hearings of the Armed Services and Appropriations Committees in the House can be opened without any danger to the national security.

When I became chairman of the Senate Appropriations Subcommittee on Foreign Operations the hearings on military aid were closed. I opened them. On those rare occasions when classified material is at issue the witness merely states that to be the case. In most of those instances the information is only technically classified, for I have read in the most authoritative public sources the precise amounts of annual military aid for a handful of Middle Eastern nations which remain classified. These hearings were opened without any loss to the security of the United States but with great public benefits in terms of timely information.

Secret hearings give enormous advantage to the advocate. In the case of the Secretary of Defense and his deputies, a sanitized version of their testimony is often made public or released by the Pentagon at the time of the closed-door hearings. The executive branch therefore gets vast publicity for its request while critical Congressional questioning behind closed doors goes entirely unreported.

There is ample precedent for open hearings. In the House, where the abuse of closed hearings is greater than in the Senate, the general rule is that hearings should be open unless a vote of the committee orders them closed. In some committees, such as the Education and Labor Committee and the Banking Committee, bills are actually marked up in open session. The country has not suffered as a result.

Establish a Congressional Office of Experts

Ex-parte hearings should be ended. There are a number of ways to do this. As the Joint Economic Committee recommended after its study of priorities and in its report "Economic Analysis and the Efficiency in Government":

An Office of Economic Evaluation and Analysis should be established as an autonomous nonpartisan staff unit within the Joint Economic Committee. This Office would be responsive to all congressional offices and would assist them in obtaining analytical studies, data, and information on policy and program alternatives.

My view of its function would be to evaluate the objectives presented by the executive agencies in support of their legislative and budget requests, and to examine critically the costs, benefits, alternative costs, and other analysis which the President provides in his budget and legislative requests. Where the President and his departments fail to present objective evidence, the Office of Economic Evaluation and Analysis could perform that function *de novo* for the Congress.

In addition, the Congress should receive either public testimony or detailed information from an independent agency such as the General Accounting Office concerning the detailed requests of the executive departments. The GAO knows where the bodies are buried. It has access to much executive-branch information. It is an honest, hardworking, and independent group. It has been of immeasurable value to me both in testimony before the Joint Economic Committee and in staff work on military foreign aid.

Finally, as the Joint Economic Committee also recommended,

Congressional committees with program responsibilities should establish an explicit schedule whereby all existing Federal programs would be subjected to a comprehensive, from-the-ground-up reappraisal at least every five years. This reevaluation would focus on the objectives of the program and its performance in meeting the objectives . . .

These reforms would apply the same standards of procedure for Congress' review of the budget as apply to the President's procedure in constructing it. Providing an open public process, objective analysis, adversary proceedings, zero-based budgeting, five-year estimates, and a review of the uncontrollables can do much to bring intelligent consideration to the priority process.

Scrutinize Trust Funds and Regulatory Commissions

There are two other areas of program inefficiency and inequity which are the source of serious misallocation of resources and impose bad distributional effects on the public. The first is those trust funds which involve investment, construction, or the provision of services. The most glaring example is the multi-billion-dollar highway trust fund. The second area is the regulatory commissions. In both cases the economic consequences of their actions are effectively removed from both Budget Bureau and Congressional review. That must be changed.

In its report entitled "Economic Analysis and the Efficiency of Government," the Subcommittee on Priorities and Economy in Government of the Joint Economic Committee gave a clear exposition of the problem in connection with the Highway Trust Fund.

The federal highway program is financed by the Highway Trust Fund. The moneys for this fund accumulate automatically from the revenues generated by the federal gasoline tax. The allocation of expenditures to the highway program is by formula and heavily favors area over population. As the trust fund is established, neither Congress nor the executive branch has any substantial annual control over the amount of money which goes into the trust fund or the amount which goes out. The expenditure generated by the trust fund amounts to between $4 billion and $5 billion a year. It is a mindless way of both collecting and spending the money. Except for an occasional Presidentially imposed freeze, the funds are essentially impervious to overall budgetary policy.

A critic of the federal highway policy, Dr. James R. Nelson, professor of economics at Amherst College, emphasized the following points in his testimony on this issue to the Joint Economic Committee.

The failure of the financing of the Federal highway program to rely on specific user charges or tolls actually accentuates the problem of highway congestion and encourages the construction of uneconomic facilities.

The prohibition against the Department of Transportation's undertaking any economic analysis of alternative transportation policies, under the provisions of Section 4-b-2 of the Department of Transportation Act of 1966, makes a sham of intelligent budgeting of billions of highway funds.

The highway trust fund effectively insulates the highway programs from policy planning, economic analysis, and Congressional scrutiny. It does this not only because funds are allocated by formula instead of on the basis of demand, benefits, and costs; it does it also because the formula is based on the past use of highways rather than on the prospective demand which should be efficiently met.

The Highway Trust Fund Frustrates Intelligent Action

One could hardly devise a system better designed to frustrate and thwart intelligent attempts to make choices or properly order priorities.

Dr. Anthony Downs, an economist and a member of the National Commission on Urban Problems (the Douglas Commission), testified before the Joint Economic Committee on the Baltimore highway and urban-renewal programs and the neglect of real costs in the projects. From 1951 to 1964 a federal highway project in Baltimore destroyed the equivalent of 21 percent of the entire housing inventory of low-income blacks. This was not included as a cost when determining whether the highway should be built. Dr. Downs estimated that the total noncompensated cost of these and other injustices resulting from both federally financed highways and federally financed urban-renewal projects will amount to somewhere between $156 million and $230 million per year over the next few years.

Dr. Downs also estimated that about 237,000 displaced persons and another 237,000 nondisplaced persons will be affected by the programs. He estimated that the potential noncompensated loss would be from $812 to $1,194 per household affected. This is 20 to 30 percent of the average household income of this income group. If these costs were calculated properly by the government, they would add 14 to 21 percent of the total costs of acquiring the real property involved in the projects.

This is just one example of the magnitude of injustice thrust on the poorest segment of society by the failure to properly calculate costs. In the case of the highway program, the law specifically prevents such calculations from being made. It is not an oversight; it is deliberate public policy. That is why the federal highway program must be brought under a system of intelligent analysis.

I therefore recommend that the Highway Trust Fund be abolished. Other trust funds which involve investment, construction, and services of these kinds should also be abolished. Some $60 billion now shoveled out through antiquated or self-defeating formulas should be brought under direct budget control and Congressional oversight.

Evaluate the Economic Impact of Regulatory Agencies

With respect to the regulatory agencies, their operating budgets are subject to Congressional and Budget Bureau review, but the decisions they make are removed from economic analysis, questions of alternative methods of achieving ends, clear statements of objectives, and cost–benefit analysis and review. Furthermore, the testimony the regulatory agencies receive is almost universally self-serving and *ex parte* in nature.

As the regulatory agencies should be removed from political pressures rather than subjected to them, their decisions obviously should not be the subject of individual Budget Bureau or Congressional review. I recommend that a comprehensive study should be undertaken of the problems of the regulatory commissions and the effect their decisions have on allocating resources and redistributing income. In addition, an Office of Economic Evaluation and Analysis, similar to the one I have recommended for Congress, should be established to serve the regulatory agencies.

Such an office's analysis of costs, benefits, alternative programs, equity and distributional effects of decisions should be required for every major decision of the regulatory agencies—the granting of a route, the issuance of a TV license, or an increase in the price of natural gas. In some cases, as in the case of granting a radio or TV license, the calculation of the massive economic benefit derived from the public privilege could lead to a public charge for the privilege.

Regulatory agencies should be given the responsibility to consider a much broader range of alternatives than the laws now often allow them to do.

Their procedures should be changed so that the public-interest point of view is directly presented to them in evidence at their hearings. It is not enough to hear only from the industries involved. A group of "public defenders" should be established to make such an advocacy before the regulatory commissions.

These proposals merely scratch the surface of the nature of the reforms needed to transform the so-called regulatory agencies into instruments which universally defend the public interest.

These are the institutional changes necessary in the executive and legislative branches of the government and for the trust funds and regulatory agencies if the programs and policies of the government of the United States are to be returned to the people of the United States.

Act in the Public Interest

Reordering priorities, simply stated, means that the government should act in the public interest and on behalf of the American people to meet their most pressing needs in an intelligent and economic fashion. The issue of national priorities merely focuses on the question "What do we want our nation to be?" as Senator Fulbright put it so succinctly.

Abroad we face the problem of war and peace. Priorities confront us with the central issue, How can military and civilian needs be balanced?

While the level of international uncertainty and danger is substantial, we also face major problems at home.

Our polarized and deteriorating cities, our poor, our racial and ethnic minorities, and our students demand the attention of the nation.

Despite our general affluence, all of the major river systems are polluted. One cannot safely swim in them, fish in them, or drink from them. The Great Lakes are dying. The air in our major cities is polluted. The housing shortage for low-income families grows worse. High interest rates and rising building costs now prevent at least half the American people from owning their own home.

The public-school system is in serious trouble. The highways and city streets are crowded with impatient automobile drivers for whom mass transit offers no real alternative.

Unemployment is excessively high and for blacks, teenagers, and some other groups is at depression levels.

The threat and sometimes the fact of riots hang over our cities. The talk of a taxpayers' revolt grows louder as inflation erodes the incomes and savings of many of our citizens. Crime and unrest grow.

That is why we have taken a self-conscious look at our national priorities, at the faults and shortcomings of federal programs, and at the way our institutions have become the agents of powerful economic groups who have shaped public policy to serve their own interests.

The simple way of changing this is to open up public functions to a public process. We should demand excellence of information and intelligent policies based on that information. We should return public institutions and public programs to the public interest.

Why should the press instead of the government have to publish the Pentagon Papers? Wouldn't the country be stronger if the Pentagon itself had released them, asked for public comment, and tried to learn from them instead of sweeping them under the rug?

Why shouldn't Ralph Nader be heard at a Department of Transportation budget hearing on the proposed auto safety program? Wouldn't lives be saved if decisions were the result of constructive public conflict rather than arbitrary bureaucratic decisions or secret ones influenced only by the highway or auto lobby?

Isn't the country stronger if proposals for foreign military aid are discussed in the press and by the public before the weapons are sent, rather than after the damage is done?

Shouldn't the President and the Secretary of Defense or the Secretary of State follow the rule on the whole that if it would embarrass them to see a truthful account of a new policy printed in, say, the Milwaukee *Journal*, the program is either of doubtful merit or just dead wrong?

Why isn't public argument and debate a better guide to public policy than secret decisions made in the war rooms of the Pentagon? Didn't John F. Kennedy belatedly realize that criticism by the press and the public would have saved him from the folly of the Bay of Pigs?

Aren't these the ways to reorder our national priorities and make democracy work?

I believe they are. I believe these are the ways to keep faith with the Nils Torgesons, the Helga Schmidts, the Casimir Jankowskis, and the Mary Finertys throughout Wisconsin and America.